Enter the REAL world of cloak and dagger

where truth is often more fantastic than the wildest fiction.

Learn the TRUTH about:

- The 1942 mission of eight German saboteurs in the United States, with never-before-revealed information from the officer who was in personal charge of the operation

- Operation Cicero, the inside story from hitherto secret British files

- The amazing intelligence work behind the shooting down of Admiral Yamamoto in the Pacific

In his years with Naval Intelligence Ladislas Farago has known most of the great spies of our time and has had access to information never before released to the public.

This exciting, authoritative book, which probes the violent, vital world of the secret agent, is the result of those years.

Other Books by the Author

Abyssinia on the Eve

Abyssinian Stop Press (editor)

Palestine at the Crossroads

The Riddle of Arabia

Axis Grand Strategy (editor)

German Psychological Warfare (editor)

The Japanese: His Character and Morale

Behind Closed Doors (with Admiral E. M. Zacharias)

WAR OF WITS

THE ANATOMY OF ESPIONAGE AND INTELLIGENCE

LADISLAS FARAGO

PAPERBACK LIBRARY, INC.
New York

PAPERBACK LIBRARY EDITION
First Printing: January, 1962

Printed in the United States of America

Preface

WHETHER IT WAS A SEQUENCE OF ACCIDENTS OR WHAT SIR Robert Howard called honest design, I have been running into the foremost "spies" of the century since the beginning of my career as a journalist exactly thirty years ago. I was fortunate enough to know Colonel Walther Nicolai and Admiral Wilhelm Canaris, Admiral Sir Reginald Hall and Sir Basil Thomson, General William J. Donovan and Admiral Ellis M. Zacharias, the six great modern directors of intelligence. I knew personally and well Captain Franz von Rintelen, Colonel George Sosnowski, Captain Sidney G. Reilly, Sir Paul Dukes, General Pavel Skoropadsky, General Walter Kriwitsky, and a host of lesser "spies." They frequently allowed me, as a writer, access to their memories and memoirs.

The purpose of this explanation is not mere name-dropping. It is, I believe, necessary to establish the credentials of anyone who writes such a book as this, and at the very outset. I have never done an hour of spying in my life, but I have watched and even directed other people in such activities and witnessed from several vantage points intelligence, espionage, and propaganda in both their technical and their adventurous forms.

My lifelong interest in the business, and my association with some of the greatest intelligence experts of our times eventually resulted in my working actively in the field. In 1942, I joined a branch of United States governmental intelligence work and spent almost four years inside this agency, working together with our opposite numbers in a similar British organization. Part of this work consisted of participation in a major intelligence and propaganda campaign against Nazi U-boats and blockade runners. Later I was connected with the operations which Captain—now Admiral—Zacharias conducted against the Japanese High Command.

After the war, I had a share in an adventure in propaganda known as Radio Free Europe; there I headed a clandestine "Desk X," combating Communism behind the Iron

Curtain. In line with the melodrama of this work, I went by different "cover" names, one of which, Colonel Bell, was to gain a modicum of prominence in the European underground. In the course of this work I had intimate contact with several intelligence organizations of various resistance movements. About these nothing more can be said, for obvious reasons.

During this decade in operational propaganda I invented at least two "characters" who managed to impress themselves vigorously on the imagination of their target audiences. One was a Commander Robert E. Norden of the U. S. Navy, whose broadcasts had, in the words of a captured German document, "a crushing effect on the morale of German naval personnel." The other was a certain Balint Boda, an omniscient and ubiquitous Hungarian forever moving surreptitiously behind the Iron Curtain, whose hypothetical body gained substance by the effectiveness of his patriotic appeals.

Thus, much that is related in this book is based on personal experience. Still more is based on material that came to me first-hand from the protagonists of some of the great espionage dramas. Secret agents have molded our destiny far more than is generally recognized. I feel that their historic role, frequently nefarious, should be brought forward from the limelight of pure melodrama into the less deceptive illumination of public discussion.

LADISLAS FARAGO

Contents

PART III . . . *Sabotage*

PART IV . . . *Counterespionage*

PART V . . . *Propaganda*

PART I

Intelligence

The War of Wits

Our very survival in the crisis of today is closely and inexorably tied to an exact, timely knowledge of what is going on in the world—everywhere in the world, and most especially behind the walls of the Kremlin. There is plenty of uninformed talk about the importance of such knowledge, and also every intelligent person is aware that efforts are being made on an unprecedented scale to acquire it by all means, some fair, some foul. The newspapers, in particular, treat their readers daily to a running spectacle in which men and women scramble for the secrets of nations, for the intimate details of their high policies, strategic plans, intentions, military capabilities, and economic potentials.

Behind the respectable façade of all great powers, their secret services work with blatant disregard for decorum and decency. Their agents seek secrets in the files of war ministries and in the vaults of foreign offices, but also in refuse cans and garbage pails. They break safes and codes, arrange kidnapings and assassinations, engineer conspiracies.

The melodrama of this conflict is widely featured. It is generally presented as a furtive war ranging on clandestine fronts, as if it were nothing but a series of plots for television scripts. And indeed, superficial facts are often close to equally superficial fiction. A stately blonde steps into a cab in Vienna and is never seen again. The briefcase of a stranger is snatched from his hands on a Hong Kong bus. From Indochina comes word that saboteurs have disabled a French destroyer. In Malaya, Her Britannic Majesty's governor general is killed on an inspection trip. In Frankfurt, the private diary of an American general is stolen from his hotel room. In Canberra, Tokyo, and Berlin, Soviet agents desert with documents to expose and incriminate the service to which they themselves owed allegiance up to the moment of their escape.

Members of Parliament complain in the House of Commons that "secret documents are even being stolen from Buckingham Palace." Phones are tapped, mail is rifled, people are trailed, homes are entered surreptitiously. Frontiers are crossed illegally and men are ambushed from Germany all the way to Australia.

Isolated though these incidents appear, they all have an intrinsic relation to each other. Combined, they form a single pattern. But the melodrama inherent in such incidents sometimes obscures their significance. For behind the plots and perfidies of individual operatives stand huge and rich organizations, the secret services of the great powers, which exist because there is a need—the need to know. Behind the melodrama and adventure there is today's grim business of survival. The total pattern is what can be called the war of wits —organized and waged because it is the function of prudent nations to watch their ramparts and bolster their defenses at the sources of danger. In this age of absolute weapons existence depends on the knowledge of the intentions, plans, and capabilities of the opponents.

Pearl Harbor taught Americans this lesson in 1941. But a sneak attack which at that time merely destroyed some elements of the United States Pacific fleet would today "take out," as the technical term goes, whole metropolitan areas. It could cripple a nation, perhaps beyond recovery, with a single stroke at the very outset of a new war.

Foreknowledge is needed to forestall such sneak attacks, to enable nations to make their policies and conduct their diplomacy in anticipation of strategic onslaughts or to provide warnings on the eve of disaster. Knowledge is needed to enable nations which are attacked to retaliate—knowledge of the enemy's hidden targets, his sensitive or weak points, the focal areas where his physical and moral resources are concentrated. In short, knowledge is needed to wage the cold war, to stage its maneuvers, to avoid its defeats and score its victories.

This is an important part of the war of wits in its organized form: this effort to acquire such knowledge. But that is merely a point of departure. In the past belligerents tried chiefly to out-gun each other; today they maneuver to out-think or outsmart each other. In this sense, the war of wits becomes a major operation by itself. The war of today, as it is waged relentlessly even in times of nominal peace, thus assumes new dimensions.

With the coming of the cold war, the ancient art of war—with its emphasis on the material and military aspects of conflict—has moved into the intellectual sphere. This is not to say that intellectual factors were absent in the conduct of past conventional wars. "In all ages," Henderson wrote in his brilliant essay on war, "the power of intellect has asserted itself in war. It was not courage and experience only that made Hannibal, Alexander, and Caesar the greatest names of antiquity. Napoleon, Wellington, and the Archduke Charles were certainly the best-educated soldiers of their time; while Lee, Jackson, and Sherman probably knew more of war, before they made it, than any one else in the United States."

But through the evolution of society itself, knowledge of war as an isolated technique has become insufficient. Wars include not only the armies which fight them in isolated theaters, but whole nations; not only the generals, but statesmen and the people; not only strategy but policy; not only military science, but diplomacy, economy, and the social sciences. The totality of war, the all-embracing, all-pervasive nature of modern conflict, tends to place greater stress on the non-military features of war and bring to the fore forces and means which stem from man's knowledge, his emotions, impulses, and urges. Up to now, stamina and courage have been recognized as the two main intangible forces of war; today we recognize that intellect and education play a more important part in it. What is more, intellect is no longer confined to aid in the conduct of conventional war, but is endowed with the power of conducting a kind of "war" of its own—what the Germans called *geistiger Krieg* or intellectual war—without resort to conventional arms, and waged with intangible weapons of its own which replace the implements of armed conflict.

This modern conflict of minds is the war of wits. In this new war, brainpower has come into its own to take its place alongside landpower, seapower, and airpower, the traditional powers of brute war. It may yet turn out that the coming of the cold war has brought an improvement in the art of war as a whole through a shift in emphasis from the material to the largely intellectual aspects of human conflict.

What Is Intelligence ?

Some seventy years ago, George Aston, then a young officer of the Royal Marines, was ordered to London for duty in a mysterious branch of the British Navy, the "Foreign Intelligence Committee of the Military, Secret, and Political Branch of the Secretary of the Admiralty." His arrival caused a mild flurry of excitement in the old Admiralty Building and, on his way to his new post, the officer was buttonholed by a puzzled Old Salt:

"I say, Aston," said the Old Salt, "are you the new *intelligent* officer?"

Much of that old confusion still survives, even if today "intelligence" is a fashionable word. It is, in fact, one of those modern expressions, such as enzymes or existentialism or fission, that form the special vocabulary of an age of organized disorder.

The word keeps cropping up in official announcements and officious pronouncements. Recently *The New York Times* printed an article about the strength of the Red Army in Germany, and the correspondent stated that his facts and figures came from "Allied intelligence sources." He did not mean to say that they came from people who were just smart by nature. He meant that his sources were individuals whose business it is to gather such information and who have special means of finding out the exact nature of certain specified things. By slipping the word "intelligence" into his dispatch, the correspondent implied that his information was not mere hearsay, or gossip floating about in European coffee houses. He meant to say that it was factual, reliable, and confidential —that it was that inner-sanctum commodity—"intelligence."

Despite the aura of mystery that surrounds it, there is nothing occult about intelligence. In one sense, the word does, of course, mean the capacity to understand and manage ideas. But in the contest of wits, both in competitive human society and in the conduct of relations between nations, it means information that is handled as a commodity by people who specialize in it, much in the manner in which news is handled by newspapermen.

The dictionary definition of this kind of intelligence is "communicated information"—in other words, information that no longer merely stays in one person's mind, but that has been passed on to somebody else. In the agencies that specialize in the activity, intelligence is defined as "evaluated information," information the credibility, meaning, and importance of which has been duly established and appraised.

As a function or activity, intelligence is the organized effort to collect information, to appraise it bit by bit, and to piece it together until it forms larger and clearer patterns which in turn enable us to see the shape of things to come. It is a perpetual effort to pierce the fog of war and diplomacy so that we may draw with bold strokes the contours of tomorrow.

"In view of the present world situation," said General Matthew B. Ridgway, chief of staff of the U. S. Army, "it is more important than ever to have complete information upon which to determine the most economical deployment of Army forces commensurate with the military situation, to minimize the possibility or advantage of surprise aggression, and to assure the most effective employment of such forces should the need arise." He added: "Adequate intelligence constitutes the fundamental basis for the calculation of risks, the formulation of plans, the development of materiel, the allocation of resources, and the conduct of operations."

The acquisition of adequate intelligence is no haphazard activity or improvised function. It is a clearly defined effort in which a great many experts and specialists are engaged, for intelligence can be effective only if it is conducted along exact scientific lines in which causes and effects are meticulously linked.

The Maze of Information

The first weapons of men were the stone, the club—and intelligence. Surviving remnants of primitive races, like the American Indians, show that a crude form of intelligence figured prominently in their arsenals. It first took the form of minor scouting. Then it developed into reconnaissance. Then came the differentiation between scouting and reconnaissance on the one hand, and intelligence and espionage on the other.

When Noah sent forth the dove "to see if the waters were abated from off the face of the ground," he engaged in a strikinglymodern form of intelligence activity—in aerial reconnaissance. The ancient Egyptians had organized intelligence services centuries before Christ, even if their deficient counterintelligence caused Sir Basil Thomson to remark: "If the Pharaoh Memptah had been given an efficient intelligence service, there would have been no exodus." Moses improvised a secret service under Oshea ben Nun on the way to the Promised Land in a somewhat sacrilegious quest to check up on the promise of the Lord.

The Crusaders went on their adventurous mission without an organized intelligence service and fared badly. Then they created one and fared better. Military classics like Sextus Julius Frontinus, Sun Tsu, and Maurice de Saxe stressed the importance of intelligence and wrote manuals for its practice. A few generals ignored their suggestions, but most of them scrupulously observed the manuals. Commenting on the mis-

9

haps of an adversary, Frederick the Great remarked: "Marshal de Soubise is always followed by a hundred cooks. I am always preceded by a hundred spies."

The crucial role of intelligence in victory or defeat was demonstrated most dramatically in a great historic event of the seventh century: in the establishment of Islam as the dominant secular and spiritual force in Arabia. In A.D. 622, Mohammed fled from his native Mecca where life had become unbearable for him. He moved to Medina with a few of his disciples and from there he led raids on Meccan caravans. In A.D. 624 he defeated a superior Meccan force in the battle of Badr whereupon the Meccans decided to get rid of Mohammed once and for all. They mobilized a force of 10,000 men against him.

The Prophet was not unduly worried. He had left efficient agents in Mecca who reported to him the plans of his enemies. But his adversaries had planted no agents with him. So when the Meccans reached Medina, they were stunned to find a trench and a wall that completely encircled the city and sheltered Mohammed from attack.

"This trench struck the Bedouin miscellany as one of the most unsportsmanlike things that had ever been known in the history of the world," H. G. Wells wrote. "They rode about the place. They shouted their opinion of the whole business to the besieged." The outraged attackers then encamped to discuss the unexpected developments. Then came the rains. "The tents of the allies got wet and the cooking difficult, views became divergent and tempers gave away, and at last this great host dwindled again into its constituent parts without ever having given battle."

The vast Meccan army was defeated without an arrow's discharge, by the failure of its commanders to gather information about the enemy. Mohammed, on the other hand, triumphed because he had exact information about the plans, disposition, intentions, and strength of the enemy. Had he not secured this vital intelligence, Mohammed certainly would have been defeated by such a superior host and whatever then existed of Islam would have been wiped off the face of the earth.

You do not have to penetrate the rarefied air of international politics to realize the importance of information and foreknowledge. We all need some sort of information at one time or another, in our business, in our private dealings, even in the most intimate phases of our personal lives. When we buy a house, we go to some length to find out everything there is to know about the neighborhood, termites, schools, stores, transportation facilities. In our daily lives, we continually seek information, if it is only to dial a number on the telephone to get a weather report. In normal times, the information contained in a weather report is freely available, but in times of war it becomes a piece of intelligence that the enemy needs for his plans.

The information that nations need for the conduct of their foreign relations is vast as to both type and subject. We live today in a highly complex world in which competition is acute and often ruthless. No nation today can any longer exist in an isolated position, sealed off hermetically from the rest of the world or protected automatically by natural barriers. Every nation must, of necessity, fit itself into the global pattern that technological progress has forced upon the world.

Communications and transportation have so shrunk the world that even a small and remote country may find itself in the direct path of military conquest or political or economic aggression. The unilateral proclamation of neutrality is no longer sufficient to guarantee the inviolability of a nation. In fact, neutrality is frowned upon by the great powers, which demand that all countries of the world choose sides.

As long as there remain nations that have expansionist aspirations and ideas of aggrandizement, or merely paranoiac grievances, other nations are in danger of being outwitted in diplomacy or infiltrated by economic and political influences, or even attacked by military force without warning.

Behind the shadow of the military threat lie, therefore, some very different aspects of intelligence which, though not so precisely definable, are equally important to a comprehensive interpretation and understanding of a nation's own position in the ever-shrinking world today. To illustrate this point, an outline of the major considerations of intelligence might appear in this form:

1. MILITARY: Offensive and defensive doctrines. War plans. Strategic concepts and tactical principles. Organization. Installations. Industrial base. Armed forces. Command structure. Command personnel. Materiel. Tactics. Morale.

2. GENERAL: Topographical and hydographic characteristics. Historical backgrounds.

3. DIPLOMATIC: Foreign policies. Alliances. Diplomatic establishment. Foreign-service personnel. Technique of conducting foreign relations.

4. POLITICAL: Ideology. Traditions. Institutions. Personalities. Areas of friction.

5. ECONOMIC:
   a. *Financial:* Monetary policies. Currency structure. Transactions. Institutions. Personalities.
   b. *Commercial:* Trade policies. Markets. Trading methods. Price policies. Personalities.
   c. *Industrial:* Structure and capacity. Manufacturing plants and processes. Raw materials. Energy resources. Labor relations. Personalities.
   d. *Mining:* Mineral resources. Production methods. Output.
   e. *Agriculture:* Policies. Crop structure. Cultivation methods. Mechanization. Financing. Specific characteristics of rural population.

6. COMMUNICATIONS AND TRANSPORTATION: Telephones. Telegraph. Wireless. Railways. Shipping. Automobiles and trucks. Highways. Aviation. Ownership. Policies. Organization. Personnel.

7. SOCIAL: Nationality structure. Classes and castes. Historical factors. Census. Personal aspects, characteristics, and mentality of peoples. Social legislation. Abnormal sociology of nations.

8. CULTURAL: Institutions. Intellectual accomplishments. Arts and sciences. Literature. Professions. Radio. Television. Press. Motion pictures.

9. INTELLIGENCE: Organization, methods, and personnel of competing intelligence systems.

Specifically, military information includes data about the military theories and prowess of individual countries, the doctrines of their armed forces, their war plans in general and their deployment and mobilization plans in particular, their strategic and tactical concepts in theory and practice. Also embodied are the tables of organization of the armed forces and their so-called Order of Battle, which, in turn, includes such general information as the location of military, naval, or air districts and such specific data as the names and ranks of offices and the insignia of units.

In addition, it includes data on weapon developments and the various arms, from the hydrogen bomb down to AA guns on PT boats and range-finders on fighter planes. It includes, too, detailed information about the strength and distribution of the armed forces in their components, the uniforms and the equipment of the troops, their health conditions, their morale, the *esprit de corps* of individual units, even such seemingly incidental information as the biographies of officers, the weak and strong points of their character, their preferences and prejudices, their circle of friends and off-duty hobbies.

12

Napoleon was keenly interested in the character traits of the commanders who opposed him. Karl Schulmeister, his chief of intelligence, had to procure for him all kinds of information about the personal lives and habits of the enemy generals. In his campaign plans Napoleon paid as much attention to the character and foibles of the generals who opposed him as to the disposition and equipment of enemy troops.

Military information on a monumental scale was procured by Sir Francis Walsingham in 1587, on the eve of the great running battle off Britain, about the plans, disposition, and strength of Spain's Invincible Armada. Since then, the war plans of nations have been the most closely guarded and the most sought-after military information. But even such seemingly general details as an army's tactics when fighting in wooded areas or a fleet's deployment of destroyers for night action are considered important.

Topographical or hydrographic information in the general category of intelligence has figured prominently throughout history. As a matter of fact, the first extant intelligence report was concerned with such information. It was prepared for Pharaoh Thothmes III in 1479 B.C., during his Armageddon campaign.

The army of Thothmes, moving on the city of Yemma, sixteen miles southwest of Megiddo, had the choice of three roads leading into the city. An approach march so close to the enemy was a delicate operation, and Thothmes was anxious to deploy his forces on the best of the three approaches. He sent out scouts, and they returned with information about the different roads. This information was then evaluated by the Pharaoh's chief of staff, who recommended that the middle road be used. Thothmes invoked the privilege of all commanders and disregarded the recommendation of his chief of staff. He moved against Megiddo by the northern road, which proved, in fact, ideal for his maneuver.

Modern military intelligence developed out of the gathering of topographical information which monopolized the interest of commanders in the nineteenth century. At that time, intelligence relating to terrain was considered more important than the knowledge of the nature and strength of foreign armies.

Today military surveys and the preparation and maintenance of maps and nautical charts still form a primary function of army and navy intelligence. Mapmaking is a continuous challenge to intelligence, an undertaking that never ceases, because the political boundaries and man-made changes of the

13

earth never cease to take place. "Man comes along," Colonel A. W. Masters of G-2 said, "and he makes changes in the roads, in the rail systems, and in the cities, and all of those things affect the military use of the map, so there have to be revisions." Maps used by the military establishment must be "adequate"—complete, up-to-date, legible, and accurate—or else they are not only useless but dangerous since they might mislead commanders who base plans on the information contained in them. "Many historical examples could be given," Colonel Masters said, "as to the effect of lack of maps or the effect of map errors." In actual fact, from its early wars to the Korean campaign, the United States has never gone to war with adequate maps. "The resulting cost in men and materiel would be difficult to assess," Colonel Masters said, "but it could be assumed that it has been considerable."

During the Second World War, the Army spent a yearly average of $80,000,000 on military surveys, topographic maps, and geodetic data. The current annual average is around $40,000,000. At the present time, there are 8,123 persons in the U. S. Army permanently absorbed by this highly specialized intelligence activity.

The U. S. Navy keeps about 7,000 nautical charts up to date and produces more than 1,000 new charts every year. On this intelligence activity alone, the Navy spends almost $10,000,000 a year.

Maps are difficult to make, and especially difficult today with certain sensitive areas closed to our mapmakers. Maps of these areas must be prepared from data supplied by costly intelligence and espionage. And even under favorable circumstances mapmaking is expensive and time-consuming: an average 1/25,000-scale military map covering an area of fifty-six square miles costs about $150,000 and requires two years to make.

General intelligence also includes information about other physical characteristics of countries, such as the potability of the water from streams or the composition of the soil. Before the Allied invasion of North Africa in 1942, information concerning the latter was urgently sought; when obtained, it led to a wholesale resoling of GI boots to adapt them to the specific nature of the soft African soil on the outer fringes of the Sahara Desert.

In addition to geography, geology, and hydrology, general intelligence is also concerned with the history of nations, particularly their wars and political fortunes, since it has been demonstrated that history does repeat itself. An ambitious historical study along these lines was undertaken by the American Navy in 1944-45. It was conducted by a branch of the Office of Naval Intelligence in preparation for a psychological warfare campaign, conducted by Captain (later Rear Admiral) Ellis M. Zacharias, to persuade the Japanese high command to surrender. Considering the way the Japanese had been fighting the war up to then, the idea that they would ever lay down their arms en masse seemed almost preposterous at the time. Their troops were severely indoctrinated against surrender. They were drilled in the Samurai tradition —in the ancient code of Bushido—which regarded surrender as a mortal shame, far worse than death. The behavior of many Japanese units in battle had reflected this indoctrination.

Information was sought on the behavior of the Japanese in defeat, and Nipponese history supplied the clues. While ancient and medieval Japan had engaged in only two foreign wars up to the time of the Meiji Restoration in the nineteenth century, its history showed an unbroken chain of struggles between individual clans. It was then found by the American specialists who sought this information that the defeated clan never died in battle. On the contrary, it always surrendered. This background information, which also described the formalities of surrender, was then applied in the Zacharias operations plan, and used in its execution.

Diplomatic information today matches military information in significance and is particularly important in a cold war in which no armies actually meet. It comprises data about the diplomatic establishment of individual nations, the personalities of their foreign ministers and foreign-service personnel, the practices and techniques of their diplomacy, their foreign policies and alliances, the manner in which they conduct negotiations, their conference techniques, details of protocol.

Britain in particular has been interested in diplomatic information for the conduct of her foreign relations, sometimes to an almost ludicrous degree. Prior to sending a diplomatic delegation to a Moroccan potentate in 1879, the British obtained detailed information on the customs of the Sultan's court and also about the Sultan himself. When this information revealed that the Sultan was inordinately superstitious, the English delegation was enlarged by the addition of Douglas Beaufort, scion of the famous family of magicians. His assignment was to perform certain tricks before the Sultan, in order to impress the ruler with the supernatural powers of Queen Victoria, thus softening him up for the diplomatic pourparler that followed.

In preparation for the Berlin conference of the Big Four

Foreign Ministers in January-February, 1954, the American State Department studied all the information on file about the conference habits of Foreign Minister Vyacheslav M. Molotov of the Soviet Union. To prepare himself for the Moscow conference in 1945, Secretary of State James F. Byrnes even studied Lenin's writings, especially his treatise on compromise.

The Soviet Foreign Ministry puts a premium on such information and regards the gathering of intelligence as the primary function of Russian diplomatic missions abroad, especially intelligence relating to the frictions between countries opposed to the U.S.S.R.

Political information is derived partly from diplomatic information, but it also includes data about the leading personalities of states, especially the chief executives, prime ministers, leaders of the opposition, and politicians in general, their character traits, associations, influence, and particularly gossip about scandals in which they might have been involved. Beyond that, political information consists of data concerning the political institutions and systems of individual countries, their philosophies and ideologies, political parties, electoral systems, the influence of minorities, and the vast areas of friction present in all political systems. Information about foreign frictions monopolized the attention of Hitler up to 1939, as long as he thought he would be able to carry out his plans of expansion without going to war.

Information of decisive importance along these lines came into his hands in the summer of 1939, during the convention of an international organization called the Nordic Federation, held in Lübeck. One of the delegates to that conference was a certain Major Vidkun Quisling of Norway, leader of an extreme rightist party, the Nasjonal Samling.

During the convention, contact was established between Quisling and Alfred Rosenberg, a Nazi publicist who functioned primarily as Hitler's chief friction expert. Quisling supplied information on the Norwegian armed forces and on his country's international policies, and then organized a Nazi underground in Norway to provide additional information, including data on the defense installations of the strategic port of Narvik. This information encouraged Hitler to invade Norway in April, 1940, and to base his operations plan on the support he expected to get from Quisling's party, which was opposed to Norway's national government to the point of aligning itself with a foreign power. Hitler's Norwegian enterprise, which added the word "quisling" to the dictionary, is

16

the perfect example of manipulating political friction in foreign countries on the basis of pertinent information.

In the twentieth century, economic information gained equal importance with military and diplomatic information. Such information covers a vast area and ranges from data on the fiscal policies of individual countries to the blueprints of patents. Of particular interest is information pertaining to the monetary condition of a country, its foreign trade, and especially its industries, natural resources, and agriculture. Information about labor is of special importance, since labor-management relations frequently produce vast areas of friction, with violent strife and bloody strikes occasionally leading to revolution. There is a reciprocal relationship between industrial and military information, not merely in the field of production for the armed forces and in the special area of war economy, but specifically in technological fields, which are important sources of information.

The location of war-essential plants is the primary concern of what is called "target" intelligence, upon which stategic bombing is completely dependent. It is assumed, today more than ever, that the elimination of an army's industrial base is certain to paralyze the army in the field, and an enormous amount of information is needed about the nature and location of the industries of other countries to enable an air force to interfere strategically in an all-out conflict.

Industrial intelligence was much in demand even before industries existed in the modern sense. In A.D. 673, a Byzantine fleet wrought havoc on the fleet of the Saracens, chiefly through the use of an unheard-of implement of war which came to be known as "Greek fire." This was a deadly incendiary compound which the Byzantine ships hurled at the vessels of the Saracens, setting them on fire, disabling and sinking them all.

The Saracens set out at once to obtain information about the new weapon, which may properly be called the atomic bomb of that age. They discovered that it was the invention of a Syrian architect who had migrated to Constantinople, but they could not obtain the secret of the compound itself. For the next four hundred years, all the enemies of Byzantium sought information on this wonderful implement of war, but to no avail. Its secret is still not completely known today, when fire is again used with telling effect in the improved flamethrowers of armies and in "napalm" bombs.

With the emergence of the people at large as the major factor in a nation's life, sociological information has gained increased importance. Such information includes detailed

17

demographic data of the exactitude of a census bureau's inquiry, material on all strata of populations and their relations with one another. It penetrates to a nation's soul, as it includes knowledge about the people's ideas, desires, ambitions, hopes, preferences, prejudices, frustrations, morale, race consciousness, aptitudes, even family patterns.

Such information was highly regarded in Germany during the thirties, when special efforts were made to prepare composite pictures of the social structures of Great Britain, France, and the United States. Social scientists were sent to these countries by the Psychological Branch of the German High Command to collect data on the various manifestations of the nations' social existence. A psychologist named Walter Beck came to the United States disguised as a refugee scholar. He was received with open arms and given a job at an eastern university. Under this cloak, he gathered information about the American people for a study he was supposed to prepare for the Psychological Branch of the Wehrmacht.

In the course of his investigations, Dr. Beck visited all parts of the United States and studied the peoples in the East, Middle West, South, and Far West. When he tried to estimate what sort of soldiers Americans would make, he was unable to form any conclusions, until he watched a college football game. There he thought he had found what he was looking for. When he compiled his report, he represented all Americans as football players. He emphasized in the report that Americans have a highly developed team spirit, that they are aggressive in contests, that they have tenacity, and, above all, that they bring a scientific approach to everything they do, from football to war. He was convinced that the old frontier spirit was still very much alive in the people of America, and cautioned against the tendency in high German circles to regard Americans as materialistic and decadent. On the contrary, Dr. Beck reported, they were idealistic and virile. He ended his report with the urgent recommendation that Hitler refrain from provoking the United States to war, and predicted that America would certainly be victorious in war, not only because of its vast industrial superiority, but also because of superior social factors which would come to the fore in an open conflict.

It is interesting to note that the scientist who was sent to Britain to prepare a similar study returned with identical conclusions, reached on the basis of totally different information. This specialist also advised against becoming involved in war with Britain. However, the psychologist who was sent to France predicted flatly that Germany would win easily in a war against France, no matter how powerful the French army might be, solely because of dominant social factors in the life of the French nation.

Cultural information has an immediate connection with social information, chiefly because it provides the data needed for the manipulation of peoples and public opinion by intangible means. Such data includes information about the press, radio, and television, as well as other media of communication; the arts and professions; and the intellectual stature of nations. In a special category of rapidly increasing importance is scientific information, demonstrated most dramatically in the development of the atomic bomb in the United States, Britain, and Canada, and in the eagerness of the Soviet Union to acquire information about this.

Scientific information is always at a premium. In 1938, a notorious professional spy named Frederick Duquesne endeared himself to the Nazis by his self-declared ability to supply such information. This man made a good living by peddling information to highest bidders, beginning a shady career in the Boer War when he worked against England, continuing it in World War I when he again acted against the British, and then topping it on the eve of World War II when he proposed to work on a substantial scale against the United States. The information he promised to supply was almost exclusively scientific in nature and included the formula for certain textiles to be used in Army uniforms to neutralize mustard gas, certain devices developed by the scientists of the International Telephone and Telegraph Company, and information on bacterial agents in warfare.

While Duquesne was a dangerous operative, much of his information was useless. There were others, however, who did succeed in uncovering eagerly sought-after details of certain scientific achievements. During World War II, the United States employed teams of scientists for intelligence missions, including the famous *Alsos* operation, whose aim was to uncover information about Germany's atomic developments. The cover name Alsos was chosen because it was the Greek word for grove—and Leslie Groves was the name of the American general who headed the Manhattan Project. The information Alsos brought back was reassuring: it showed bungling, departmental jealousies, government interference, and relatively little scientific achievement.

Only once were the operatives of Alsos really afraid that the Germans might have made important progress in the development of an atomic bomb. They discovered that the Germans were hoarding thorium, an element that could be used

19

in an A-bomb project in a well-advanced stage. From the moment of that discovery, the thorium mystery monopolized the attention of Alsos, since it might have held the key to some genuine and promising German effort. At last the thorium was traced to a certain German chemical firm, but nothing in this firm's set-up indicated that it was working on anything remotely resembling an atomic bomb. In actual fact, it was manufacturing toothpaste—thoriated toothpaste. In order to monopolize the market, this firm was hoarding all the thorium it could lay its hands on. This information about Operation Toothpaste was almost as important as if Alsos had found the thorium used in an A-bomb project, because it satisfied the Allies that the Germans were not using it for that threatening purpose.

It is quite obvious that information on the communication and transportation networks of foreign countries is of extreme importance in calculating the military potential of those countries. Comprehensive intelligence information is compiled on the rail nets, including such details as the number of tracks in railroad stations and marshaling yards and the location of switches and railroad crossings, in addition to major information about signal systems, junctions, key stations, and rolling stock. The importance of this information is demonstrated by the fact that in time of war a special corps of intelligence agents is assigned to its collection—people called "train watchers" in the lingo of intelligence. Their job is to observe the movement of troops and goods on rails, to record changes in the network, to keep track of schedules.

Like the weather report, the ordinary timetable is a casualty of war. It usually disappears on the day hostilities commence, since the movement of trains suddenly becomes military information to be carefully concealed from an enemy whose air force and sabotage troops are only too anxious to interfere with schedules.

The practical significance of such information was demonstrated in a most dramatic manner in June, 1944, during the Allied landings in France, when exact information about the French rail net enabled General Eisenhower to have the lines cut wherever it became necessary to retard the movement of German troops on their way to the Normandy battlefield. General Eisenhower later declared that the special operation based on this information was worth fifteen divisions in keeping the Germans away from the combat zone.

The state of chaos within the railway system became so serious that, by the beginning of July, 1944, it took the Germans eight days to go from the German-Swiss border to

Paris, a journey that normally requires seven hours. All told, nine German divisions were thus prevented from reaching the Normandy battlefields. When the 11th German Panzer Division was brought from the Russian front to reinforce the troops in France, it took them three times longer to cover the 450 kilometers in France than had been required to travel the 1,650 kilometers separating Russia from the French frontier. In order to effect this delaying action, the Allies needed information about the French rail network before they could organize the little band of rail cutters and bridge wreckers within the French resistance movement. Without adequate and accurate information, in which the exact location of a single switch often assumed key importance, the attempt to destroy German communications would have been doomed to failure, if it could have been made at all.

Last but not least, intelligence needs information about intelligence. Since the organized collection of information is among a nation's most competitive activities, those engaged professionally in intelligence work are never idle but must try forever to infiltrate competitive organizations. Such infiltration is difficult and risky and is virtually impossible without the most detailed and up-to-the-minute information about the opponent's organization. This information usually includes data about the opponent's method of collecting information, the items he is interested in (sometimes called the "shopping list" in the business), and, above all else, his personnel, both in the home office and in the field.

It is at this point that those who collect information may be most effectively destroyed. For knowledge of the opponent's intelligence enables one to manipulate information, to conceal certain items and dilute others, to put out bogus information, and so to destroy the value of information by destroying its accuracy. However, inaccurate information will occasionally avalanche and involve those who disseminate it as well as the intended victims.

The Need To Know

Obviously, a vast amount and enormous variety of information is needed to guard a nation against surprises—strategic attacks like that at Pearl Harbor, diplomatic coups like the conclusion of the pact between Stalin and Hitler in 1939, or economic moves like the devaluation of key currencies, as of

21

the franc in 1930 and the pound sterling in 1949—and to supply the data on the basis of which a nation can form its policies, draw up its plans, and organize its moves.

Information is needed by the governments of all nations, and within these governments there are departments designed primarily for dealing with intelligence in all its forms.

Policy makers—the President of the United States, the Prime Minister of the United Kingdom, the premiers of France or Germany, and a few men in the Kremlin—require intelligence to carry out their work. Yet intelligence rarely goes directly to them. Intelligence services normally collect such vast amounts of information that no president, prime minister, chief of state, or secretary of state could possibly examine and evaluate it all and be able to distinguish between the essential and the trivial.

All this information, essential and trivial, factual and conjectural, has to pass through a large and intricate machine, which processes the raw material, filtering it and culling from it those individual items having a direct bearing on the policy under study by the policy makers at the time.

Let us see how this process works by looking at a specific example of some historical importance. In December, 1944, the policy makers of the Western Allies were deeply concerned with the seemingly stubborn determination of Japan to fight on to the bitter end, despite the gradual weakening of her war-making capacity in the face of our victories. The Joint Chiefs of Staff were extremely pessimistic and advised the White House that an invasion of the Japanese main islands would be necessary to subdue that country. They were convinced that Japan would never surrender. This gloomy advice was accompanied by the recommendation that the policies of the United States and Britain be based on the assumption that the war in Japan would continue until 1948 or 1949. This somber estimate of the situation was based not so much on hard military intelligence as on the innate cautiousness of General George C. Marshall, which dominated the Joint Chiefs of Staff and which had great influence with President Roosevelt and Secretary of War Henry L. Stimson. Both President Roosevelt and Mr. Stimson were deeply impressed with General Marshall's estimate and developed a policy for the fight against Japan which seemed to complicate the war and prolong it.

The results of this policy were the costly invasions of Iwo Jima and Okinawa. A large-scale invasion of Kyushu, one of the main islands of Japan, was scheduled to take place in the fall of 1945 with a force of millions and casualties estimated at one million men. The official Anglo-American attitude stiffened toward Japan and especially toward the Emperor.

These were tremendously important decisions in themselves, yet they were by no means all. Again upon the advice of the Joint Chiefs, a policy decision was reached to invite the Soviet Union into the Pacific war and to make considerable concessions in Europe for her participation in Manchuria. In its consequences, this policy had more serious results than any directly concerning Japan.

Whatever information lay at the bottom of these policy decisions, it was inadequate, one-sided, and highly biased. It was almost exclusively military information, consisting of such orthodox forms of intelligence as the order of battle and combat narratives, which are the chief sources of a *military* commander's information.

In December, 1944, however, a great quantity of political, diplomatic, and economic information arrived in Washington which should have placed the Joint Chiefs' estimates in an entirely different light. Included in this information was intelligence from two excellently informed diplomatic sources: the Vatican, and the envoy of a neutral country stationed in Tokyo. Both supplied the information that the Emperor himself had decided to explore the prospects of surrender, and that a peace party existing within Japan's highest echelons enjoyed the support of the Emperor and of top-ranking Naval officers.

The first definite information on this score reached Washington on Christmas Eve of 1944. From then on, additional evidence poured in. A special branch of the Army obtained reliable information indicating that Japan was being strangled by our blockade and was rapidly reaching the end of the road. Information was then obtained from a number of sources about Japanese peace-feelers, including direct appeals from Tokyo to Moscow asking the Kremlin to act as a mediator between Japan and the United States.

While the information on hand was considerable in volume and impressively persuasive, it was scattered among a great number of agencies. Some of it was in the Office of Naval Intelligence; some was in the Army's so-called Magic operation, which translated the codes of foreign governments; some was in the Office of Strategic Services; and still more was in a special intelligence branch of the Army attached to the assistant secretary's own office. Strangely enough, no information was forthcoming from the State Department, which is normally the chief clearing-house of diplomatic intelligence.

23

And there was no centralized agency that could have coordinated this scattered information.

Then, in February, 1945, an organ was created by Secretary of the Navy James Forrestal to concentrate this information, to evaluate it, and to prepare the necessary recommendations for the policy makers. To head this organization, Captain Zacharias was ordered to Washington. He was ideally suited for the assignment, since he had had three decades of intelligence experience and was the U.S. Navy's foremost expert on Japan. From then on, the scattered information became centralized. Captain Zacharias summarized the information in twelve major points, reducing it from reams of reports to a single closely typed page for the eyes of the President. When the information was processed for the policy maker, this is how it looked:

INFORMATION: (a) The Japanese main islands are now isolated *except from the continent* and are faced with threats from all directions.

(b) Our present and future position outside of the Japanese main islands will afford means of exerting all coercive pressure necessary.

(c) Certain members of the Japanese High Command realize that the war is irretrievably lost; the others of the High Command recognize the seriousness of the present situation, which is bound to deteriorate in the future.

(d) The plans for victory of the Japanese High Command are contingent upon continued unity of thought between the [Imperial] Army and Navy and upon an all-sacrificing prosecution of the war.

(e) Great conflict of opinion exists within the High Command as to the past, present and future conduct of the war.

(f) Field commanders in highest echelons are blaming the High Command for inept leadership in the war.

(g) Great difference of opinion and dissension exists among commanders in the field and at sea.

(h) For the first time since the Russo-Japanese war, the Premier has been instructed to participate in the deliberations of the High Command, thus establishing an immediate link between the political and military leadership of the empire, carefully separated since 1886.

(i) For the first time in 24 years, criticism of the government and the High Command is openly voiced.

(j) The Axis pact of September 27, 1940, was signed by Japan by the narrowest margin and only after extensive bribery in Tokyo and distribution of large sums of money.

(k) There are a great many highly placed individuals in Japan who realize that war with the United States meant "the finish of the Japanese empire and a great loss to the United States."

(l) It is known that foreign broadcasts are monitored in Japan and transcripts have a comparatively wide distribution.

24

Captain Zacharias then proceeded to make a policy recommendation on the basis of this information and also to draft an operations plan for the execution of that policy. This policy goal was worded as follows:

To make unnecessary an opposed landing in the Japanese main islands, by weakening the will of the High Command, by effecting cessation of hostilities, and by bringing about unconditional surrender with the least possible loss of life to us consistent with early termination of the war.

This summary of information, the policy recommendation, and the operations plan were then submitted to the Secretary of the Navy and through him to President Roosevelt in the White House. The document was on the President's desk at the time of his death. He had made a few penciled changes in it, a sign that he had read and considered it, but he never approved it. On May 8, 1945, however, it was studied by President Truman and, then, part of the Zacharias plan, based on hard information, became the policy of the United States government.

This, then, is an example of how information is coordinated, collated, orchestrated, evaluated, and summarized for presentation to the policy makers, and how such information then influences the major policy decisions of nations. Now let us see how an incidental piece of intelligence resulted in an isolated but major strategic move. In 1942, a prominent political scientist of the University of Pennsylvania, Dr. Robert Strausz-Hupe, was working in Washington on certain population studies in which President Roosevelt was personally interested. He and his staff surveyed all problems of peoples, including, of course, the question of food supplies.

The problem of food supplies in Japan was given special attention, since it was early recognized as one of the bottlenecks of the entire Japanese war effort. Dr. Strausz-Hupe surveyed all aspects of the problem and came to an important subsidiary problem: the question of agricultural fertilizer. He examined the sources of Japan's fertilizer supply and found that most of it came from the French possessions in North Africa.

Our invasion of French Morocco and Algeria and our control of the sea lanes cut off this source, but Strausz-Hupe found upon studying certain information emerging from inside Japan that there was no shortage of fertilizers in Japan, despite the loss of the North African sources. He then proceeded to ascertain all possible new sources of supply. He succeeded in pinpointing a Pacific island called Nauru, the surface of which abounded in leached guanos and phosphatized rocks. He assumed that supplies from Nauru were compensating for Japan's lost fertilizer imports from North Africa.

This information was then communicated to the military authorities, with the recommendation that Nauru be subjected to heavy aerial attack to knock it out as Japan's source of fertilizer supply and thereby to interfere with the food production of the country. The soundness of Strausz-Hupe's assumption was established when information was gained through aerial reconnaissance. Navy scouting planes took many pictures of the island and the usual examination of these aerial photographs revealed a number of interesting items. First, they showed a cluster of new installations. Second, they showed a number of cargo vessels loading at newly constructed piers. Third, they produced convincing evidence that Nauru had become the major source of Japan's fertilizer supply.

This information was then submitted to the Joint Chiefs, with a definite recommendation of action against Nauru. An operations plan was drafted and its execution assigned to the Navy. Energetic bombardment followed, and soon Nauru was knocked out. In time, information was obtained that showed a gradual deterioration of Japan's fertilizer stocks and a concurrent crisis in food supplies. The information that lay at the basis of this important operation was obtained by the orthodox means of library research and the unorthodox methods of aerial reconnaissance. The two combined to supply the intelligence needed for an important military operation. Of course, the details of the intelligence were never presented to the Joint Chiefs. They were merely given the results of the intelligence study and the findings of the reconnaissance, together with the recommendation based on both.

The far-reaching repercussions of the Zacharias and Strausz-Hupe operations, then, illustrate the need for knowledge of other countries in such areas as political, economic, diplomatic, social, and cultural matters. The Zacharias estimate was based on up-to-date information and also on a thorough knowledge of modern Japanese history. The summary combined political and military information, but, more important, it supplied data on the mood of the people, which is a social aspect, and on historic backgrounds, which is a general aspect of intelligence. The Strausz-Hupe estimate was based on information about certain basic needs of the population, on economic and geographical data, and on a great

26

number of related factors across the entire spectrum of intelligence.

In the political area, knowledge of important personalities of the country under study is of crucial importance. This is called biographical intelligence. This type of information may be collected separately or within the various specialized intelligence systems. Thus, the diplomatic establishment has its own biographical file on foreign personalities, quite separate from the military establishment's, which maintains dossiers on the leading commanders of foreign armies, navies, and air forces. In lower echelons, biographical information is accumulated even on tactical personnel, such as crew members of U-boats and officers of companies in the combat zones. Information of this kind enabled us during World War II to address appeals to officers of all ranks opposing our forces and to make these appeals very personal indeed. A broadcast to a young lieutenant who commanded a machine-gun nest in Okinawa might mention his wife and children in Japan, and broadcasts to U-boat personnel could make use of similar intimate data, culled from the mass of biographical information accumulated in Britain's Division of Naval Intelligence and the U.S. Office of Naval Intelligence.

While such tactical exploitation of biographical data is useful, this information assumes decisive importance when used on the top level of national governments. With Stalin's death it became imperative to know as much as possible about the personality of the man who would succeed him. Intelligence in the past has supplied a picture of all personalities within the Kremlin. Certain information was available about all the probable successors to Stalin, including data on their character traits and personal lives. Consequently, intelligence did not have to start from scratch when the appraisal of Stalin's successor became necessary and urgent.

Previous intelligence operations had given a cursory picture of the men who were likely to take his place, among them Georgi Malenkov. Once Malenkov was designated as Stalin's successor, intelligence concentrated on him. Scattered data was pulled together and orchestrated until the picture of Malenkov appeared in sharp focus.

This information is needed because the personalities of political leaders play a major role in the formulation of policies. Before Roosevelt went to Teheran, he engaged in an elaborate effort to find out everything he could about the personality and character traits of Stalin. All intelligence agencies had to supply data for this study. In addition, Roosevelt interviewed persons who knew Stalin and tried to find out from them certain specific aspects of his character. He then based his whole approach to Stalin on this data. He became supremely confident that he would be able to "handle" Stalin, because he knew not only his ideas, but also his whims, methods of negotiation, and various indelible personal traits.

And so, although information may not be of immediate importance, it must nevertheless be on file when needed, if only to round out a picture and thus aid in the formulation of policies and the direction of moves. Information may be available about certain mines in East Germany, but it need not be "live" information required for immediate action. Then, specific information may become available that will serve as tinder to start up the dormant fire. This information may reach us in a variety of forms and from a variety of sources, occasionally even from what would be normally regarded as a low tactical source.

Thus, an exile from East Germany who has worked in one of the mines may arrive in West Berlin with information that uranium has been discovered there. He knew it at first hand. He himself worked in that mine until his escape. Since uranium is essential in the Soviet Union's atomic developments, the mine found to contain this vital raw material acquires strategic importance. In such a case, all the available information is pulled together and additional information is obtained. This information may not be needed for immediate action against the mine. But it supplies crucial data for a greater pattern that shows, for example, the status and progress of atomic developments in the U.S.S.R.

We have seen before how important topographical information is, data on terrain and hydrographic information consisting of exact charts of seas and inland waters. The Sicilian charts lay neglected for decades in the hydrographic branches of the U.S. and Royal navies. But, when the decision was reached to invade Italy in 1943, these charts came to life and supplied much of the essential data needed in the drafting of the operations plan, actually influencing the operation itself. This type of information was considered so important that during the war special teams were sent surreptitiously into the Pacific area to acquire such data under the very noses of the enemy.

An isolated bit of scientific information may start a chain reaction in intelligence that explodes in a major operation which influences the course of history. On March 28, 1945, a go-between of the Soviet intelligence network in Canada had a luncheon meeting with one of his informants, a young scientist named Durnford Smith. The go-between tried to get information from Smith about the latest radar developments, but the scientist told him, "Radar is no longer important. What is really important today is the Anglo-American-Canadian effort to develop atomic energy for military purposes."

This was the first word Soviet intelligence in Canada had received on the momentous decision of the Western Allies to build an atomic bomb. The go-between reported Smith's remark to a Colonel Zabutin, resident director of Soviet intelligence in Canada, who in turn reported it to General Kuznetsov, director of the Center, as the U.S.S.R.'s central intelligence service is intimately called. The information was then called to the attention of Stalin himself and the enormous intelligence machinery of the Soviet Union was set in motion to acquire the details of this important development.

The Canadian branch of the network was instructed to obtain samples of the uranium used in the atomic bomb. The American branch was ordered to procure certain technical information: the scientific principles of the bomb, its trigger mechanism, its blueprints. Others were instructed to get information about the policy developments within the Allied governments in the wake of this historic discovery.

From scientists like Klaus Fuchs, Alan Nunn May, and Bruno Pontecorvo, from technicians like David Greenglass, from diplomatic informants whose identities are still unknown, Soviet intelligence received all the information Russia needed to determine the country's policies in the light of this development and to supply her own scientists with the necessary process for building their own A-bomb. All this was accomplished within three months. Since information is really useful only if available when needed, speed of acquisition is an essential aspect of intelligence. The success of Soviet intelligence was due to a perfect combination of the factors of accuracy, explicitness, and speed—the true criteria of good intelligence.

Scattered information is useful by itself. But to make it dynamic, it has to be pulled together piece by piece and developed to form distinct patterns for the enlightenment of higher echelons. This coordination of information is an important function of intelligence.

All intelligence is pulled together in concentrated form in a closely guarded and highly restricted area within the military establishments, foreign offices, and the executive departments of chiefs of states. This area is called the Map Room, not only because it contains a collection of maps, but because much of the intelligence accumulating there is spelled out on maps and charts to visualize and relate it directly to the areas involved, and because huge maps dominate the interior decoration of these rooms. In international emergencies the Map Room is called War Room or Plot Room; that of the Joint Chiefs of Staff in Washington is called Situation Room.

It is a place of intelligence coordination where skilled officers form patterns of topical information on a minute-by-minute basis to the staccato rhythm of tickers. It has its own communication set-up and small army of dispatch riders who rush reports and estimates to this terminal nerve center of a nation's intelligence network. To the Map Room troop the policy makers and strategists to acquaint themselves with the situation as far as it concerns them. They review the scene presented on the maps and charts and listen to briefings by area specialists and experts who are called in to augment or explain the information supplied by the staff. The Map Room produces a vibrant thrill all its own. In it the humdrum world of intelligence acquires dynamism and drama with undertones reminiscent of Hollywood's concept of this romantic activity.

Another coordinating function of intelligence is the preparation of summaries and estimates, including those prepared for the highest policy makers and strategists. They are called "national estimates." This particular function is performed by carefully chosen specialists trained explicitly for this activity, or by committees in which several intelligence agencies are represented. In the summary or estimate intelligence reaches its most concentrated form and attains direct kinetic influence. The crucial importance of this function is clearly recognized by all countries. The Soviet Union maintains a special intelligence agency for this function, the so-called Confidential Bureau situated within the Kremlin and headed by one of the U.S.S.R.'s outstanding intelligence experts, at the time of this writing General Panyushkin, a former ambassador to the United States and China.

In Britain during the Second World War, the preparation of intelligence summaries for the War Cabinet was a job assigned to Professor Arnold Toynbee, the eminent historian. In the United States, summaries and estimates are prepared on various levels, most important being those handled by the Joint Intelligence Group of the Joint Chiefs, and by a special branch of CIA, headed by a Deputy Director for Estimates. The top-ranking official in CIA in charge of estimates is Dr. Sherman Kent, a former professor of history at Yale. The estimates prepared by CIA are presented to the

President and the National Security Council by the Director himself, who stands by to supply additional information or details if they are needed.

The Organization of Intelligence

Although the importance of information was recognized even in antiquity and organizations have existed throughout history which specialized in the management of information, intelligence remained a haphazard, improvised activity until the nineteenth century, when so many aspects of man's world changed.

Retreating from Moscow, Napoleon, traveling at top speed, covered the distance between Vilna and Paris—a distance of 1,400 miles—in 312 hours. This had been the speed of communication since time immemorial. This was the maximum rate of travel between Rome and Gaul in the first century A.D., and between Sardis and Susa in the fourth century before Christ. Then suddenly this classic rate was speeded up. Striking new inventions were added to facilitate human intercourse. The coming of the railway and the steamboat accelerated travel. In 1832, the electric telegraph came into being. In 1851, the first submarine cable was laid between England and France.

Man's interests were broadened and his powers enhanced; and the importance of intelligence in turn increased. The progress of technology improved its facilities. Gradually intelligence became an organized effort, promoted and stimulated by ambitious rulers to aid in not only the formulation but the execution of their plans. Napoleon III made political intelligence a permanent fixture in his government. In Britain, diplomatic and economic intelligence became fixed instruments of national policy. Then, during the Civil War in the United States, military intelligence, too, acquired organized form.

Although domestic in scope, the Civil War was really the first modern war in history. It applied for the first time many of the technological means developed since the turn of the century. Troops were moved by rail. The signal corps utilized the telegraph. A balloon was employed for aerial observation. Ironclad ships revolutionized naval tactics, and a practical step was made toward the development of the submarine. Major victories were scored simply because information

31

was available to the commanders and they could make their arrangements with exact knowledge of the enemy's plans, dispositions, and strength.

The first great triumph of modern intelligence was General Beauregard's victory over McDowell at Bull Run. The source of this intelligence was an aristocratic widow named Rose Greenhow, who maintained a fashionable salon on Washington's Eye Street. She was a descendant of Dolly Madison and a relative of Stephen A. Douglas. Politicians, diplomats, and generals flocked to her parties. She picked up whatever information she could and sent her reports to the generals of the Confederacy. The information about McDowell's plans came to her from one of her regular guests, a Union general. It was promptly forwarded to Beauregard, who used it in planning for his subsequent victory at Bull Run.

Recognition of the decisive value of intelligence persuaded both sides to establish active intelligence services. The American example was followed abroad. Britain established its Military Intelligence Service in the immediate wake of the American Civil War, then added a Naval Intelligence Service in 1887. In 1866, military intelligence was institutionalized in Prussia in preparation for the campaigns against Austria and France. France followed suit with the establishment of the Second Bureau of the General Staff, and Russia with the Seventh Bureau of the General Staff, both specializing in the collection of all forms of information for military and politico-diplomatic ends.

Today all countries have their intelligence services. They may be different in their organizations, efficiency, and methods, but they all have the same three basic functions.

As we have already seen, in the various examples listed above, these functions are:

1. the collection or procurement of information;
2. the evaluation of the information, which then becomes intelligence; and
3. the dissemination of intelligence to those who need it.

There is also a fourth function, called by the generic term counterintelligence. This activity is dedicated to the concealment and protection of one's own information from the intelligence operations of an adversary. Heretofore we have dealt with a single form of intelligence, the gathering of necessary information about other countries, called positive intelligence.

This fourth function, counterintelligence, is known as negative intelligence, and may be defined as the effort to protect our own secrets and to apprehend those who try to gain unauthorized access to them. This is the defensive function of intelligence. In most countries of the world, these two activities are joined under one roof. Britain's Military Intelligence, the famous MI, has a branch called MI-5 which is the United Kingdom's major negative-intelligence agency. In France, the Second Bureau practices both positive and negative intelligence. In Germany, the now defunct *Abwehr*, as the High Command's central intelligence service was called, had three major departments: one for positive intelligence, another for such intelligence operations as sabotage and subversive activities, and a third for negative intelligence.

The United States and the Soviet Union are the only major countries in the world today which keep these two activities apart. The Intelligence Department of the Red Army, which is the Kremlin's *de facto* central intelligence agency, specializes exclusively in positive intelligence, while other agencies are maintained for negative intelligence.

In the United States, the top-ranking intelligence service is the Central Intelligence Agency, in which positive intelligence predominates. Negative intelligence is assigned to the CIC and the Federal Bureau of Investigation which, in turn, are not intended to conduct any positive intelligence.

At this point we are concerned with positive intelligence, and with the bureaucratic and less melodramatic aspects of intelligence proper. When information is procured solely by surreptitious means, by secret agents who disguise their true missions, the activity is called espionage. Reports of spies form an integral part of the intelligence summary, but spies only rarely represent an integral part of the inner intelligence organization. We will deal with espionage and negative intelligence in later chapters.

The purpose of a modern intelligence service was spelled out most lucidly by Allen W. Dulles, director of the American Central Intelligence Agency. This important service, which represents the most efficient centralization of intelligence functions ever attempted in modern times, came into existence after World War II, when the need for such an organization became evident. The CIA was established under the National Security Council by the National Security Act of 1947, and was approved on July 26, 1947. CIA itself was placed within the framework of the National Security Council. The duties of the Council are "to assess and appraise the objectives, commitments, and risks of the United States in relation to our actual and potential military power, in the interest of national security, for the purpose of making recommendations to the President; and to consider policies on matters of common interest to the departments and agencies of the Government concerned with the national security, and to make recommendations to the President."

The primary function of the Central Intelligence Agency, then, is to supply the data that the National Security Council needs for these recommendations to the President. According to Mr. Dulles, the Central Intelligence Agency performs five interrelated functions, described by him in what may be regarded as the classic definition of the purpose of a central intelligence service:

For the purpose of coordinating the intelligence activities of the several Government departments and agencies in the interest of national security, the Agency, under direction of the National Security Council:

1. Advises the National Security Council in matters concerning such intelligence activities of the Government departments and agencies as relate to national security.

2. Makes recommendations to the National Security Council for the coordination of such intelligence activities of the departments and agencies of the Government as relate to national security.

3. Correlates and evaluates intelligence relating to the national security, and provides for the appropriate dissemination of such intelligence within the Government using, where appropriate, existing agencies and facilities.

4. Performs, for the benefit of existing intelligence agencies, such additional services of common concern as the National Security Council determines can be more efficiently accomplished centrally.

5. Performs such other functions and duties related to intelligence affecting the national security as the National Security Council may from time to time direct.

The Central Intelligence Agency is not the only intelligence service of the United States Government. There are special intelligence services within the Army, Navy, and Air Force, and scattered among other government departments. But the Central Intelligence Agency is the top-ranking intelligence service of the United States, if only because it serves the highest organs of the state and has a dominant influence, through the information it supplies, on the recommendations to the President, from which the policies and actions of the United States then emerge.

As Mr. Dulles pointed out, collection, evaluation, and dissemination are the major functions of the Central Intelligence Agency, as they are of most modern intelligence services.

To perform these functions, intelligence services operate

with carefully drawn tables of organization. These are sometimes quite elaborate, as was the case with Germany's *Abwehr,* active during Hitler's reign, which had a labyrinth of departments, sections, divisions, and subdivisions, and employed 15,000 persons at its peak in 1938. The CIA is also organized along elaborate lines, with different divisions for the conduct of various forms of intelligence, for evaluation, for clandestine activities, and for distribution. Hanson W. Baldwin, military editor for *The New York Times,* estimated that it employs from 9,000 to 15,000 persons.

Intelligence organizations have a tendency to grow around their waists and to put on weight as they get older. However, experience shows that smaller and more tightly organized services are capable of functioning more efficiently, since they have less waste, duplication, and bureaucratic diffusion, none of which is conducive to effective intelligence work. My own experience convinces me that the smaller an intelligence organization is, the better it will function, provided, of course, that its personnel is first-class.

On many grounds, the PID, or Political Intelligence Division of Her Britannic Majesty's Foreign Office, is the most efficiently organized intelligence service of all. Supervised by the Permanent Under-Secretary of State for Foreign Affairs and headed by its own director, usually a man of exceptional qualifications, this branch of the Foreign Office is small and compact, serving as a clearing-house of information by making use of the various regional and functional divisions of the mother department.

Britain's Military Intelligence, the MI, is organized into about twelve branches (the number of branches varies with exigencies), in which the various intelligence functions are handled by specialists. As we have already seen, MI-5, quartered in the War Office in Whitehall, specializes in negative intelligence, under a civilian head. MI-8 specializes in so-called communication intelligence, i.e., the reading and translating of foreign codes and ciphers. MI-11 is in charge of clandestine or "black" propaganda. A semi-autonomous branch, called Special Intelligence, has supervision over strategic espionage and over the more secret phases of intelligence work. It is usually headed by an Army general, who is regarded as one of the top-ranking personalities within the British intelligence network.

In addition to PID and MI, Britain has at least thirteen additional intelligence agencies, including the Admiralty's Division of Naval Intelligence and the Air Ministry's intelligence department. Britain's counterpart of CIA is the Joint Intelligence Bureau of the Ministry of Defense, specializing in coordination, analysis, and evaluation, rather than in collection. It is headed by a Director under whom are a Deputy Director, three Assistant Directors, seven Principal Research Officers, twenty-one Senior Research Officers, and their staffs. The Joint Intelligence Bureau maintains a special branch for high-level political and military intelligence in the secret (or espionage) category. A majority of the department heads in JIB are senior officers of the armed forces. The primary function of JIB is to supply policy and strategic intelligence to the Cabinet together with national estimates.

In the Soviet Union, this function is performed by "RU" or Intelligence Department of the Red Army, situated in an old baroque palace at 19 Znamensky in Moscow. It is headed by a colonel general, who has the title of Director, and a major general with the title of Deputy Director. Under them are several major regional divisions, in charge of colonels, each with the title of Organizer. It also has a number of functional branches. This Department is called "the Center" in Soviet intelligence parlance.

The different regional divisions specialize in given areas, as the Western Hemisphere, the Far East and South Asia, Western Europe, and so on. Within each, individual countries are handled by subdivisions. Among functional branches are the Communications Branch, which handles the Bureau's own lines of communications, the Cryptographic Branch, which specializes in the translation of codes and ciphers of foreign governments, and the Authentication Branch, which supplies forged documents, manufactures bogus passports, and performs other functions similar to those of any other intelligence service.

There is also a semi-autonomous division called the Political Division, under the personal supervision of the Director, and charged with the evaluation of incoming intelligence.

In the United States, intelligence services are also organized along regional and functional lines, which means that they have separate branches for individual countries and others for the various technical functions of an intelligence service. The U.S. Office of Naval Intelligence, for example, has two major divisions, one specializing in positive intelligence, the other in negative intelligence or counterintelligence.

At the positive end, the ONI has a chief and a deputy chief, under whom there are major divisions for foreign intelligence, for technological intelligence, and for special activities, such as interpretation of documents, prisoner interrogation, psychological warfare, and similar functions. The foreign intelligence division is organized by desks, the major navies of the world each having its own desk, while the minor ones are lumped together under single officers. Communications intelligence is separated from ONI. It is handled by the Navy's Bureau of Communications, which has a special division for the reading and translation of foreign codes and ciphers. This is one of the most efficient intelligence organizations of its kind in the world.

The table of organization of central intelligence services is itself classified information, but we know from the Office of Strategic Services that the positive intelligence work of such central intelligence authorities is organized in three major divisions. One is concerned with research and analysis, or the exploitation of reference material in the public domain. The other is secret intelligence, which is engaged in the collection of information by surreptitious means. The third is morale operations, which is a branch designed to conduct propaganda in all its known shades, white, gray, and black.

The CIA itself is organized into five major divisions. Three of them collect or procure information by the various means of intelligence, both overt and covert; one conducts research and analysis and indexes evaluated information; and one division appraises all incoming information and prepares estimates on a daily, weekly, and monthly basis. These are complex functions, and the complexity of modern intelligence is reflected even in the physical set-up of CIA. It occupies more than twenty buildings and warehouses in Washington, some housing offices which in outward appearance resemble any Washington government office, others accommodating the various training establishments and the diversified apparatus without which no efficient intelligence organization can function.

Because the problems of positive intelligence are entirely different from those of negative intelligence, both functions operate best as separate organizations. Furthermore, the combination of both activities in the hands of one director might tempt him to use his organization, with its enormous power, to exploit the liberties of his fellow citizens.

The ideal central intelligence service should be headed by a director general, with three deputy directors to head the three major divisions of the organization: one to be in charge of information procurement, another in charge of evaluation and distribution, and the third in charge of administration.

The deputy director for procurement would thus direct a considerable organization of his own, in which basic separations are made between intelligence proper, secret intelligence, and intelligence operations. The first is concerned with research and analysis, i.e., the exploitation of published material and references accessible publicly, the monitoring of foreign broadcasts, the study of foreign newspapers and magazines, liaison with other governmental and private agencies collecting information, and the interrogation of citizens returning from travels abroad. This division should maintain a picture library, a very important tool of effective intelligence. Even amateur snapshots of such open and innocent scenes as bathing beaches often contribute essential topographic and hydrographic information.

Secret intelligence would logically handle undercover work or the acquisition of confidential material not easily accessible. It would direct outright espionage and would have as one of its tasks the job of infiltrating foreign intelligence organizations. It would also prepare, within its own organization, the technical facilities needed for undercover work and supply whatever documentation or authentication might be needed for secret agents working in the field.

Intelligence operations means exactly what the term denotes: the operational use of intelligence. It functions in five major branches. The business of one is liaison with friendly foreign organizations whose cooperation is essential for this kind of work. The second is in charge of sabotage operations. The third is devoted to the organization of guerrilla warfare, the supplying of tactical commanders, weapons instructors, radio operators, and other technical personnel essential for guerrilla action behind the enemy's lines. The fourth specializes in psychological warfare, while the fifth conducts conspiratorial warfare, or what may be called the dynamic subversion of an opponent's political organization.

An evaluation branch, headed by its own deputy director, would have important functions, including the publication of intelligence reports which might be of interest to wider circles within the government organization; for example, combat narratives, prisoner interrogation transcripts, analyses, and the like, and periodicals such as the brilliant *Weekly Intelligence Report* of the Admiralty's Division of Naval Intelligence, or the American *O.N.I. Weekly*. A special branch on a high level would be in charge of intelligence summaries, in which information is pulled together for the benefit of the policy makers.

A major section within this division should be responsible for the vital task of getting the evaluated information into the hands of those who could make the best use of it. This division would also have a liaison branch for the enlistment of experts and specialists needed for the best possible evaluation of individual items of intelligence. It would also serve as a link to the evaluators in other intelligence agencies, including those maintained within the military establishment.

The deputy director in charge of administration would handle the general management of the whole service (CIA actually has a General Manager), and supervise personnel, security, and finances, which assume special importance in an intelligence organization in which substantial funds are handled confidentially.

Two important activities of the intelligence service might also be placed under the deputy director for administration. One is training and indoctrination, which should be a subsection of personnel. The other is communications, which is not concerned with the translation of foreign codes and ciphers, but solely with the maintenance of the organization's own lines of communications. This branch is best placed centrally in administration where it is easily accessible to all those dependent upon its facilities.

Internal efficiency in an intelligence service is of exceptional importance for smooth and fast operation and is essential to effectiveness. Such efficiency might not be possible in an organization that overflows its banks, and consequently the diversification of the various activities must not be taken to mean that an intelligence service should have a great many employees in each function of the basic organization.

My experience in the Special Warfare Branch of ONI during World War II persuaded me that relatively few people are needed to make an intelligence organization efficient and effective, if the right people can be found for the right jobs. Thus Op-16-W, as the Special Warfare Branch was called within ONI, had an officer in charge, plus an executive officer who handled all administrative matters and supervised all activities. The branch had one officer in charge of liaison with operational agencies, and another to serve as a link to collection agencies. The latter doubled as a radio commentator, addressing German U-boat crews several times a week during the war.

Three regional sections, or "desks," were then maintained, one for Germany, another for Italy, and a third for Japan. The German desk consisted of three persons; the Italian desk, a single WAVE officer; the Japanese desk, two officers and three civilians.

The whole branch shared a single yeoman and two civilian stenographers. Its total annual budget amounted to less than the purchase price of two torpedoes.

Yet this branch was engaged in both the collection and the evaluation of intelligence, and also in various intelligence operations. It functioned efficiently and effectively, probably because it was small and closely coordinated.

In intelligence, quality is far more important than quantity, especially in organization.

In the field, an intelligence service may assume various forms. It may be organized within the offices of so-called service attachés, i.e., military, naval, and air attachés, or be set up as independent units, serving as foreign branches of the home office. Such organizations are usually headed by resident directors and maintain branches of their own, either to procure information about the country to which they are assigned or to stimulate the flow of information by developing and cultivating informants.

The Price of Intelligence

How much does intelligence cost or, to put it pragmatically, how much do nations spend on this important instrument of policy and security? It is quite difficult to answer this question in specific terms, because most countries prefer to keep their intelligence budgets under wraps. A distinction must also be made between the costs of orthodox intelligence, which may be fairly low, and the price of secret intelligence, which may be substantial. It is impossible to separate the budget of straight intelligence from expenditures on espionage, so the following account of the financial aspects of the trade will explain both.

In Elizabethan England, Sir Francis Walsingham had constant financial trouble maintaining his secret service and actually bankrupted himself in the end by investing his own money when he could squeeze no more funds from the thrifty queen. Cromwell, unlike the queen, expended large sums on his intelligence service as was attested by Samuel Pepys, who wrote in his diary on February 14, 1668, "Secretary Morrice did this day in the House, when they talked of intelligence, say that he was allowed but £700 a year for intelligence, whereas, in Cromwell's time, he [Cromwell] did allow £70,000 a year for it."

The financial affairs of today's British secret service emerge from obscurity just once a year, on Budget Day in the House of Commons. The Budget includes appropriations for "Her

Majesty's Foreign and Other Secret Services." In 1954 this was item No. 21 in Class I of the central government's appropriations under "Civil Estimates and Supplementary Estimates." It amounted to the sum of £ 3,000,000, highest in the whole history of the British secret service. Even this high figure is deceptive since it reveals only allotments from public funds. The bulk of Britain's intelligence revenue comes from private funds, such as dividends of the Anglo-Iranian Oil Company, some of whose shares are held by the Admiralty.

On the level of the individual, the glamour of intelligence is not reflected in the salaries paid to its practitioners. It was estimated that Britain employs 3,000 persons in secret service, most of them detailed from the armed forces. The secret agents of Britain draw an average salary of £ 1,500 a year (or about $4,400 at the current rate of exchange). Everything is paid in cash and such earnings are not reported to the tax authorities. Allowances are limited and agents are explicitly told to keep their expenses within bounds. While the British secret service in principle insists on paying for everything it gets, it is rarely willing to pay more than £ 1,000, even for data it is most anxious to have.

Before World War I, Germany appropriated only 450,000 marks (about $180,000) a year for all secret service activities within the Imperial Army, including counterespionage. At that time the Seventh Bureau of the Czarist Army was spending 12,000,000 rubles (about $5,000,000) a year. Russia was traditionally generous with money spent on intelligence, and the Soviet Union continues this expensive generosity. The total Soviet intelligence budget of today is impossible to calculate, but it may be safe to say that it amounts to several hundred million dollars—indeed *dollars*, since Soviet intelligence conducts all its financial transactions in American currency.

Probably the highest "fee" ever paid to a single agent—sums in excess of $100,000—was paid to Colonel Alfred Redl, chief of the Austro-Hungarian secret service who doubled as a spy for Russia. In more recent years, Soviet intelligence paid about $60,000 to an agent named Lucy (Rudolf Roessler) who operated in Switzerland from 1941 to 1943 and again from 1947 to 1953.

In the Soviet Union, professional intelligence specialists are paid only the regular salaries of their military ranks, while Communists and fellow travelers receive but nominal compensation, their chief motivation being devotion to the cause.

In its summary on the motivation of Soviet agents, the Canadian Royal Commission stated, "Thus it is apparent that despite the relatively cheap method of inducing most new recruits to join the espionage network through non-monetary motivation courses provided by Communist study groups, nevertheless fairly substantial sums of money were in fact paid out by [Colonel] Zabutin [the Soviet military attaché in Canada], particularly to senior agents."

In the United States, there is only one such openly designated sum, the item called Activity 2100 in the U.S. Army's budget. It covers the total expenses of U.S. Army intelligence, including Activity 2131, its sole secret intelligence project. In the 1954-55 fiscal year, the U.S. Army asked for $54,454,000 to cover the expenses of intelligence. During the three fiscal years of 1952, 1953, and 1954, the U.S. Army spent a total of $176,400,000 on intelligence, or less than one half of one percent of the total Army budget.

The Army's budget reveals three additional intelligence items, totaling $88,363,000. This sum includes appropriations for the National Security Agency (not to be confused with the National Security Council), a top-secret intelligence organization about which nothing is spread on the record.

The budget of the Central Intelligence Agency is not known. General C. P. Cabell, Chief of Staff of CIA, wrote in a letter on September 4, 1953, "The budget of CIA is held very tightly; only four or five members in each House are shown the appropriation figures." CIA's appropriations are hidden in allotments to other agencies and the Bureau of the Budget does not report its personnel strength to Congress. "The amount is a classified figure," Senator Mike Mansfield of Montana said, "but published estimates of the annual appropriation run from $500 million to $800 million."

In the armed forces, intelligence officers draw the regular pay of their ranks. Civilian intelligence specialists are paid by Civil Service scales, from $5,000 to $12,000 according to their individual ratings.

The sum total the powers now spend on their secret services may amount to as much as two to three billion dollars a year. However, nothing may be gained by speculating on this score. It is safer to say that intelligence still represents but an infinitesimal part of the budgets. It should be remembered that the best intelligence is not always bought with money and that the amount of money expended does not necessarily reflect the quality of the intelligence effort or the results it may eventually produce.

The Collection of Intelligence

Collection represents the culling of information from overt sources, such as foreign newspapers, books, radio intercepts, and other material of a similar nature. On the other hand, "procurement" as used in intelligence parlance describes an aggressive effort to acquire certain specific information which may not be readily available. To this end a number of means may be used, including secret intelligence and espionage. In the vast majority of cases, however, even the procurement of intelligence is to a large extent a bureaucratic effort, a job that intelligence officers and specialists can do at their desks, without the adventure and melodrama that is popularly associated with the gathering of intelligence information. In fact, it was estimated that approximately ninety percent of all information accumulated within intelligence services comes from overt sources, even though some special knowledge and skill is often needed to produce the information. Today, the proportion of intelligence about Iron Curtain countries which comes from overt sources is, perhaps, half of the total.

Once an intelligence service is organized, it begins collecting the various kinds of information needed by its government: military, political, economic and industrial, scientific, social, and cultural information. The collection of diplomatic information, that pertaining to the conduct of international relations, is to a large extent the function of the State Department, whose own Foreign Service, the organization composed of career diplomats, is supposed to obtain such information through the conventional diplomatic channels.

Collection in an intelligence service is not performed haphazardly. It is the result of a thoroughly considered plan directed at the gathering of information of a specific nature. In this light, collection of specific information is undertaken by specialists who possess thorough knowledge of the subject to which they are assigned. Such knowledge may come from the specialist's educational background, from his familiarity with a foreign country, or from a professional knowledge of a particular subject.

For example, a specialist assigned to the collection of industrial information will logically have had some practical or scientific experience within the industrial field. As a result of this method of assignment to a familiar field, the specialist's personal knowledge assures a familiarity with the subject under study, thereby eliminating the necessity for giving him time-consuming education within that phase of industry under study at the time. A specialist assigned to the gathering of information in any particular field moves with an ease engendered by knowledge of his surroundings.

For example, a person collecting information of a military nature should have a thorough knowledge of his own army and a similar knowledge of the army under scrutiny. Military knowledge is his specialty, and he will not be responsible for the collection of information outside of this immediate field. Any basic knowledge that the specialist already possesses is at the disposal of his own intelligence service, and it is the collection of additional knowledge within this field through largely overt means that is his primary function.

The collector, contrary to the popular conception, is not one who actually infiltrates by surreptitious means into the military or industrial organization about which he seeks information. He is, on the contrary, an official who is attached to a special desk where he scans such primary sources of information as newspapers and magazines, scientific and technical journals, radio transcriptions, books, official government publications, and financial and industrial bulletins issued by private firms. The collector, in scanning these media, looks for any information immediately or potentially relating to his individual specialty. When he finds an item corroborating information previously known to him or to his service, or containing information not previously known, he records it for future reference. Out of these very scattered items develops an enormous backlog of information, which ultimately forms that pattern from which policy is determined at the highest level of government.

Occasionally, items of great immediate importance are discovered, even if only by reading between the lines, which is one of the collector's special skills. Such information is then passed swiftly to the proper authorities on a higher level. Collection is a continuous function in which even the most trivial item, though usually not of such an immediate nature, goes into the weaving of a pattern that ultimately influences the policy of the government. This form of collection is known as research and analysis. It is supplemented by intelligence reports sent in by spies and agents, and by information supplied by other agencies, such as military attachés stationed abroad, consular agents and diplomatic personnel, and other informants. In wartime, collection is aided by censorship intercepts, such as letters and postcards, which are read and copied by the censor, partly to prevent classified information from reaching unauthorized hands, and partly also to collect information.

There is also oral intelligence, in which persons possessing certain desired knowledge are interviewed. Such sources include specialists outside of the intelligence service, visitors to one's own country from abroad, and citizens returning from trips abroad.

An outstanding example of the effectiveness of research and analysis was supplied by a German journalist and military expert whose remarkable intelligence case became celebrated throughout the world. On March 20, 1935, this man, an author named Berthold Jacob, was kidnaped by agents of the German secret service from Switzerland. Jacob had written extensively about the German army that was then in its initial stages of rearmament. He had published a little book which spelled out virtually every detail of the organization of Hitler's new army. This book of 172 pages described the command structure, the personnel of the revived General Staff, the army group commands, the various military districts, even the rifle platoons attached to the most recently formed Panzer divisions. It listed the names of the 168 commanding generals of the army and supplied their biographical sketches.

When Hitler was shown the book, he flew into a rage. He summoned Colonel Walther Nicolai, then his adviser in intelligence matters, and asked, "How was it possible for one man to find out so much about the Wehrmacht?" Nicolai decided to find out the answer to this question from Jacob himself. An agent named Hans Wesemann was assigned to contact Jacob and lure him into a trap. Wesemann set up shop in Basel, in Switzerland near the German border, in the guise of a literary agent. He masqueraded as a refugee and struck up friendships with several exiles from Nazi Germany. Then he got in touch with Jacob in London and invited him to come to Switzerland to discuss a literary deal.

Jacob went to Basel with his wife and was received by Wesemann. They deposited Mrs. Jacob at a hotel, then went to a fashionable restaurant to lunch. At one point during this merry meeting, Jacob had to excuse himself to go to the men's room. His absence permitted Wesemann to slip a sedative into his drink. The unsuspecting writer returned in high mood and lifted his doctored glass for another toast.

Wesemann sat back in his chair and watched Jacob doze under the impact of the Mickey Finn. He then apologized to the waiter for his inebriated companion and asked him to help

45

carry Jacob to a waiting car. A moment later Jacob was on his way to Germany.

Berthold Jacob arrived in Berlin shortly before midnight, acutely aware of his predicament. He was driven straight to Gestapo headquarters in Prinz Albrecht Strasse and taken to a room on the second floor where a commission of officers and civilians awaited him. At their head was Colonel Walther Nicolai.

The moment Jacob was pushed into the room, Nicolai pounced upon him with the question: "Tell us, Herr Jacob! Where did you get the data for your confounded book?"

There followed an explanation that sounded like an exposition of brilliant intelligence work. "Everything in my book came from reports published in the German press, Herr Oberst," Jacob said. "When I stated that Major General Haase was commanding officer of the 17th Division and located in Nuremberg, I received my information from an obituary notice in a Nuremberg newspaper. The item in the paper stated that General Haase, who had just come to Nuremberg in command of the recently transferred 17th Division, had attended a funeral.

"In an Ulm newspaper," Jacob went on, "I found an item on the society page about a happier event, the wedding of a Colonel Vierow's daughter to a Major Stemmermann. Vierow was described in the item as the commanding officer of the 36th Regiment of the 25th Division. Major Stemmermann was identified as the Division's signal officer. Also present at the wedding was Major General Schaller, described in the story as commander of the division who had come, the paper said, from Stuttgart where his division had its headquarters."

This virtually ended the interrogation. Fortunately for Jacob, Nicolai respected good intelligence work. His admiration for the job Jacob had done secured for the writer humane treatment, in addition to which Jacob's wife left no stone unturned to secure her husband's release. The Jacob case became a diplomatic incident. Switzerland demanded that Germany release Jacob at once. The German Foreign Office was embarrassed and made a search for Jacob. He was discovered in the Gestapo jail. Some months later Jacob was returned to Switzerland where he related to me the details of his adventure.

Nicolai reported to Hitler on his findings. "This Jacob had no accomplice, my Fuehrer, except our own military journals and the daily press," he said. "He prepared his remarkable Order of Battle from scraps of information he discovered in obituary notices, wedding announcements, and so forth." He then added in a low voice in which there was suppressed a distant trace of admiration, "This Jacob is the greatest intelligence genius I have ever encountered in my thirty-five years in the service."

The case that at first looked as if it would explode into the greatest espionage scandal ever to rock the German Army was resolved. There was not a spy in it as far as the eye could see. It was a scoop scored by an outstanding civilian whose tools were a pair of scissors, a pot of glue, a file of index cards—and the mind of an intelligence officer.

I first witnessed the process of collection some twenty-odd years ago and, though it was a simple and relatively easy process, it impressed me even then as supremely efficient and effective. At that time, I was employed in the Berlin office of the New York *Times*, under whose auspices was a local agency called "Wide World Pictures," which sold news pictures to German clients. One of these clients was a tall, distinguished-looking, greying man called Herr Goetz. He arrived in our office every morning at 10 A.M. and went through all the pictures pouring in from Wide World's foreign branches and from its headquarters in New York. Hundreds of pictures went on sale every day, pictures of people, places, and events. Herr Goetz would spend a couple of hours every morning examining each fresh crop with great care. Then he would pick a few photographs and buy them "for his personal use," as he put it, at five marks each, their regular commercial price.

After Herr Goetz had come in this way for a number of years, familiarity inevitably developed. He relaxed gradually until we became friends. One day, for reasons known only to him, he revealed to us the true nature of his interest in our pictures. He was a major in *Abwehr*, the intelligence service of the German High Command, and he bought the pictures as a short cut in the collection of information.

"It would require no little effort," he once told me, "and perhaps a pretty penny, to get reliable information about, let's say, structural changes in the ships of the Royal Navy." He picked up a photograph that had just come in from New York and said, "But here is a picture of H.M.S. *Leander*, an excellent picture, don't you think, of that ship all decked out, during a courtesy visit to the Chilean port of Valparaiso. Now, we know a lot about *Leander*. She's the old lady of the new *Ajax* class of light cruisers. She was launched in 1931 in Devonport. We know all about her armor and her speed, her displacement and cruising range. As a matter of fact, we used to think she was pretty lightly armed for her size. I'm going to buy this picture of the *Leander*, take it to my office, and compare it with older pictures we already have on file. I want to see if anything has been changed in her superstructure. We may find that nothing has changed. But then again, there might be some really important changes. It's quite possible that the caliber of her guns has been increased, her turrets moved or altered, or her silhouette modified. If any of this is true, let me ask you, where could you get such information for five marks?"

He went on, "This was how we found out that cruisers of the *Effingham* class had had the caliber of their main guns reduced, and that the armor on the battleships *Renown* and *Repulse* had been increased." He picked up another picture sent to us from Wide World's Paris office. "Here," Major Goetz said, "is a train wreck near Chateaureaux in France. Who cares? But there is a tunnel in the background and we might want to determine its dimensions." He turned to another picture, "How do you like this photograph? The usual stuff, you say? Maybe! Bank Holiday in Brighton. It is an unusually good shot of the whole beach, considering that it's only a news picture taken from a little commercial plane."

A few months after this amazingly candid explanation, Wide World sent me to Danzig on an assignment, and I returned with a scoop—pictures of a tiny island fortress called the Westerplatte, maintained by the Poles in the very heart of the Free City. Just at this time the Westerplatte figured prominently in the news. It was a bone of contention, since Danzigers protested vehemently that this Polish dagger was pointing threateningly at them. In Danzig, I requested permission from the high commissioner to take pictures in the Westerplatte and when permission was refused I took them anyway. It was a journalistic achievement for which I was given a bonus by Wide World. The pictures appeared in virtually every major paper in the world. Herr Goetz showed his personal appreciation by buying copies of every one of them.

Five years later in New York, on September 1, 1939, I stayed up the entire night to listen to the fantastic bulletins announcing the outbreak of the Second World War. Suddenly I felt a chill when I heard the first official communiqué of the Wehrmacht, revealing that the war had begun with the old battleship *Schleswig-Holstein* bombarding the Westerplatte.

Photographs taken by professional cameramen, journalists, amateurs, or tourists are today eagerly sought by all intelligence organizations. They make the collection of information a simple and rewarding job. In intelligence parlance, these pictures are "Aunt Minnies," after the familiar relative who usually appears in such snapshots, with head half obscured and limbs magnified by bad focusing. But behind "Aunt Minnie" there may be a winding road, the particular bends of which are of interest to the topographer. Or high up above "Aunty's" head, on a protruding cliff, there may be a quaint little whitewashed church with a distinctive steeple, invaluable as a marker for target intelligence.

In intelligence work, snapshots and picture postcards are collector's items. Some of them, in demand when the lives of troops may depend on the intelligence they supply, may be worth more than a Rembrandt. Seven such pictures formed an important portion of the advance information the 1st Marine Division had when it went into Guadalcanal in August, 1942. They came from someone who had visited the Solomons in times of peace and then had given the prints to a friend in Washington when OSS's predecessor, the so-called Coordinator of Information, requested that citizens send in snapshots taken abroad. The collection of such "photographic ground intelligence," for example, is one of the few really centralized efforts in Britain's widely scattered intelligence network. It is localized in the Admiralty, which is the custodian of the photographic library of the entire British intelligence system.

Snapshots, news pictures, and picture postcards are but one group of the overt sources that supply the clues intelligence needs. Since the acquisition of information is the primary function of intelligence, it is also the most voluminous phase of the entire activity.

Among the most important basic intelligence sources, as said before, are foreign newspapers and periodicals, particularly specialty and trade journals, intercepts of radio broadcasts beamed to home audiences abroad, books of all kinds, especially yearbooks and reference books, and virtually any printed matter available on the counters of bookshops. Most valuable, however, are informants, or contacts, those individuals who supply information either voluntarily or involuntarily, sometimes even under duress. In the first category are patriotic citizens who might have obtained certain valuable information in the course of their routine activities, travelers returning from trips abroad with observations of immediate value to intelligence, and, especially in these days, refugees from countries behind the Iron Curtain.

Publicly available printed matter—from single issues of newspapers to encyclopedias—represents the chief source from which information is usually culled. Some of the most rewarding missions have taken intelligence officers not into the vaults of general staffs but into the reading rooms of public libraries. In this respect, Soviet intelligence is in a much more advantageous position than any intelligence service in the West, if only because so much of the sort of thing that is labeled top secret in the U.S.S.R. is published freely in the United States, Great Britain, and France. The Western press, in particular, is an inexhaustible mine of information that continually feeds a wealth of information to the alert intelligence specialist who knows how to read between the lines. Recently one five-line item printed by the Associated Press was actually revealed as the sole source of a Soviet intelligence report when the dispatch of a Soviet agent was intercepted by the Sûreté in Paris. This particular item reported the crash of two Lancaster bombers of the RAF during maneuvers in the Mediterranean near Malta, adding only that the seven members of one Lancaster's crew had been rescued. These five lines supplied welcome information to the agent. They told him that the Royal Navy was holding exercises around Malta, and that it was operating with land-based planes. Additional data was concealed between the lines, intelligible only to the trained intelligence specialist.

Scientific and trade journals of the West supply specific information, as do encyclopedias and handy reference books like the *World Almanac* in the United States, *Whitaker's Almanack* and *The Statesman's Year-Book* in the United Kingdom, and the *Petit Larousse* in France. On pages 724 to 734 of the 1954 edition of the *World Almanac*, for example, Soviet intelligence specialists can find, openly printed, vital information about the armed forces of the United States.

Among other data, the *World Almanac* also prints the exact number of nurses in the U.S. Air Force. This type of information was actually sought by the German intelligence service in the United States in 1938-39 and was one of the assignments of German spies in this country. In addition, the *World Almanac* describes in great detail the education and training of American officers, the operation of the selective service system in the United States, the pay scale of the Army, Navy, Air Force, and the women's branches of the armed forces. Although such information may not appear to be exceptionally valuable or conclusive by itself, it is useful to the intelligence specialist because it supplies the clues from which major deductions may be made. As an intelligence manual of the U.S. Army put it, "from the character, the measures, the situation of an adversary, and the relations with which he is surrounded, each side will draw conclusions by the law of probability as to designs of the other, and act accordingly."

Congressional hearings on American weapons developments, especially the use of the B-36 bomber as a strategic weapon, revealed to the Soviet Union virtually the entire American military doctrine. The hearings that followed General Douglas MacArthur's dismissal provided invaluable tactical clues, for both the North Koreans and Red Chinese, to the way the United Nations planned to prosecute the war in Korea.

In a similar manner, the debates in the House of Commons and in the French National Assembly furnish invaluable data to the Soviet intelligence service, for it has only to procure the records of those debates to obtain hard intelligence concerning those nations. Especially important information emerges from the so-called "question periods" in the House of Commons, during which members ask pointed questions about the state of Britain and members of Her Majesty's Government are required to answer just as unguardedly.

No such information ever emerges from behind the Iron Curtain, where even the legitimate functions of foreign press correspondents are regarded as espionage. Production figures of industries, even though they may not have any military significance, are labeled as state secrets, as are virtually all data concerning the state affairs of those nations.

By contrast with Western practice, the Soviet press prints little of direct intelligence value and great care is taken in general to withhold information from other overt sources as well. When I was in Moscow in 1937, I visited a foreign bookstore on Kuznetsky Most and tried to buy some thirty books printed in the English language, apparently intended for foreign readers. My selection completed, the clerk asked me whether I planned to take the books abroad. When I told him I did, he consulted a catalog and announced that only two of the books were approved for export—a slim volume about Stalin as a military genius, written by Marshal Voroshilov, and a report on a Russo-Japanese clash on the Amur River. The Soviet Union bans on principle the exportation of any book which may even remotely or inferentially contain intelligence data. It goes so far as to prohibit the exportation of the official journal of librarians on the theory that the reviews printed in it, or a mere listing of the books published in the U.S.S.R., might supply unintended information. Most of the Russian periodicals, and even some newspapers, are in this proscribed category, the ban representing an intense effort to withhold this important source of information from foreign intelligence specialists.

The Soviet effort to control these sources of possible information is unprecedented. It was unheard of in other totalitarian countries, even during the war. As a matter of fact, during World War II, a considerable part of our intelligence came directly from German, Italian, and Japanese periodicals. Recognizing the value of this source, the Allied intelligence services set up joint purchasing agencies in Europe and Asia which either bought the enemy's papers the moment they hit the newsstands or subscribed to his periodicals through neutral channels. They were then sent by plane to London, Washington, and New York. We thus received not only the daily papers of the enemy but also his scientific journals with gratifying promptness and regularity. At my desk in Washington, I was able to read Hitler's own *Völkischer Beobachter* within two days of its publication in Germany, and I culled an astonishing amount of hard intelligence from it, items no country can effectively conceal as long as newspapers are published on the open market.

Today, despite iron-clad censorship, ingenious intelligence specialists still can find valuable items in the strictly controlled Communist press. There is little the Communists can do about it. Since the press is an important instrument of their propaganda, they must continue to publish all kinds of printed matter. Often nothing is to be gained from an evaluation of items collected in this way, but the fact remains that even the thickest wall has its fissures.

One need not be a trained cryptanalyst in the breaking of codes and ciphers to obtain information from thin air. You need only tune in on the home beam of, let us say, Radio Moscow or Radio Prague to get a lot of valuable information. The exceptional value of such broadcasts was recognized by Britain shortly before the Second World War, and a special branch was established within the B.B.C. to monitor all foreign radio broadcasts directed at home audiences. Shortly afterwards, a similar agency was established in the United States, under the aegis of the Federal Communications Commission. Later called Foreign Broadcast Monitoring (Intelligence) Service, the special agency was transferred to the CIA where it now forms an important organ of collection. A daily digest of all such intercepts is printed, and the information is made available to a wide circle of officials. My own experience showed this to be an invaluable source of information.

Forming a third group of collection sources are the so-called informants. They may be "confidential informants," who supply information deliberately and voluntarily, out of sympathy with one's own cause, or they may be "incidental informants," who drop information carelessly and unwittingly. It is a primary task of good intelligence to seek out potential informants in both categories, then develop or cultivate them and keep them on tap. A seemingly innocent luncheon with an unsuspecting informant may yield more valuable information than an intelligence operation employing espionage agents.

If the battle of Verdun in 1916 ended in victory for the French, it was at least partly due to the indiscretion of an unwitting informant whose boastful remarks about the coming offensive were picked up by the various antennae of Allied intelligence. In January, 1916, an American merchant was traveling unhindered in Europe, since the United States was then still neutral. He visited Warsaw and accepted an invitation to a dinner during which a high-ranking German staff officer happened to be seated beside him at the table.

The German was interested in having an American as his dinner companion and proceeded to abuse the United States for her support of Britain and France. "But it won't do any good," he said, "because, you see, the war will be over very soon." He then proceeded to tell the American that there would be a decisive and all-out German offensive in the direction of Verdun that would certainly end the war. He went so far as to mention D-day of the offensive—February 20, 1916.

The American returned via London and while there related the Warsaw conversation to someone in the American Embassy. He was advised to report it to Admiral Sir Reginald Hall, director of the Division of Naval Intelligence, and regarded by Americans in London as the most outstanding intelligence officer in that field. The American went to the Admiralty but found that Hall was at home with a cold. He repeated the conversation to Hall's assistant, a young South African named Hoy, who, in turn, rushed to Hall with the information.

Hall invited Captain de Saint Seine, the French naval attaché, to his house and relayed to him the American's report. The captain left at once for France and, on the morning of January 11, reported to Marshal Joffre personally. As in the case of most unsolicited information collected from an unevaluated source, there were some doubts. Why should a high-ranking German staff officer, it was naturally asked, reveal such a secret to a stranger? However, there was intelligence already on hand that seemed to corroborate the American's story. French scouts had found that the Germans were building roads in the woods around Gremilly and Étain and in the scenic Bois de Caures. Then the sudden arrival of five German divisions from the Serbian front was reported by other informants.

Finally convinced of the authenticity of the American's information, Marshal Joffre issued orders to begin immediate preparations to meet the German onslaught. Hall and Hoy spent February 20 in their office, awaiting word from France that would confirm the American's story. The day passed, but all remained quiet on the Western Front. Hall grew restive and, since he did not cherish the prospect of appearing a gullible fool in French eyes, he went home deeply disturbed, even considering the possibility that the American had been a "plant" to mislead the French. Then at 6:30 next morning, Hoy called on the telephone. "A message from France, sir," he said. "At 0415, sir, the Germans opened up in front of Verdun, all the way from Brabant to Gussainville, with the greatest artillery barrage of the war." The battle of Verdun was on, exactly as reported by the American informant.

The recognition of the value of informants persuaded the intelligence services to deal with them systematically. Britain in particular has made the patriotic informant the backbone of her intelligence set-up. She maintains a relatively small nucleus of professional intelligence officers, and only a few specialists who may be called espionage agents, but depends on informants to supply the bulk of the information she needs. This works well in practice. "Britain's intelligence set-up," wrote E. H. Cookridge, "has never been seriously jeopardized. This is the best testimonial possible to her system of relying on the part-time agent to a great extent. A schoolmaster on a holiday, a businessman seeking markets, or a retired civil servant living abroad because of its attractions to a man dependent on a modest pension can all do useful work."

The other primary form of acquiring information, procurement, includes the gathering of data by both overt and covert means. To distinguish between the collection and the procurement of information, we may think of the latter as involving the gathering of data by going after it, in other words by contriving to acquire it rather than by culling it from various sources at the collector's desk. This may involve interviewing any person who can contribute specific information, during which interrogation he knows the purpose of the collector's visit and willingly supplies the information. It may also entail

54

traveling to and within a certain area for the purpose of witnessing or studying it at first hand, or observing a subject open to survey without recourse to surreptitious methods.

Here the primary motive of the inspection may be concealed, but the object under scrutiny is open to observation by any and all. In this form of procurement, information of great importance is available to a specialist without his having to resort to clandestine means. In this category fall such events as the opening to public inspection of naval vessels, air derbies, military displays, and industrial expositions.

When Sir George Aston, one of Britain's great intelligence experts, was a young officer in Naval Intelligence, he regarded it as his duty to procure information through personal observation on every subject on which data could not be obtained by the simpler methods of collection. He frequently left his desk in the Admiralty and undertook special trips abroad, concealing neither his real name nor his rank, withholding only the fact that he was an intelligence officer on a procurement mission. When new fortifications were built in the French port of Dunkirk, it became imperative that his office observe the new lay-out, and also ascertain whether the fortifications had already been garrisoned. Since such information could not be obtained through routine overt sources, Aston decided to procure it personally.

In Dunkirk, posing as a British officer on a vacation trip, he climbed a lighthouse to get an "aerial" view of the fortress lay-out. Then he roamed around in the port, trying to see for himself where the troops, if any, were. Upon his return to his hotel in the town, Aston found a stranger waiting for him. "Monsieur," the man accosted him, "I know that you are a British spy. I also know the purpose of your visit." The man concluded with a Gallic flourish, "I am in a position to sell you the information you seek for a paltry 10,000 francs."

Aston answered with equal flourish, "Monsieur, first of all, I am not a British spy. Secondly, I am here on a vacation and I am not trying to find out anything. And, thirdly, monsieur, I already know what I came here to discover."

Aston had made his discovery by those simple methods of deduction that helped both Sherlock Holmes and the British secret service to some of their greatest triumphs. He knew that the soldiers of France had general-issue boots whose hobnails were arranged in a certain pattern. The ground around the new forts was muddy and revealed the prints of thousands of boot-nailed soles. Aston regarded this as sufficient evidence that the forts had already been garrisoned.

Personal observation does not always yield completely satisfactory results, as Aston was to learn occasionally on his inspection trips. From an announcement in a French newspaper he learned that there was to be an exhibition of new French weapons in Paris. Aston hurried to Paris to visit the exhibition. He inspected at leisure the various models on display, but whenever he attempted to sketch one or another a policeman would approach him and caution him to abandon his art.

As if permitting him special favor, the policeman then took him to a huge gun in the center of the exhibition and allowed him to make a sketch of it. Upon his return to England, Aston discovered that the gun had been a dummy, built of cardboard especially for the benefit of visiting intelligence officers.

Some time before the United States entered the Second World War, special agencies were created for the cultivation and exploitation of informants. One of them, called Oral Intelligence Group, was set up in New York to interview anyone with information that might be of use at one time or another. Members of the group buttonholed experts and returning travelers and plied them with questions with the utmost skill.

One of the specialists in Oral Intelligence was a middle-aged matron named Emmy Rado, a far cry, indeed, from the *femme fatale* of spy fiction. Swiss by birth and married to a prominent psychoanalyst, she qualified ideally for the job because she could speak German, French, Italian, Danish, and English, and knew how to coax information from people. Mrs. Rado studied the passenger lists of incoming ships, picked names and addresses from them, and wrote letters inviting strangers to call on her at her office. She was particularly interested in refugees.

One day such a refugee came to see her. He was a somewhat erratic and excitable man who knew only a few English words, but he repeated again and again, "Must see Roosevelt." When Mrs. Rado talked to him in French, he revealed that he was really a man with a mission. He had come to the United States as a special emissary of an anti-Fascist group in North Africa, bearing a message for President Roosevelt.

"Where are you from, monsieur?" Mrs. Rado asked.

"From Bône," the man said.

"What's your profession?"

"I'm a hydraulic engineer." It so happened that Mrs. Rado was at that moment intensely interested in Bône. A few weeks earlier, a directive from Washington had requested that Oral Intelligence collect information about Bône from its North

African informants. America was preparing for the landings in North Africa but had woefully little information about the port of Bône. And here was an informant who had helped to build the port and who knew many of the technical details of the installations.

Mrs. Rado persuaded the man to sit at a drafting board and reproduce maps and blueprints from memory. The man worked for three days, and, when he was finished, the harbor's defenses were down on paper. Mrs. Rado promptly dispatched them to the War Department, where the operations plans were being drafted.

When in November, 1942, British troops under Anderson took Bône, the stranger returned to Mrs. Rado in triumph. He was convinced that his information had reached President Roosevelt after all. He had a letter of thanks, beginning with "Greeting" and bearing the President's own signature, inviting him to join the armed forces of the United States.

When engaged in procurement, the intelligence specialist must sometimes leave his desk and go out into the field to secure information by personal observation. The classic example of this method was supplied by a German general named Zeitzler during World War II, not long before he was appointed chief of the Army General Staff. In the early winter of 1941, General Zeitzler donned civilian clothes and went personally to Greece to reconnoiter the terrain across which his tanks were soon to roll.

Today, such inspection trips are undertaken regularly by service attachés, and it might be remarked that they rarely visit out-of-the-way inns just because the food is reputed to be good. In fact, a service attaché or professional intelligence officer never makes a trip with his eyes closed or for his own private pleasure. Even his furloughs serve definite purposes. He usually spends his vacation in places that have some significance in his work.

One might naturally think that collection and procurement would be more easily performed during periods of peace than in times of war, but the exact opposite is true. Wars cannot be conducted behind closed doors. Ordinarily the real secrets of a country are not easily accessible, but during wartime the exigencies of the conflict make their exposure inevitable.

At the outset of the Pacific war, we had virtually no information on the Japanese navy beyond what was publicly available, and only inadequate or faulty hydrographic charts of many strategic Pacific islands. Either these islands had been altogether uncharted and unsurveyed, or there was only a narrowly restricted knowledge of their characteristics. An effort was made between the two world wars to get an American colonel onto one of the closed Japanese islands. Although his mission was not completely camouflaged and he traveled as a bona fide tourist, his trip ended in tragedy. His ashes were returned by bowing Japanese to the American authorities in Tokyo, with the explanation that the colonel had died during his voyage and his body had been cremated with all the solemn pomp of the Shinto ritual. A post-mortem was impossible.

The important work left undone in peace became pressing when war broke out. Guadalcanal, in particular, was a symbol of the careless indifference of peace and the urgent curiosity characteristic of war. It became the symbol of the ease with which intelligence can be conducted under wartime conditions when no holds are barred and nothing can be kept under wraps.

This famous island at the southern tip of the Solomon archipelago looked on the map like a bacillus under a microscope. The Guadalcanal operation was code-named Pestilence. It was to be the first offensive move of the American forces after more than eight months of humiliating retreat. Pestilence was scheduled for August 1, 1942, and the military planners at Pearl Harbor who had to draft the assault looked up Guadalcanal in the various intelligence files—and found precious little. They discovered only two good books about the Solomons; one in English had been published in 1893, the other in German had come out in 1903. They were not much help.

The American planners were fairly confident that British Intelligence would be able to supply some information, the Solomons having been in British hands since 1893. They had had plenty of time to survey the islands and chart the waters around them. But the charts were even older than the books. There was one based on Captain Edward Manning's journey in 1792. Even the newest was more than a hundred years old.

When the Japanese occupied Guadalcanal in May, 1942, they had excellent charts, so the idea occurred to Colonel Frank B. Goettge, G-2 (intelligence officer) of the 1st Marine Division, to get theirs instead of making our own. On July 1, Colonel Goettge flew to Australia and established contact with the intelligence authorities there. It soon developed that the situation was not as bleak as it seemed at Pearl Harbor. Although nothing had been done during the years of peace, considerable effort had been made to establish an intelligence network in the Solomons after the outbreak of hostilities in Europe in 1939. German raiders and blockade-runners were expected in the general area and a system of coast watchers had been established to report on them. The Australian Navy had a young lieutenant stationed on Tulagi and Guadalcanal, and there were four trained coast watchers or "Ferdinands," as they were called after the peace-loving bull.

Goettge sent two of his officers to "Ferdinand" headquarters and found that the officer, Macfarlan, and coast watchers had everything he needed. By then, in fact, Macfarlan had his own houseboy working in the Japanese camp and bringing back reports every week-end. "Ferdinand" had a string of agents all over the island, funneling information back from the jungle. While the Australians thus supplied information from under the enemy's nose, Goettge in Australia was interrogating refugees from Guadalcanal, missionaries, planters, and workers. What had been so woefully neglected during the carefree years of peace was nearly compensated for within a fortnight. Plans for Pestilence could be drawn up with knowledge of the enemy's disposition and strength on Guadalcanal, and the Marines could be supported with good intelligence when they stormed ashore.

If ever proof were needed that faulty intelligence or lack of intelligence results in confusion, delays, and high casualties, the invasion of Tarawa, in November, 1943, supplied this proof. In taking Tarawa, the Marines suffered the loss of about 1,000 men in dead and 2,000 in wounded. About twenty percent of all casualties were suffered during the first hours of the landing, as a direct result of a complete breakdown of intelligence. "The natural defenses of Betio were almost as formidable, and as little known, as those installed by the enemy," wrote Gilbert Cant in *The Great Pacific Victory*. "The atoll of Tarawa had not been the subject of an oceanographic survey since the visit of Lieutenant (later Commodore) John Wilkes, U.S.N., in 1841. His charts were still in use, 102 years later. In the meantime, the coral polyp had been busy, making Wilkes's charts inaccurate."

Since the landing craft could not traverse the reefs, whose existence had been unknown to our intelligence, the men had to wade ashore or be ferried to battle in little "alligators," cruelly exposed to enemy fire. American authorities were shocked. After Tarawa, collection of intelligence was vastly improved and new charts were made. In "Terrible Tarawa," three thousand American casualties served to point up the importance of intelligence.

Sources of Information

Indiscreet war which cannot keep its secrets supplies three categories of sources from which invaluable information can be obtained. In the first category are the prisoners captured in combat. In the second are the documents taken from the bodies of the dead after battle, from the raided headquarters of the enemy, and from his sunken ships. The third major source of information is reconnaissance. There is a fourth source, the constant monitoring of the enemy's radio traffic, but with that we will deal later when we discuss cryptography.

The use of prisoners of war as sources of information is as old as warfare itself. The first detailed account of a campaign in which prisoners were so used comes down to us from the thirteenth century before Christ, from the campaign of Pharaoh Rameses II against King Hattushilish III of the Hittites. In that campaign, prisoners were used in two ways. The Egyptians used them to obtain information about the Hittite forces. The Hittites used them in an elaborate ruse to plant misleading information with the Egyptians.

In 1271 B.C., the army of Rameses marched 400 miles in about a month and reached the upper Orontes, but with no sign of the enemy. Finally, two Hittite soldiers showed up in the Egyptian camp. They volunteered information that the army of Hattushilish was still some distance away and that it was full of mutinous soldiers who appeared anxious to desert to the enemy. Rameses thought that this intelligence sounded too good to be true, but he ordered patrols to reconnoiter the area and bring back prisoners to corroborate the desertion story. The patrol returned with two bona fide prisoners whose interrogation produced evidence quite different from the story of the alleged deserters. These prisoners reported that the Hittites were waiting with their infantry and chariots in the immediate vicinity of the Egyptian camp, that they were "more numerous than the sands of the sea," and that there was no dissatisfaction among the soldiers of Hattushilish. Rameses drew up his battle plan entirely on the information which he received from the new prisoners, in the exact manner in which such information was used thirty centuries later in World War II and in the Korean War.

Information that is obtained from prisoners of war ranges

all the way from the lowest tactical to the highest strategic level. A prisoner brought in by a patrol may disclose nothing more important than the identity of his regiment, but he may also be the source of information that ultimately influences the course of the war, or history.

By sheer numbers, prisoners represent a vast reservoir of information in modern war. During World War I, there was a total of 7,750,919 missing or prisoners of war captured by both sides, which meant that about twelve percent of the mobilized forces ended up in prison camps. The number of prisoners during the first two years of World War II totaled more than four million men; by the end of the war their number exceeded the fantastic total of fifteen million officers and men. In the Korean War, the enemy captured nearly 10,000 United Nations combatants, of whom almost 8,000 were Americans. Not only was information of inestimable value obtained from these prisoners, but they were also used in propaganda campaigns whose repercussions still plague us long after the war.

Prisoners of war supply an amazing amount of information involuntarily and not because they entertain any traitorous sentiments or thoughts. Capture and captivity undermine the soldier's power of moral resistance and create a psychological vacuum in which a man is hardly accountable for what he says or does. This state of mind is recognized by belligerents, and they maintain elaborate organizations to exploit it through various methods of ingenious interrogation. Under international law, a prisoner is not required to submit to questioning. He is obliged only to disclose his name, rank, and serial number, and nothing beyond that. The 1927 Geneva Convention specifically prohibits any organized interrogation of prisoners of war, but this provision of the law is violated right and left even by the ethical signatories of the convention.

The moment a man is captured, he is usually subjected at once to what is called "shock interrogation," when his power of resistance is at its lowest ebb. This is designed to establish whether the man knows anything at all. If he does, he is sent to a special interrogation cage where whole teams of interrogators go to work on him to obtain as much information as possible. If a man seems to have special knowledge, he is sent on to interrogation centers specifically organized for the purpose, and he is kept there until no information is left in him. Only then is he assigned to a camp where he will sit out the war.

During the Second World War prisoner interrogation was

developed by both sides to the point where it became an exact science. A number of gadgets were constructed to aid the interrogators. Stool-pigeons and decoys were used to get information from prisoners which they would not give in direct examination. Special interrogators underwent intense training, and teams were organized in which every interrogator was an expert on certain subjects.

The ordinary soldier usually cannot provide very valuable information. He is not privy to the secrets of the war, and he rarely has knowledge of more than the most routine functions of his own outfit. However, the interrogation of generals sometimes yields information of inestimable value about the plans and dispositions of the enemy. Field Marshall Sir Bernard (later Lord) Montgomery penetrated the most closely guarded secrets of his chief adversary, Marshal Erwin Rommel, when one of Rommel's top commanders, General Ritter von Thoma, fell into his hands. Thoma was not subjected to the usual interrogation. Instead, he was invited to Montgomery's for a series of friendly conversations which eventually provided all that the field marshal wanted to learn. In a somewhat more direct manner, the Russians learned virtually every secret of Hitler's Russian campaign from the generals of the VI Army captured at Stalingrad. In Britain, German generals were kept in a special camp where they not only submitted willingly to interrogation on a very high level but participated in exercises involving sandboxes and miniature military models, in the course of which they revealed intimate details of the Wehrmacht's tactics.

In the winter of 1942-43, during the battle of the Atlantic, Hitler's ferocious U-boat war against Anglo-American shipping was going badly for the Allies. On January 15, we suffered a most grievous defeat. Seven vessels of a convoy of nine tankers were sunk by wolf packs of U-boats, with the forfeit of millions of barrels of high octane gasoline that was needed urgently by the air forces in North Africa.

There were indications that the situation would grow worse. Allied agents reported that the Germans were experimenting with an acoustic torpedo that would be guided to the target simply by homing on the sound of the propellers. The Allies were groping in the dark. There is, of course, an eventual defense for all offensive weapons, but no such defense can be devised before the details of the enemy's new weapon are known. All efforts to obtain details of the mysterious new torpedo had ended in failure. There was uneasiness in the Allied naval high command as the admirals waited nervously for the first report establishing German perfecting of the deadly weapon.

Then, in February, 1943, a U-boat was sunk by an American destroyer somewhere in the Atlantic, and survivors were brought to an interrogation center near Washington. The prisoners had already been exposed to shock interrogation, and it was known that the group included a petty officer who had recently served at the German Navy's torpedo station in Kiel where the acoustic torpedo was being perfected. Immediately upon his arrival in the Washington cage, the man was taken in hand by a torpedo specialist of the ONI interrogation team, and before long this young reserve officer, whom war had made into a torpedo expert, was satisfied that the German petty officer knew all the secrets he was after.

A period of hide-and-seek ensued. The officer did not want to expose his own special interest in the new torpedo, and the German was reluctant to volunteer any information. But he was obviously impressed with the apparent knowledge his interrogator had of Germany's torpedo developments; and by using shrewd psychological methods to soften up his quarry, the officer soon had the man exactly in the state he wanted him. He taunted him by deprecating German torpedoes. This was too much for the proud German. To show how advanced his navy was in this field, he not only volunteered information on German torpedoes in general, but fell to boasting about the new secret weapon, the acoustic torpedo itself.

By then, a kind of intimacy had developed between the interrogator and the man. The officer pretended to be incredulous and scoffed at the man's story of a new torpedo. The German flew into a rage, finally offering to draw a blueprint of it. He was given the necessary equipment and within a few hours drew from memory an exact blueprint of the dreaded new weapon. The blueprint was rushed to Ordnance, and pilot torpedoes were constructed to its specifications. They worked. From then on it was simple to devise the defenses. When later the Germans fired their first acoustic torpedo, the Allied ships were well equipped to counteract them. The weapon the Germans thought would decide the battle of the Atlantic in their favor proved almost completely ineffectual.

This was a piece of intelligence that apparently no spy could obtain in the field and no amount of secret intelligence could turn up. If someone had come to an Allied agency in a neutral country with the design of the torpedo, he would have earned a fabulous sum for the secret. Yet it was obtained in exact blueprint form without the aid of a single spy. It was obtained by a young American sitting at a desk somewhere in Washington with another man whom the fortunes of war had made his prisoner. No unfair pressure had been applied. The Geneva Convention had not been violated. The German had actually volunteered the information.

I tried to do the impossible and compute the cost of this operation. Counting everything, including the expenses of the man's rescue from the sea, I came to a sum that was far below $1,000. Yet this piece of intelligence probably saved ships worth hundreds of millions of dollars.

Another major source supplies the hardest intelligence of all. This is the mass of documents that the gust of war inevitably scatters in all directions. Every high command is well aware of the dangers that the possession of its classified documents represents in unauthorized hands. Strict instructions are issued which prohibit the carrying of highly classified documents into a combat zone, prohibit the writing of diaries, and forbid the maintenance of files where they might fall into enemy hands. But human nature and the exigencies of war somehow combine to foil these excellent regulations. Certain documents obviously have to be carried into advanced areas, and some paper work is inevitable even at the front. No amount of warning will keep men from writing secret diaries. The Japanese, in particular, were avid diarists, and thousands of diaries fell into our hands during World War II, including some kept by top-ranking generals. Occasionally, however, the shoe is on the other foot. A few years ago, the diary of an American general fell into the hands of Soviet intelligence, causing grave embarrassment on this side of the fence and audible rejoicing on the other.

The Second World War was remarkable for the wholesale capture of vital documents. In 1940, the Germans captured the entire secret archives of the French general staff. Among the documents were protocols of conferences and arrangements the French had made with Britain's Imperial General Staff. France was then already knocked out of the war, so those documents concerned with French plans and dispositions were only of academic or historic interest. But Britain was still fighting, and the capture of the French archives caused inestimable damage to the British war effort.

Wherever Americans fought the Japanese on land, highly classified enemy documents came to the Allies by the ream. The Japanese gave far too wide distribution to very highly classified documents and even sent such precious papers regularly to commanders in the field. They probably acted on the vainglorious theory that we would never get near them. Furthermore, the Japanese had been indoctrinated in only the most superficial methods of destroying vital documents in emergencies. The result was that early in the Pacific war, when only low-level Japanese command posts were in the path of our advances, we succeeded in capturing documents of amazingly high-level strategic significance.

In August, 1942, we were testing Japan's newly formed outer defense perimeter with a probing invasion of Guadalcanal. While the main operation centered on the Solomons, two U.S. submarines, the *Argonaut* and the *Nautilus*, ferried combat teams of Colonel Evans F. Carlson's 2nd Marine Raider Battalion from Pearl Harbor to the island of Makin. The purpose of this operation was to harass the handful of Japanese on that outpost, to divert attention from Guadalcanal, and to give the troops some combat experience.

Alerted by intelligence reports compiled from loose talk overheard in the United States, the Japanese prepared defense positions against the anticipated "invasion." But when Carlson's Raiders landed, the enemy abandoned those prepared positions in unexpected haste and scattered inland. Some fighting developed, but such was the efficiency of the Marines that within forty-eight hours no living Japanese was left on the island. Going through the motions of a mop-up, the Marines blew up a radio station, burned substantial quantities of aviation gasoline, collected rations of canned meat and crackers—and paid a visit to the commandant's house. In Fletcher Pratt's lively description of the Makin raid, this phase rated exactly ten words. In actual fact, however, this incidental call on the absent commandant's house made the Makin raid one of the most rewarding enterprises of the whole war.

The Marines found the commandant's house deserted, although some warm dishes on a stove indicated that it had been only recently abandoned. The commandant himself had already joined his ancestors. But piled high in his office were stacks of highly classified documents, including operations plans, battle-order data, intelligence reports, combat narratives, virtually everything one would expect to find, not in the command post of such a remote outpost, but in a topechelon headquarters.

Baskets of the papers were carried to the waiting submarines and, when they reached Washington, they revealed many closely guarded and otherwise inaccessible secrets of the Japanese high command. After that, documents in increasing number and importance fell into our hands wherever we went. By the time Saipan was reached, there was scarcely a Japanese document that did not have at least one copy in some file in Washington.

Like no other war in history, the Second World War opened up the files of the vanquished. At first, Germany was the beneficiary of such revelations, but, when the tide turned, she was on the losing side in this respect as well. When the end came, the complete files of the German General Staff, Foreign Ministry, and every other government department were captured by the Allies, including such invaluable historical documents as the original of the famous Schlieffen Plan itself, the blueprint drawn up before World War I for the military defeat of France. It was in this connection that an eminent German historian said after the war, "We not only lost the war, but we also lost all the secrets of our history and lost our national memory."

I recall how hard we used to work to establish the order of battle of the German Navy from telltale evidence that came to us through overt sources and prisoner interrogation and particularly through secret access to entries in the logs of individual U-boats. Then, in 1944, a U-boat surrendered, and everything that we had tried to piece together by painful and painstaking effort fell into our hands in a single day. The commander of the U-boat put into an Allied port that day with all the equipment that it normally carried absolutely intact. After that, it was no longer necessary to grope in the dark for information about the U-boat command. Everything that was needed floated in with the surrendering vessel, including code books and the German Navy's order of battle.

If ever a single document influenced history, it was a seemingly routine order signed by General Gerd von Rundstedt during the Battle of France in 1940 that fell into the hands of the helpless British and enabled England to evacuate her forces from Dunkirk on the eve of the French collapse. The story of this remarkable intelligence scoop may be told here for the first time.

Toward the end of May, 1940, the destruction of the Allied armies in Europe seemed merely a matter of days. The Belgian, French, and British armies were being pushed relentlessly to the English Channel. In the theater of operations there remained only the port of Dunkirk as a means of escape. The fate of the British Expeditionary Force appeared to lie, as Chester Wilmot expressed it, "in the hollow of Hitler's hand."

Evacuation seemed a possibility, but Prime Minister Churchill was advised that, at the most, only about thirty thousand men might be saved—less than one tenth of the forces involved. Churchill feared that it would soon be his "hard lot to announce the greatest military disaster in our long history." Confronted with what seemed imminent doom, and specifically and more immediately with the Panzer divisions of General Gerd von Rundstedt's Army Group B, the B.E.F. stood almost still, awaiting the *coup de grâce*. Rundstedt's tanks were barely fifteen miles away.

On the evening of May 24, Hitler suddenly intervened in the operation. He decided to change the center of gravity by pressing the advance on Paris, and to leave the British to their fate. He gave orders to halt Rundstedt's Panzers, a senseless and inexplicable order that no British commander or intelligence officer could have hoped for. Yet the order was issued, and, at dawn of May 25, it was carried to the Panzer commanders between Bethune and St. Omer by Colonel von Tresckow, one of Rundstedt's staff officers.

Colonel von Tresckow's command car skirted perilously close to the shattered British lines, and the unexpected happened. It was ambushed and fired on by a stray British patrol. The driver was killed and the car set on fire. Colonel von Tresckow jumped out of the car and escaped on foot, leaving his briefcase in the burning car. And in the briefcase was the momentous order that was to halt the advance of Rundstedt's Panzers.

The British patrol sneaked up to the car and snatched the briefcase from the flames. It was intact. A few hours later, its contents were examined by British intelligence officers. They were reluctant to believe what they saw. But the captured document was rushed to General Alexander and then to General Lord Gort, commander in chief of the B.E.F. Incredible as it must have seemed the British had but one alternative in their desperate situation—to accept it as a miraculous reprieve. Gort issued orders to strengthen his southern flank. Then he speeded up the march of the troops on Dunkirk.

Hitler's generals remonstrated with him, and with Rundstedt who had concurred wholeheartedly in the Fuehrer's order. But the order was not changed, and the British gained time to strengthen their defenses. The reembarkation proceeded virtually unmolested by German tanks. During those days, General Franz Halder, chief of staff of the German Army, wrote in his diary, "Bad weather has grounded the Luftwaffe and now we must stand by and watch countless thousands of the enemy getting away to England right under our noses."

By June 4, 338,000 Allied troops had been rescued from

the beaches—the nucleus around which, in Churchill's words, "Britain could build her armies of the future."

This was security at its worst where the Germans were concerned, but intelligence at its best on the British side. Colonel von Tresckow's conduct is difficult to explain, impossible to justify. He was not supposed to carry a document of such importance into the combat zone. He should not have carried it in a briefcase but should have carried it on his person, if he carried it at all. And he was grossly negligent in abandoning the briefcase when his car was set on fire. When he showed up at Bethune without the written order, he was called before a hastily summoned board of inquiry. He explained the incident and gave his word of honor that he had with his own eyes seen the order consumed by flames.

While prisoner interrogation and the capture of vital documents are primary sources of information for intelligence services, the real eye of the belligerent command is the airplane. General H. H. Arnold, the late great air chief of the U.S. Army, once said, "Introduce one lone airplane into the fifteen decisive battles of the world, and the course of history would have been changed." Aerial observation by balloon was first used in the American Civil War, and balloons were still used widely in World War I. By 1939 they all but disappeared from the skies over battlefields because they had become too vulnerable to the modern plane, which itself took over from the balloon the important task of observation, adding to it the more modern photo-reconnaissance and so-called "intelligence command missions."

The air force flies on observation missions for the ground command, to scout from the air the disposition of the enemy, his front lines, the location of his reserves, his maneuvers, his lines of supply and communications—in other words, the whole complex war-making machinery of the enemy in the active theater of operations. The entire enemy country is open to the observation planes. Planes have even been used to observe the habits and customs of the enemy population. They have been sent out to determine whether factories black out at night, whether business is being carried on as usual, whether the people still gather at racecourses or athletic fields, whether the schools in cities are still open or whether children have been evacuated to the country. This kind of observation produces so-called "morale intelligence" on the moods of the enemy's population, an important factor in calculating his total war potential.

There were times in the early days of aviation when commanders were dependent on returning pilots' reports of their personal observations. Later, the camera was placed in the plane, and today much of the aerial observation is recorded on film or photographic plates. While formerly troops in woods were hidden from the aerial observer, color photography has effectively countered such camouflage. Today, maneuvers and movements on the ground are almost impossible to conceal from the air observer and his camera. Frequently, commanding generals board observation planes and fly over the enemy, even while battles are in progress, to see for themselves. According to the most modern military theory, intelligence is bound to suffer some loss in the second-hand transfer of information. Commanders have come to favor personal observation from the air in order to compensate for this inevitable loss.

Aerial or photo reconnaissance, conducted for the benefit of the air force itself, is designed to establish the exact location of targets, to photograph them so that blown-up pictures may be available during the briefings of crews prior to bombardment missions. Bombardment units have their own intelligence kits, called "objective folders." These envelopes contain all available information about enemy targets and are kept in readiness in the event of the outbreak of hostilities.

One of the Second World War's outstanding intelligence scoops involving aviation observation was associated with a pretty, blue-eyed English girl named Constance Babington-Smith. She performed single-handed a major intelligence operation when she discovered one of the war's most valuable targets without leaving her underground office in a secret R.A.F. headquarters. The aerial target was Peenemünde, a German island in the Baltic, where Hitler was conducting experiments with the rocket bombs and guided missiles with which he hoped to decide the war in his favor.

These experiments had begun as early as 1933 and had been concentrated at Peenemünde since 1936. But British intelligence was unaware of this phase of Germany's war preparations and failed to evince interest even when information did leak out about the top-secret project. Between 1939 and 1943, a number of confidential informants tried to alert British intelligence. One report came in the form of an unsigned letter mailed in Norway. Another came from an old Dane in Nykøbing. Many others came in and were promptly lost in the fog with which blundering intelligence sometimes conceals its mistakes.

Somehow these reports were all filed and forgotten, without any action following them up. When the reports became more persistent, British intelligence simply dismissed the information as German "plants" or propaganda in line with Goebbels' efforts to advertise non-existent secret weapons. Whatever it was, Britain had to pay a heavy and bloody price for the complacency and indifference of its peacetime intelligence organs. It was only partly compensated by intelligence, which eventually and belatedly became concerned with the problem. Even then, the impact of this German "absolute weapon" would have been greater had not Miss Babington-Smith made her discovery.

She was one of a group of young officers whose job was the examination of reconnaissance photographs brought back by the R.A.F. from missions over Germany. One day in May, 1943, she scrutinized a picture taken the day before during a flight over Peenemünde. She used a stereoscope and a measuring magnifier, and, with these simple instruments, she discovered a small curving black shadow and a T-shaped white blot above it. It occurred to her that the curving black shadow was a kind of launching ramp, and that the T-shaped white blot was a small airplane placed on the ramp for launching.

Her superior accepted her hypothesis and ordered immense enlargements made of the photograph. In the enlargement, both the ramp and the little "plane" became clearly visible. Only then was British intelligence mobilized to procure additional and detailed information about Peenemünde. What followed was more or less routine intelligence work in which the old spy reports emerged as important clues, with new ones added to complete the picture. Peenemünde was then bombed by the R.A.F., and the production of flying bombs was retarded at least six months.

The Process of Evaluation

With the collection and procurement of information, the basic function of the intelligence service is essentially completed. Evaluation of this information is a superior intellectual task. It not only assesses the probability, credibility, and reliability of information, but it estimates its general importance and relates it to the general situation for the benefit of higher echelon policy makers.

Although it might seem imperative to leave the function of evaluation to the intelligence service, this is not always done.

Often only preliminary evaluation is made within the intelligence organization, leaving eventual evaluation to recipient agencies or to organizations specially created for this function.

Preliminary evaluation is usually done at the level of the lower echelons, mostly by the most immediate recipients of incoming data at the appropriate desks. They confine their evaluation to a rating of the information. Such ratings assess (a) the reliability or trustworthiness of the source, and (b) the probability of the information.

The reliability of sources or informants is usually rated with letters from "A" to "D." The letter "A" indicates that the source is highly reliable, and the letter "D" that it is an unreliable or untested source.

The probability of the information is rated with numerals from "1" to "4." No. "1" indicates that the information on hand is highly probable, accurate, and corroborated; number "4" that it is improbable or inaccurate.

I have rarely seen intelligence reports rated "A-1." The reluctance to bestow such a high rating on a report is usually due to a wholesome, but sometimes exaggerated, skepticism of individual evaluators. A "B-2" rating is considered pretty good. Even a rating of "C-3" is respected. Frequently, on the other hand, "D-4" reports turn out to be completely reliable and accurate. The whims of intelligence are inscrutable.

Evaluation continues on increasingly higher levels; the eventual attitude of the highest policy maker or supreme commander to a report or a piece of information represents only a more or less final form of evaluation.

While collection may not be particularly difficult, evaluation is. It requires broad knowledge, imagination, and intuition. It is often the banana peel on which hapless intelligence organizations slip up.

The decisive importance of evaluation has been demonstrated, both in its positive and negative consequences, virtually at every step of history. Stalin's negative attitude toward the reports of his secret service which indicated an imminent German attack in 1941 is not characteristic, because it was irrational and was motivated by Stalin's personal prejudices and innate suspiciousness.

The same information Stalin received was also accumulated by various British intelligence services. By the middle of March, 1941, there was ample information on hand in London to indicate that a German attack on the Soviet Union was definitely planned, and that it was due within three months. This was, in fact, the consensus of British intelligence of-

71

ficers on lower echelons. But then the information was relayed to the Joint Intelligence Committee, composed of representatives of the services, whose function was to sift the information and evaluate it for the Prime Minister and the War Cabinet.

The Joint Intelligence Committee surveyed the information and dismissed it on purely rational grounds, concluding that an attack on the Soviet Union would be a senseless enterprise on Hitler's part. They decided that, despite convincing data, a German invasion of U.S.S.R. was unlikely, chiefly because it did not seem reasonable. The Committee overlooked the fact that reason was not a Hitler characteristic.

Probably because the Committee disturbed the circles of his own thinking, Mr. Churchill decided to act as his own intelligence officer in this momentous case, and he gave orders that all raw reports concerning Barbarossa, the operation's code name, be sent directly to him without bothering him with further deductions and evaluations.

On March 30, 1941, a report reached his desk from a highly trusted agent in the Balkans, reporting the movement of five Panzer divisions into the deployment area of the projected operation, and involving about sixty trains. This report convinced Churchill that Germany was indeed preparing for the invasion of the U.S.S.R., and, although he still thought such a development too good to be true in view of Britain's plight, he concluded that the invasion was certain to come and that it was imminent.

Although relations between Britain and the Soviet Union, then Germany's "non-belligerent" partner, were strained, Churchill decided to share this information with Stalin. Churchill's message was delivered to Vishinsky on April 19 and given to Stalin on April 23. It is possible that it merely solidified Stalin's suspicion of similar reports presented to him by his own secret service and persuaded him that the whole flood of warnings was but a British plot.

In October, 1950, intelligence reports from Korea indicated, and actually predicted, that Red China would intervene at any moment in the war there. These reports received a high probability rating on lower echelons, but they were dismissed as improbable both by General MacArthur and by the intelligence committee in Washington to which they were referred for high-level evaluation. This evaluation prevailed, and it influenced policies, decisions, and moves made on the White House level, eventually causing embarrassment despite the explicit and timely nature of the warning.

The pitfalls of intelligence are many and varied. Discussing these dangers with jovial bluntness, Allen W. Dulles, one of America's greatest intelligence specialists, and at present director of the Central Intelligence Agency, once remarked: "It is often harder to use the product than to get it. The receivers of intelligence generally start out by discounting a particular report as false or a plant. Then, when they get over that hurdle, they discard what they don't like and refuse to believe it. Finally, when they do get a report they both believe and like, they don't know what to do about it."

The problem of evaluation represents a standing controversy among the students of intelligence. Some say, and I am inclined to side with them, that information should be evaluated somewhere within the intelligence organization that acts as the clearing-house of all information. There it may be evaluated by the chiefs of desks on their own level, if only because they have the broadest knowledge of their particular field, or by a branch whose function is general evaluation.

Others question the wisdom of leaving evaluation to those who collect the information. "Human enthusiasm is such," an observer remarked, "that it is difficult for me to believe that secret intelligence will be objectively evaluated by its collectors." Having separated its collection agencies from its analysis and evaluation section, the CIA has tried to prove in practice that effective evaluation work can be done within an agency that is also engaged in collection of information.

The Dissemination of Intelligence

Even the best intelligence is totally useless if it remains in the files of the intelligence service. This fact is fully recognized by the agencies themselves, who generally regard the distribution of evaluated information as one of their three basic functions. This part of their activity is called "dissemination of intelligence." It is usually handled by a separate branch of the service dedicated solely to this function and called the Dissemination Branch. The function of dissemination has many manual or technical aspects, such as the printing or mimeographing and the actual physical distribution of reports. Yet dissemination is essentially an intellectual activity involving great responsibilities, if only because it is the job of the men doing it to see that the proper information reaches the proper desks.

Intelligence material reaches the Dissemination Branch in

its classified form. Documents are given specific classifications to indicate their degree of secrecy. The scale of classifications begins with "Confidential." Next is "Secret." The highest classification is "Top Secret." Special documents involving highly confidential matters or operations are given individual classifications and often the term used in classifying such documents is itself in the classified category. During World War II, for example, the translations of the U.S. Army of foreign codes were classified "Magic." The operations plan of Overlord, the code name for the invasion of France in 1944, was classified "Bigot" and the men who were allowed access to such information were called "Bigoted."

The classification determines *ipso facto* how wide-spread the distribution of individual documents may be. An unclassified report, of course, may have unrestricted distribution, even though no official of any government is expected to hand over even unclassified papers to unauthorized persons. A report classified "Confidential" has a limited distribution but still may go to a great number of people who must be cognizant of its contents.

A document classified "Secret" has a far more limited distribution but it may still go to several hundred persons, but papers with the classification "Top Secret" are seen by only a few people, often no more than two or three. Even the physical transportation of such highly classified documents is severely restricted and prescribed. They are carried only by exceptionally trustworthy messengers specially cleared for the job, or in the armed forces by officer personnel who are required to carry side arms in transit. I recall the case of a "Top Secret" document of World War II that had a distribution of only seven specifically marked copies, and required that a brigadier general distribute them to their recipients, including the writer. Actually, the precautions taken with this particular document were out of all proportion to the value of the information it contained.

Even before such highly classified documents reach the Dissemination Branch, they are paraphrased or rewritten to prevent the identification of the codes used in their transmission and to safeguard the sources of their origin. Sources in general are indicated by established covers. "Top Secret" documents are numbered, and each copy is phrased differently. All these measures and many others are used to protect the sources of information even from the personnel of the Dissemination Branch.

Although it is widely recognized that dissemination is a crucial phase of effective intelligence work, it is very often the weakest link in the intelligence chain. Dissemination branches are frequently staffed by minor clerical personnel who carry out their responsibilities in a mechanical fashion. They give a perfunctory reading to the document at hand and then designate its recipients from a prearranged distribution list. As a result, certain vital intelligence material may never reach the person who could probably make the best use of it or, if it does, may reach him too late.

The sacroscant chain of command, observed religiously within bureaucratic organizations, also tends to interfere with efficient and effective distribution of intelligence. An intelligence report may originate on a rather low level of the hierarchy. The official who then handles it is supposed to pass it on through channels, which means that he gives it to his own immediate superior, who in turn relays it upward. Sometimes inefficient routing within the Dissemination Branch and the shackles of the chain of command combine to prevent vital items from reaching the final policy maker or commander in time for necessary action.

In December, 1944, an important piece of information was routed to a low-level official in one of the American intelligence agencies, simply because a distribution list showed him to be "cognizant" of the particular subject treated in the report. This report, however, contained intelligence of the utmost immediate importance to the highest policy maker, in this case President Roosevelt himself. It was a report from Tokyo, from a highly respected neutral source, advising us that Emperor Hirohito had established contact with the peace party in Japan and was actively working to create the preconditions for a possible cessation of hostilities. The official who received the report was quick to recognize its importance and possible influence on policy, but the chain of command separated him from the President by at least ten intermediate steps. Although the report was passed on at once, with a note urging that it be brought immediately to the attention of the President, it never actually reached Mr. Roosevelt's desk. It was sidetracked somewhere in the shuffle.

Although handled as separate functions, the close reciprocal relations between the three interlocking activities of an intelligence service—collection, evaluation, and distribution—are clearly evident. The efficient functioning of these three basic activities is essential if intelligence is to be effective and play its proper part in the great decisions that regulate international affairs.

The Influence of Intelligence

The highest form of positive intelligence is what may be called policy intelligence. The end purpose of all intelligence functions is to inform the policy makers at the highest level of impending moves of foreign governments, so that they may shape their own government's policies in the light of that knowledge.

On a somewhat lower level is strategic intelligence, which is designed to assist the higher military, naval, and air staffs in the development of their strategic plans and military policies. On an equal level is political intelligence, upon which diplomatic staffs depend for the formulation of their policies, negotiations, and treaties.

On a somewhat lower level is what may be called operational intelligence. The word "operational" is used here to identify the manifold interests and activities that fall somewhere between strategy and tactics. The term was originally coined in 1792 by an erratic Prussian military genius named Dietrich Heinrich von Bülow, who felt that a specific word was needed to express "lower strategy and higher tactics." He used the term "operation" to identify the coordination of several tactics for culmination within a single action, or the coordination of several minor actions toward the fulfillment of an intermediary step in the formulation of a definitive policy.

Accordingly, operational intelligence is designed to serve those who conduct the nation's diplomatic or military business on a high level in the field, but who have no policy-making power. Ambassadors and supreme military commanders fall into this category as the ultimate executors of a nation's policies abroad.

On the lowest level is tactical or combat intelligence, information of a localized or specific nature for use by all diplomatic and military echelons.

It may be said here that there is no critical division between the individual branches of intelligence, but that there is a very close reciprocal relation between them, since in the total intelligence activity each lower branch funnels its information upwards into policy intelligence.

Intelligence attains its greatest significance when it serves the purposes of the policy maker, and to the same extent national policy is dependent on intelligence. In this close relationship between national policy and intelligence, only a perfect equilibrium between the two can provide for the security of the nation.

In the middle thirties, high-level intelligence exerted its influence on Britain's national policy and grand strategy, and actually reshaped it. Some time in 1934, British intelligence received reports from its agents in Germany that Hitler was rearming in defiance of the Versailles Treaty and was secretly building an air force. To supplement the work of those agents already in Germany, the British Air General Staff developed a project to obtain absolutely reliable information from the Germans themselves. A number of young officers of the Air General Staff were instructed to feign friendship for the Third Reich and to worm themselves into the confidence of high Luftwaffe officials, for the purpose of getting whatever first-hand intelligence they could on the Luftwaffe's doctrine, strategy, tactics, personnel, and equipment.

The project succeeded beyond all expectations. A group commander even managed to get himself invited to Germany, where he was shown some of the Luftwaffe's most secret installations. He was eventually received by Hitler, who frankly disclosed to him confidential details of the Reich's aerial rearmament.

Influenced by reports about this surreptitious activity, His Majesty's Government decided to increase the Royal Air Force. However, this increase was only half-hearted. It was limited to seventy-five squadrons, of which forty-seven were bomber squadrons. At that time, the dominant R.A.F. doctrine still favored an offensive strategy. The British Cabinet had been persuaded by its air advisers that the four-engined heavy bombers of the R.A.F. would provide a war-winning weapon.

However, there was within the R.A.F. another school of thought, one that favored a defensive strategy concentrated in fighters and such electronic devices as radar, which was then in its earliest stages of development. This doctrine was represented most vigorously by Air Marshal Sir Hugh (later Lord) Dowding. Called "Stuffy" by his intimates and subordinates, he was a professional officer of the finest character, technical accomplishment, and imagination.

Dowding based his views on intelligence reports that indicated that Germany was increasing her Luftwaffe along offensive strategic lines, emphasis being heavy on bomber types.

Then, in March, 1935, Britain acquired, in a startlingly direct manner, a piece of policy intelligence of the greatest

77

importance. Foreign Secretary Sir John Simon visited Hitler in Germany and was told by the Fuehrer personally that Germany had already achieved air parity with Britain. Hitler also told Sir John that he "intended to go on building until he had an air force equal to those of Britain and France combined."

This "gratuitous warning," as Chester Wilmot put it, jolted the Baldwin Cabinet. They decided to increase the Home Defense Air Force to 121 squadrons with 1,512 first-line aircraft by April, 1937, and to accelerate the development of defensive electronic devices. Thus, the intelligence Sir John brought back from Germany and the corroborative material supplied by British agents brought about the abandonment of a previous military policy and determined the drafting of a new one.

Subsequently, additional information was obtained by British agents confirming the offensive character of the new Luftwaffe and bearing out the assumption that it was designed as a threat to Britain, either as a deterrent in preventing her from interfering with Hitler's designs, or as the decisive weapon in the event of war. Additional information was obtained through the arrest of a Luftwaffe spy in Britain, a suave intellectual named Hermann Goertz. The mission of this agent was to gather information about the R.A.F.'s fighter fields ringing London. The planners of the Luftwaffe needed this intelligence for the strategic air war they were drafting against Britain.

When such details became known in Downing Street, Sir Hugh Dowding was appointed commander in chief of the Fighter Command. Britain's defense in the air was entrusted to him, and, in due course, the defensive strategy he had advocated superseded the original offensive strategy.

This thrilling chain of intelligence developments, and the evolution of policies and strategies based on that intelligence, yielded historic results in the Battle of Britain when it came in August and September of 1940. The combination of superior fighter aircraft and scientific and technical equipment that had been developed as a result of the alarming information from Germany saved Britain from defeat when Göring's offensive Luftwaffe did, as predicted by British intelligence, mount its all-out onslaught against the British Isles.

If ever intelligence had a decisive influence on the military strategy of a major power, and if ever it succeeded in staving off disaster, England's survival was the historic case. There was nothing haphazard about these developments, or about the close correlation between intelligence on the one side and policy and strategy on the other. The intelligence maneuver that was designed to penetrate Hitler's plans was a superbly organized effort, in which all the branches of intelligence were employed. The information they produced was then carefully evaluated, and Britain's political leaders had the foresight to respect the information and the evaluation. The result was victory.

The United States was confronted with the necessity of making a similarly crucial policy decision in 1947 when the cold war began to take definite shape. The year before I had sat in on the deliberations of an intelligence group at which I heard the question raised for the first time, "Is the Soviet Union preparing for aggression?" Then subsidiary questions were posed, "Is the Soviet Union going to start peripheral conquests, in countries like Greece or Turkey or Germany?" and "Is she willing to risk a world war over ner plans?"

It became the job of American and British intelligence to answer these questions on the basis of the hardest possible information, and then to prepare a long-range estimate of the situation on the basis of all the collected and collated information. This was a problem on the highest strategic level, since the policy of the United States would evolve from the answers intelligence gave to those questions. In a real sense, the future of the free world depended on the accuracy of the answers supplied by intelligence.

Nor did intelligence have to start entirely from scratch. It had a pretty good idea of Soviet intentions, and the idea had come straight from the horse's mouth.

During the last days of World War II in Europe, Allied troops captured intact the archives of the German Foreign Office. For years after that, American and British intelligence officers studied these papers and tried to educe from them information that had a meaning for the future.

Among the papers were the documents covering Germany's relations with the Soviet Union, including the period of intimacy between August, 1939, and June, 1941. And in this group of documents, American intelligence experts discovered the record of Soviet Foreign Minister Molotov's conversations with Hitler and Ribbentrop between November 12 and 18, 1940. They were exceptionally frank conversations of men who saw no reason to conceal their thoughts. You might call them most realistic conversations, if exclusive preoccupation with power politics or *Realpolitik* can be called truly realistic.

The intelligence experts discovered among the papers the drafts of a secret protocol, drawn up by the Soviet Foreign

79

Commissariat, for signature by Germany and the U.S.S.R. This draft, dated November 26, 1940, is probably the frankest revelation of a country's political aspirations ever to fall into the hands of another nation.

In the draft, the Soviet government stated in so many words that "the focal point of the aspirations of the Soviet Union south of Batum and Baku [is] in the general direction of the Persian Gulf." Turkey, Bulgaria, and the rest of the Balkans were described as other such "focal areas of Soviet aspirations," and the draft proposed that "in case Turkey refuses to join the Four Powers, Germany, Italy, and the Soviet Union agree *to work out and to carry through the required military and diplomatic measures.*"

While there had been cases in the past when the aspirations and intentions of foreign powers were disclosed through indiscretions or effective secret intelligence work, never before had the ruthlessly aggressive plans of a scheming world power been so thoroughly exposed on such a comprehensive scale. The capture of the archives and the subsequent discovery of these specific documents represented a rare intelligence scoop, which was further enhanced by the brilliant investigation and evaluation of Soviet policy by British and American intelligence officers.

At the very outset of its investigation Central Intelligence could expect, on the basis of the Kremlin's own secret plans, that Soviet aggrandizement would be in the direction of the Balkans, Turkey and the Straits, and Iran.

That this was by no means a theoretical project, and that it was not abandoned with the discovery of the documents, was evidenced by another intelligence scoop scored by the British secret service in Turkey and Greece. These two countries are traditional arenas of British intelligence activity. Some of Britain's most intrepid secret service maneuvers have taken place there, as far back as the eighteenth century. During the war, Prime Minister Churchill established a special secret service detail to watch the development of Communist influence in Greece. This group succeeded in infiltrating the various Communist organizations and intercepted directives received by those organizations from Moscow. The directives showed that the Soviet Union was prepared to translate into action the aspirations of its diplomatic draft of November, 1940, and to annex Greece and Turkey in the manner outlined during the Molotov-Hitler conversations.

These intelligence papers were also placed at the disposal of American Central Intelligence, where they supplied another set of indices for the formulation of answers to the crucial questions. The entire apparatus of Central Intelligence was then directed at the procurement of information on the issue under study. Before long, Central Intelligence had a mass of data, ready for sifting and evaluation.

The process was brought to a preliminary close in February, 1947, when a Soviet move on Greece and Turkey was reported imminent. Central Intelligence was asked to prepare an estimate of the situation, which was presented to the White House, on March 3, 1947, together with an evaluation of the situation prepared by the State Department. The result was the Truman Doctrine, the *direct* outgrowth of information gained through exceptional intelligence work.

After that, the White House requested that Central Intelligence make a comprehensive survey of the situation and present a definitive estimate, on which the future policy of the United States vis-à-vis the Soviet Union could be safely based. With this assignment, intelligence came of age in the United States.

In due course, the Central Intelligence Agency completed its estimate of the situation, based on the most painstaking preparatory work in the history of intelligence, and involving extensive scientific investigation of both open and covert intelligence material. The CIA regarded its analysis as foolproof and was determined to stand by this estimate for better or for worse. It answered the basic question in the negative, stating firmly that the Soviet Union would not within the foreseeable future, risk a global war, and that it would not interfere directly, by military means, with American action in the cold war.

President Harry S. Truman and Secretary of State Dean Acheson accepted the estimate of the CIA, although competitive estimates, especially those prepared by the Air Force, contained a more alarming picture. The Air Force predicted that the Soviet Union would automatically risk war to counter American moves in Europe and even described such a war as imminent.

The entire international policy of the United States since March, 1947, when in an address before a joint session of Congress Mr. Truman announced American aid to Turkey and Greece, has been predicated on (a) the original estimate of the CIA, and (b) its running intelligence summaries, which have presented a day-by-day implementation of the original estimate.

On the basis of the CIA's definitive estimate, the United States defied the U.S.S.R. with the Berlin airlift, confident that the Soviet Union would not seize upon this American move to counter the Soviet blockade of Berlin as an excuse for unleashing World War III. Also on the basis of the CIA estimate, the United States decided (a) that there was sufficient time to rearm, (b) to organize the defenses of Europe, (c) to expedite the development of the hydrogen bomb, (d) to prepare what Dean Acheson called a "position of strength," without which dealings with the Soviet Union appeared impossible.

The final decision of President Truman to intervene in the Korean War, convinced as he was that the U.S.S.R. would not expand it into a global war, was also based on the intelligence summary evolved by the Central Intelligence Agency. The CIA apparently was never shaken in its belief that its estimate of the situation was correct, even on a long-range basis.

I was myself involved in an operation which may be cited as an example of strategic political intelligence. I think it is important to present it in some detail, if only because it opens up several other views of the unspectacular desk work in intelligence and introduces still another important phase of the intelligence effort, the order of battle.

The enemy's order of battle is something every military, naval, and air intelligence service regards as its primary function to collect. It is a list of his forces, their dispositions, insignia, designations, organizational structure, and officers. It provides the basic raw material used by the commander in the field in the preparation of his plans.

British intelligence developed the compilation of the order of battle into an art. And, despite the enormous difficulties that the collection of information entailed in the Pacific war, the United States Army succeeded by some seeming magic in compiling the battle order of the Japanese army with some comprehensiveness.

I used the little red-bound volume of Military Intelligence as my sole source of information in answering a question of great operational importance, "How good was the much-vaunted Kwantung Army that the Japanese had in Manchuria?" In estimating Japanese military strength, it was assumed by the Joint Chiefs of Staff that the Kwantung Army was an extremely efficient, well-commanded, effective force. It was theoretically self-contained and autonomous. It was further assumed by Allied intelligence that the Kwantung Army was intact despite the war, and that it was kept in Manchuria as a strategic reserve which could continue the war, if necessary, from there, in the event that the main islands of Japan were lost.

For some strange reason, this phantom army in Manchuria held the same kind of fascination for G-2 (the intelligence branch of the U.S. Army's General Staff) that Hitler's new German army had for the American military attachés stationed in Berlin. Influenced by the respectful estimates that G-2 prepared on the military potential of the Kwantung Army, G-3 (Operations) drew up plans in which the distant and idle army loomed very large indeed.

The forces of the Western Allies were deemed insufficient to deal with both the Japanese armies in the active theaters *and* the Kwantung Army. So it became an obsession with the General Staff to draw the Soviet Union into the war and to assign to the Red Army the defeat of the Kwantung Army in Manchuria. In the summer of 1943, the War Department prepared "a very high level strategic estimate" to guide President Roosevelt's relations with the Soviet Union. It was called "Russia's Position," and stated, among other things: "Finally, the most important factor in relation to Russia is the prosecution of the war in the Pacific. With Russia as an ally in the war against Japan, the war can be terminated in less time and at less expense in life and resources than if we reverse the case."

When President Roosevelt went to the Yalta Conference in the early winter of 1944-45, he was handed what amounted to an ultimatum by his military advisers. "We desire Russian entry at the earliest possible date," the démarche read, "consistent with her ability to engage in offensive operations and are prepared to offer the maximum support possible without prejudice to our main effort against Japan."

The late Secretary of State Edward R. Stettinius, who was with Roosevelt at Yalta, spoke of "the *immense pressure* put on the President by our military leaders to bring Russia into the Far Eastern war." As usual, the strategy of the General Staff was based on intelligence and evaluation.

However, there were those who regarded this intelligence estimation as faulty and the evaluation erroneous. Among those who disagreed with the plan to bring Russia into the war were W. Averell Harriman, the American Ambassador to the Soviet Union, Major General John R. Deane, the American Military Attaché in Moscow, the high commanders of the Navy, and its Secretary, James Forrestal. But these men had no concrete information with which to back up their opposition. I knew that Mr. Forrestal and Vice Admiral Charles M. Cooke, Jr., Admiral King's chief of staff, were seeking for such information, and it became a determination with me to find it.

In the summer of 1944, after the capture of Saipan in the Pacific, I was astounded by a bit of incidental intelligence which stated that among the units we had destroyed on the island were the 50th Infantry and 135th Infantry. The Japanese battle order, according to G-2, listed it as part of the Kwantung force, stationed in Manchuria.

I checked, and there was no mistake on either score. The 135th Infantry was a part of the Kwantung Army and it was destroyed on Saipan, several thousand miles from its official garrison. This was the first indication I had that the Kwantung Army had been broken up, though it was only a straw in the wind. I immediately acquired a list of all the Japanese divisions we had encountered on the various Pacific islands, from Guadalcanal to Peleliu to Tinian, and from it I made a startling discovery. The Kwantung Army, as represented by our G-2, was nothing more than an imaginary force. None of the Imperial units which once formed that fine army were still in Manchuria to wage a dreaded separate war. Those crack divisions, "the cream of the Japanese army," as Colonel Carlson of the Marines called them, had all been transferred to the various theaters of active operations, to the Pacific islands, to China, and to the Philippines. A large percentage of the original force had been destroyed by us as we advanced from island to island. Others were pinned down thousands of miles from Manchuria.

I then began to collect intelligence on the new Kwantung Army. With the help of the British battle order of the Japanese army, I found that it consisted of third- and fourth-rate divisions, some of them maintained only at brigade strength and made up of inferior troops that Tokyo had scraped from the bottom of its manpower barrel.

Here was operational intelligence of the utmost importance, calculated to radiate its influence upward, to strategy and even to policy. It was obvious that if the Kwantung Army was only a phantom force, then the Allies did not need the Red Army to deal with it. And if the Red Army were not needed in the Far East, then Soviet intervention in the war against Japan was not required.

I was on a rather low echelon of intelligence, and the problem arose as to how this information could be channeled to the higher-ups. My immediate superior in the chain of command was a lieutenant commander, the executive officer of my branch. He reported to the officer in charge, a commander, who in turn reported to the Director of Naval Intelligence. Next in the chain of command was the subchief of Naval Operations. In turn came the Vice Chief of Naval

Operations and the Chief of Naval Operations, Admiral Ernest J. King, commander in chief of the United States Fleet. His superior was the Secretary of the Navy, and there the jurisdiction of the Navy ended. And this was clearly an Army matter.

At that time, the military leaders of the War Department believed implicitly in their intelligence. In the field, General Douglas MacArthur supported it to the hilt. On February 25, 1945, during a conference with Forrestal in Manila, MacArthur stated that "we should secure the commitment of the Russians to active and vigorous prosecution of a campaign against the Japanese in Manchukuo of such proportions as to pin down a very large part of the Japanese army."

On the other hand, Assistant Secretary of War John J. McCloy opposed this view. His opposition was based on information received from another intelligence unit of the War Department, under Colonel Alfred McCormack, which had reached conclusions similar to my own findings. But McCloy failed to make his influence felt, and the estimate of G-2 prevailed to the bitter end. Years later, in March, 1947, Mr. McCloy recalled this incident. "He said," Mr. Forrestal recorded in his diary, "this for him [McCloy] illustrated most vividly the necessity for the civilian voice in military decisions even in time of war."

Despite my own low position in the intelligence hierarchy, I prepared a memorandum of my findings and ventured to offer certain conclusions. I stated without equivocation that according to the most reliable information the Kwantung Army no longer existed as an efficient and powerful force. I stated as my second premise that its replacements consisted of inferior troops incapable of defending Manchuria. I concluded that Manchuria seemed unlikely to be slated as the battleground for a last-ditch stand of defeated Japan, and that these premises made Soviet intervention in the Far Eastern war appear unnecessary.

I had no means of ascertaining the fate of my memorandum. If it ever did get across to the Army, I do not know in what pigeonhole it wound up. However, I tried every possible way to publicize my findings and conclusions. I discussed them with higher-ups, and then I volunteered to survey them in a closed meeting of the American Military Institute, a scientific organization.

The meeting took place in a conference room in the National Archives in the fall of 1944. The chair was occupied by Colonel Joseph I. Greene, then editor of the influential *Infantry Journal*. After the meeting, I gave him a copy of my memorandum, and he volunteered to get it into the hands of General George Marshall. But still there came no signs that the War Department's high opinion of the Kwantung Army was dimmed.

In December, 1944, Captain Ellis M. Zacharias returned to Washington to serve in a confidential capacity directly under the Secretary of the Navy. I immediately acquainted him with my memorandum and, through him, the gist of it reached Secretary Forrestal. He used the report as one of the guns in the battery of his arguments against Soviet intervention in the Far East.

When it became known that President Roosevelt was planning to meet with Stalin at Yalta, and that position papers were being prepared for him to acquaint him with the backgrounds of the matters to be discussed, I managed to get copies of my memorandum to Harry L. Hopkins, and also into the office of Admiral William Leahy, the President's chief of staff. I have no means of knowing whether or not the memorandum ever reached his desk. But I do know from what happened at Yalta that it never made the slightest impression on the negotiations. General Marshall remained firm in his acceptance of G-2's estimate and urged the President to bring the Soviet Union into the Far Eastern war.

This attitude did not change even when the atomic bomb became a reality. According to Forrestal, "when President Truman came to Potsdam in the summer of 1945, he told [General Dwight D.] Eisenhower he had as one of his primary objectives that of getting Russia into the Japanese war." This determination was based on a canvass of his highest military advisers in Potsdam, but it was contrary to the advice of Secretary of State James F. Byrnes, "who was most anxious to get the Japanese affair over before the Russians got in." General Eisenhower also "begged" Mr. Truman "not to assume that he had to give anything away, . . . that the Russians were desperately anxious to get into the Eastern war and that in Eisenhower's opinion there was no question but that Japan was already thoroughly beaten." Ambassador Harriman also "begged" Mr. Truman to keep the Russians out of the war against Japan. But the opinion of General Marshall, seconded by Secretary of War Henry L. Stimson, prevailed. As events proved, it was based on erroneous intelligence.

The Russians did get into the war and the highly touted Kwantung Army crumbled away before them. When the Japanese divisions fighting in Manchuria were later identified it developed that the G-2 battle order was wrong and that the British battle order was right. It also developed that the conclusions I had drawn on the basis of the British battle order were correct.

Tactical Intelligence

Tactical intelligence is information of a local or specialized nature. It is generally of no immediate importance to the policy makers or to the commanders in war time. It is information that may subsequently be used to supplement and expedite a particular intelligence problem, and it deals essentially with facts and information of a minor nature which are only a limited aspect of the comprehensive intelligence operation.

In times of war, its military version is called combat intelligence, involving information about the enemy in a tactical sense. Comprehensively it is concerned with every military aspect of the enemy or potential enemy and with any form of information that has a direct bearing upon the prosecution of the war. It comprises such incidental knowledge as the location of gun emplacements, bridgeheads, invasion points, the caliber of enemy rifles, troop movements, the personal characteristics of enemy leaders, or the enemy's military tactics.

In time of peace, tactical information is continuously and vitally needed by the chiefs of political and diplomatic organizations, and in war it is essential information for all commanders—from the commander in chief down to the leader of a squad.

Since this is the most common form of intelligence, there are any number of cases—actually millions of them—that show tactical or combat intelligence in practice. My own favorite example is a quaint scoop from the Palestine campaign of World War I. It had nothing to do with carefully planned organized intelligence. It was entirely spontaneous, the product of that rare combination of erudition, ingenuity, intrepidity, and adaptation that in combat intelligence inevitably yields the best results.

On February 14, 1918, the British 60th Division was ordered by General Allenby to attack Jericho and drive the Turks across the Jordan. In preparation for the main attack they were to capture a small village named Michmash that was perched on a high rocky hill in the path of the drive. A brigade was detached to storm the hill and take Michmash by frontal attack from the substantial force of Turks holding it firmly.

When the name of Michmash was mentioned during the briefing, the brigade major felt somehow that it sounded familiar. Then he remembered. It was mentioned in the Bible. The major retired to his tent and by the light of a candle began to study the Bible, looking for the dimly remembered reference to Michmash. He found it in I Samuel, chapters 13 and 14.

The passage reads:

> And Saul, and Jonathan his son, and the people that were present with them, abode in Gibeah of Benjamin: but the Philistines encamped in Michmash. . . .
>
> Now it came to pass upon a day, that Jonathan the son of Saul said unto the young man that bare his armour, Come, and let us go over to the Philistines' garrison, that is on the other side. But he told not his father. . . . and the people knew not that Jonathan was gone.
>
> And between the passages, by which Jonathan sought to go over unto the Philistines' garrison, there was a sharp rock on the one side, and a sharp rock on the other side: and the name of the one was Bozez, and the name of the other Seneh.
>
> The forefront of the one was situate northward over against Michmash, and the other southward over against Gibeah.
>
> And Jonathan said to the young man that bare his armour, come, and let us go over unto the garrison . . . it may be that the Lord will work for us: for there is no restraint to the Lord to save by many or by few.

Here was an important bit of combat intelligence about the approaches to Michmash. The major read on about how Jonathan climbed through the pass until he and his armorbearer came to a place high up. The Philistines who were asleep awoke. They thought they were surrounded by the armies of Saul and fled in disorder. Saul then attacked with his whole army. It was, according to the Bible, his first victory against the Philistines.

The major roused his brigadier and showed him the passage in the Bible. "This pass," he said, "these rocky headlands and flat piece of ground are probably still there. Why don't we try to do what Jonathan did?" The brigadier agreed. Scouts were sent out to reconnoiter the ancient land. They found the pass exactly where the Bible described it, with the plateau above Michmash illuminated in the moonlight. "Very little has changed in Palestine," the brigadier said, "throughout the centuries."

The plan of the attack was promptly changed. Instead of

a whole brigade, the brigadier sent a single company against the sleeping Turks in Michmash. The few sentries the company encountered were silently eliminated and the biblical plateau was reached without incident shortly before dawn. The Turks awoke, as had the Philistines before them, and, thinking they were surrounded, "the multitude melted away."

The name of the young British major who was helped to this neat scoop by his knowledge of the Bible was Vivian Gilbert. "We killed or captured every Turk that night in Michmash," he said afterwards, "so that, after thousands of years, the tactics of Saul and Jonathan were repeated with success by a British force."

There can be, of course, no airtight separation between the various forms of intelligence, however they might be viewed. An item of seemingly general tactical significance may turn out to be of enormous strategic importance, and it may even have a direct bearing on final policy. Information about two strange new devices which arrived on Tinian in the summer of 1945, would have been a piece of combat intelligence had the Japanese been able to procure it. Yet the possession of this particular bit of information would have had enormous strategic implications to the Japanese High Command, since those two devices were in actual fact the atomic bombs destined for Hiroshima and Nagasaki.

Data about the arrival of certain Panzer divisions on the Western Front near Eupen-Malmédy in November, 1944, would have been regarded as *prima facie* combat intelligence, since the location and identification of enemy units in active combat areas is a tactical task of intelligence. In this particular case, however, such information would have had enormous operational significance, because those unidentified divisions formed part of the new German VI SS Panzer Army, organized and deployed specifically for what was soon to become the Battle of the Bulge.

We saw previously how an order by General von Rundstedt, which halted the Panzers converging on Dunkirk, had such a decisive influence when it was captured by a British patrol. Yet this coup was strictly within the framework of combat intelligence. Thus it is that intelligence in its practical application cuts boldly across categories and influences. A minute item may turn out to be of stupendous value, while what at first blush appears to be a major piece of information might prove to possess only minor tactical significance.

Pitfalls of Intelligence

Despite the size of the apparatus, the scientific scaffolding of the activity, the money expended on it—despite the conceit and arrogance of some organizations—intelligence is very far from being infallible. It is by no means a foolproof defense against unpleasant and damaging surprises in international relations, and the chances are that it never will be.

The modern history of intelligence is crowded with failures, blunders, and wrong estimates. Their respective secret services assured the Kaiser in 1914 and Hitler in 1939 that Britain would stay out of the war, and advised Prime Minister Neville Chamberlain on April 3, 1940, on the very eve of the conquests of Norway, Denmark, the Low Countries, and France, that Germany had "missed the bus." The Japanese secret service misled its government about the war potential of the United States. American intelligence failed to provide a definitive warning on the eve of Pearl Harbor. Stalin's secret service misinformed him about the power of the Finns in 1940. Marshall Göring's intelligence persuaded him the U.S. Air Force would never be able to develop a long-range fighter, and persisted in this estimate even when such planes had already been assembled on British flying fields.

Mussolini was constantly fooled by his secret service and went into all his wars, against Ethiopia, Greece, and the Allies, with inadequate or erroneous information. British intelligence only learned of the arrival of Field Marshal Rommel in North Africa fifteen days after a whole Panzer division of the Afrika Korps had landed. Allied intelligence never spotted the negotiations which led to the Russo-German pact of 1939. During the ensuing Polish campaign, Allied intelligence failed to ascertain that Germany had only 23 divisions in the West facing 110 French divisions, and that Hitler was ready to call it a day if the Allies started a real war in 1939.

Between the end of World War II and the outbreak of the war in Korea, American intelligence was guilty of five major blunders.

1. *It failed to predict the fall of Czechoslovakia.* Our intelligence assured the government that the crisis of 1948 was a routine change of government and not a seizure of absolute power by the Communists.

2. *It failed to predict and then to evaluate the meaning of Tito's defection.* We had no advance warning of impending events in Yugoslavia and no inside information on the circumstances of the break. The absence of hard facts prevented the U.S. government from acting promptly and exploiting the first serious emergency within the monolithic Communist orbit.

3. *It failed to anticipate the rapid disintegration of the Kuomintang in China.* "All our intelligence services save G-2," wrote Reid and Bird, "discounted the capabilities of the Communists to overrun China."

4. *It failed to provide accurate information on developments in Palestine in 1948.* The military abilities of the Arabs were embarrassingly overrated by the various intelligence groups. According to Secretary Forrestal, even such an astute observer as George F. Kennan was misled by State Department intelligence, exaggerating the strength of the Arabs and the weakness of the Jews.

5. *It failed to predict an uprising in Colombia in April, 1948.* This failure embarrassed the American Secretary of State who went to Bogotá to attend a conference of American states and found a revolution under way.

In 1950, the United States was caught *avec des pantalons bas,* as a French newspaper put it, when North Korea invaded South Korea. Remembering Pearl Harbor, Congress was understandably disturbed and invited Admiral Roscoe Hillenkoetter, Director of CIA, to explain this latest breakdown of American intelligence. Hillenkoetter produced a number of intelligence reports which his agency had received and circulated, all of them describing ominous moves and preparations north of the 38th parallel. Hillenkoetter persuaded Congress that insofar as Korea was concerned, CIA was "on the ball," even though other agencies of the government had failed to appreciate its warnings and were surprised when war came on June 25, 1950. In actual fact, however, Hillenkoetter had appeared in executive session before the Foreign Affairs Committee of the House two days before the outbreak of hostilities, on June 23, 1950, to report on the state of the world as CIA saw it. Congressman James G. Fulton of Pennsylvania then asked Hillenkoetter specifically about Korea and the likelihood of trouble there. The Admiral firmly assured members of the Committee that, insofar as his organization could tell, all was well in Korea and no trouble was expected then or in the foreseeable future. War came thirty hours later.

While the outsider is inclined to exaggerate the errors of

the secret service, there is a tendency on the part of intelligence services themselves to minimize their failures and cover up their blunders. Both attitudes are wrong, of course, and dangerous as well, if only because they tend to obscure the real potentialities of intelligence. In the words of Admiral Hillenkoetter, CIA's job involves "the systematic and critical examination of intelligence information, the synthesis of that intelligence information with all available related material and the determination of the probable significance of evaluated intelligence." But he added, "To *predict* the intentions of the enemy, real or potential, you would need a crystal ball."

The emphasis is on the word "predict." It implies deduction or rather an oracular venture even when it is based on masses of factual data. Yet prediction is an essential and inevitable function of intelligence. It is an integral part of its estimates and is necessary even though it involves risk. A prediction may be right and it may be wrong. Intelligence is on firm ground only when it makes its prognostication on the basis of exact knowledge of an opponent's proven intentions. There are at least four such cases on record, yet in three of those cases policy makers failed to accept the estimates of their intelligence services and act on the basis of corroborated information. In such cases, of course, it is the policy maker and not the intelligence service that must bear the responsibility for the consequences.

The pitfalls of intelligence are dramatized in its failures. It is, however, important to bear in mind that the errors of intelligence are not necessarily due to any basic deficiency of the service, but rather to the inevitable risks and difficulties inherent in this complex activity.

The failures of intelligence may be due to a number of causes. There may be too little or too much information on hand on which to base estimates. It may not be humanly possible to procure information about an opponent's intentions, or there may be too much information available, making selection difficult. On the eve of the Allied landings in North Africa in 1942, German intelligence had ample information about our intentions and so advised Hitler. The problem then became to acquire exact intelligence about the location of the prospective landings. Specific intelligence was obtained in substantial quantities, and selection left to the evaluators of the German High Command. In this particular case, the German High Command chose the wrong reports and expected the landings to take place near Bengasi and Dakar.

In December, 1941, we definitely expected Japan to start

a war, since convincing evidence had been produced in quantities by our intelligence organs. Yet when the reports were evaluated and estimates prepared, the wrong predictions emerged, and the striking area was fixed far from Pearl Harbor. In the hindsight of today this error is magnified and presented as a proof of the deficiencies of intelligence. In actual fact, such deficiencies cannot be remedied no matter how the facilities of intelligence may improve. The human tendency to err is an unavoidable pitfall in intelligence, and no technical competence is capable of eliminating it.

There are, however, other pitfalls which can be avoided: undue timidity, or undue recklessness, in collection and evaluation; or evaluation biased by deep-seated prejudices or preconceived notions. In March, 1948, for example, the Defense Department received information from General Lucius D. Clay in Germany indicating the imminence of a Soviet invasion of Germany. There was a tendency in Washington to accept the information at face value and to make the necessary arrangements to meet the onslaught. Secretary of Defense Forrestal, however, refused to act on the intelligence alone. He summoned the chiefs of the service intelligence agencies to his office and remained closeted with them for two days in an effort to determine the significance of what appeared in the surface-evaluated information.

It was then merely by the sheer force of Forrestal's personality and under the threat of serious danger that he succeeded in fusing their best thinking on the subject and producing an estimate that proved correct. Majority agreement was reached, with the Air Force dissenting, that the suspicious troop movements represented a build-up for the blockade of Berlin rather than preparations for a full-scale invasion.

Another pitfall is created in the inferior position of intelligence within the government organization. Colonel Nicolai pointed out that in the German Imperial Army, "in which the feeling of subordination was very strongly developed," the chief of the intelligence service was "by far the youngest departmental chief of the High Command"—a mere major. Anyone who is familiar with the sacrosanct institution of the chain of command knows how little influence even a colonel has in the greater order of things. "I must emphasize these personal considerations," Nicolai wrote, "because they help to make credible the difficulties which our Intelligence Service met with in its work."

In the United States, too, key intelligence officers have been hampered in their work and reduced in their influence by their inferior ranks. Thus, for example, the fleet intelligence officer in Hawaii at the time of Pearl Harbor was a mere lieutenant commander. Throughout the military organization, old-line senior officers imposed strict subordination on their intelligence officers. The latter were prevented from influencing strategies and policies, despite the fact that by virtue of their preoccupation they knew first and best the trends and data on which such strategies and policies should be based. The echelon of intelligence is still far removed from the echelon of the policy makers and military planners. This distance alone reduces the effectiveness of even the best intelligence.

Worst of all is a condition common to all intelligence set-ups, in the United States as well as the U.S.S.R., in Britain as well as China. It is duplication within the intelligence effort. Tighter organization and a clearer demarcation of jurisdictional boundaries could ameliorate this situation, but we are still far from even a tolerable situation in this respect. In Britain, for example, intelligence activities are scattered among no fewer than fifteen intelligence agencies converging on the Joint Intelligence Bureau of the Ministry of Defence. While JIB is nominally the central intelligence agency of Her Majesty's Government, it shares its work with the Foreign Office, the Admiralty, the War Office, the Air Ministry, the Colonial Office, the Ministry of Commonwealth Relations, the Board of Trade, the Ministry of Supply, the Ministry of Civil Aviation, the Ministry of Transport, the Central Office of Information, the Medical Research Council, and the Department of Scientific and Industrial Research. Each has its own autonomous intelligence department.

The situation is not better in the Soviet Union where there are at least five major intelligence organizations, working parallel and even competing with one another. In the United States duplication is rampant with the work distributed among as many as twenty-five agencies. Aside from CIA, the State Department, the Army, Navy, and Air Force each has its own major and more or less autonomous intelligence department. In addition to these, there are a number of committees, conferences, and groups in operation. And the Joint Chiefs of Staff depend on their own Joint Intelligence Group.

This is a dangerous situation. It is not calculated to enhance the efficiency and effectiveness of intelligence. Contradictions, already existing by the very nature of the activity, inevitably develop from such decentralization. The situation is further complicated by the departmental jealousies which are rampant within intelligence services. The situation appears most detrimental when it comes to the appraisal of information. Corroborative evidence is as important in intelligence as it is in courts of law, but the scattering of intelligence interferes with effective corroboration. A piece of information may become available to but one major agency and then lack of corroboration may detract from its persuasiveness. Or a piece of misleading information may be fed to several intelligence agencies causing higher authorities to regard such information as "fully corroborated."

Centralization of intelligence is, however, only a partial remedy of this condition. There may be pitfalls even in this centralization, if only that assigning too much power and responsibility to a single agency leaves none at large to check up on it. When considering the potentialities of intelligence the pitfalls mentioned must always be borne in mind, and in thinking of intelligence as a first line of defense its limitations must be taken into account. Any absolute dependence on intelligence is itself a pitfall that must be avoided.

The Human Equation

The greatest, most intrepid operator in the business of intelligence is a mysterious American whom Radio Moscow calls "Colonel Lincoln." Not much is known about the man. He is said to be Robert T. Lincoln, the middle initial "T" standing for Throckmorton. He was born in Slippery Rock, Arkansas, on October 10, 1909. He used to be a rum-runner.

No superlative is strong enough to do justice to the skill of this man. He fought and won single-handed battles in the mountains of Iran against a whole army of Soviet operatives. He penetrated to Atomgrad, the mysterious Russian atomic city, and returned with a complete hydrogen bomb. He calmed unruly tribes in Afghanistan, and, on a Pacific island, disarmed a band of Japanese conspirators who plotted the assassination of General Douglas MacArthur. He also discovered Hitler alive in a cave in Patagonia some time after the world was satisfied that the dictator was no longer living.

Lincoln is known by a score of aliases and is frequently seen in a number of different places simultaneously. He is a champion marksman, a daredevil pilot, an expert mountaineer, a wizard in codes and ciphers, and a man of a hundred faces.

In every respect, Lincoln is the right man for the job. He

is modest and has a passion for anonymity. He is selfless and intensely patriotic. He is daring and resourceful.

There is just one thing wrong with Colonel Robert Throckmorton Lincoln. He does not exist.

He was conjured up over an after-dinner drink one night in Teheran by Ambassador John Wiley and his political officer, Gerald Dooher. It was 1948 and the two men were listening to the Moscow Radio. They were suddenly reduced to helpless laughter by a Soviet tale about a ubiquitous American agent. They decided to put their heads together and accommodate the Russians. The product of this whimsical conspiracy was Robert Throckmorton Lincoln, who emerged full-grown in all his classic and majestic proportions from the combined imaginations of the two inspired Americans.

Coming from nowhere, Lincoln was suddenly everywhere —to the bewilderment and dismay of the Moscow propagandists. His fame, given publicity by his creators, spread like wildfire. His name and exploits were on everyone's lips. It was soon quite common to meet people, especially in bars, who swore that they had actually seen Lincoln, or worked with him, or bunked with him.

When Supreme Court Justice William O. Douglas went mountain-climbing in Asia, Moscow charged that he, too, was an American secret agent and linked to Lincoln. When the associate justice of the Supreme Court came back to the States, reporters asked him to comment on the charge. "Oh, yes," Mr. Douglas said, "Lincoln was my constant companion on every one of my own secret missions."

Then the bubble burst in April, 1950. Cyrus L. Sulzberger of the New York *Times* was in Teheran and he picked up a lead about the fabulous Lincoln. The result was an article that announced Lincoln's death. It was not on the obituary page. Bob Lincoln was exposed as an amusing fraud! Some of us were very sorry to see him go and wished that men like him really existed. However, it seems that Sulzberger's scoop did not kill off Lincoln altogether. He continues to show up from time to time on Radio Moscow which claims that Sulzberger's story was printed to camouflage the fact that Lincoln is still as active as he ever was.

To be sure, the Lincoln myth is not all myth by any means. The colonel may be pure fiction (who knows?), but he is genuine, too, because he represents the epitome of the intelligence officer as he exists in the popular mind.

The people who thought up Lincoln made him active in all branches and categories of secret service. He was made what may be called the intelligence officer proper, a member of the "landed aristocracy" who donates his skills to his government without pay. He was made a secret intelligence agent, only slightly less important than the intelligence officer. He was a spy whose pedigree is perforce spurious. He was a saboteur, a conspirator, a guerrilla leader—a protean adventurer in the thrilling drama of intelligence.

This is not too unrealistic, since such zigzagging transfers and interlocking assignments do occur once in a while in actual practice. In Britain, for example, such jacks of all secret service trade were Baden-Powell, Dale Long, Lawrence, Paul Dukes, and, more recently, Keswick, Hutchison, and Picquet-Wicks, residents of the mysterious Norgeby House. In the United States, too, intelligence officers were frequently given assignments in the field, and may still be at large, walking boldly where even Lincoln never trod.

However, there are not many of them. With growth and specialization has come a stricter distribution of labor, and the casting of the right man in the right role has become the order of the day.

An intelligence specialist is like John Erskine's man—he has the moral obligation to be intelligent. But he need not be exceptionally brilliant or a creative thinker. The qualities sought in the rank and file are not so much inspiration, imagination, and bursting initiative as a professional knowledge of a particular activity, patience, application, persistence, and thoroughness. "The determination of facts relating to the enemy," Colonel Walter C. Sweeney wrote in his pioneering *Military Intelligence*, "the object of the labors of Intelligence Service personnel, is not arrived at by inspiration nor by any divine gift from a higher power. It is gained by the application of hard and patient work to the matter in hand, based upon knowledge, experience, and common sense. There is no mystery about it, only painstaking and systematic study of the recorded information. There is no royal road to success in the work of the Intelligence specialist."

Directors of Intelligence

The intelligence service need not be a phalanstery of geniuses —as long as there is a genius at its head. In the history of the secret service, great epochs have been linked directly and intimately not to any collective brilliance of the organization but to the individual brilliance of the chief. The history of the British Secret Service by no means shows uninterrupted efficiency, and there have been times when it was in rather bad shape, as well as others when it shone brightly. Those periods of greatness were marked by the appearance of exceptional personalities at the head of the Service.

Sir Francis Walsingham (1530-90) was such a genius during the reign of Queen Elizabeth, as was John Thurloe (1616-68) under Cromwell. After them, for about two hundred years, the luster of the Secret Service dimmed, not because England was unchallenged abroad, but simply because no great chiefs were developed at home.

In more modern times, the halcyon days of British intelligence were linked to such names as Sir H. M. Hozier (Winston Churchill's father-in-law), Sir Henry Brackenburry, Sir John Ardagh, and General Cockerrill, the genius who changed the art of intelligence into the exacting science it is today. Similarly the greatness of France's Deuxième Bureau is linked to General Dupont, who headed it during and after World War I and laid out a network of agents that reached from the Rhineland deep into the U.S.S.R.

The German Secret Service flourished under Bismarck's Wilhelm Stieber and Hitler's Wilhelm Canaris, and Soviet intelligence attained its greatest efficiency under such exceptional "spymasters" as Beldin, Davinov, Ulitsky, Fitin, Ossipov, and Kuznetsov.

These Russians were Marxist intellectuals raised in the Communist Party who had close personal ties with the party leaders. But otherwise they were hardly different from the great European chiefs. Common to all were exceptional organizing ability, the ability to inspire loyalty in subordinates, an innate flair for secret service work, a prodigious memory, a sense of history, an almost universal knowledge of complex technological matters, insatiable curiosity, and that aseptic intellectual ruthlessness and cold cynicism that Ambrose Bierce, bitingly satirical writer of horror stories, thought comes from a study of mankind.

The United States has found exceptional personalities as secret service chiefs whenever they were needed. The first man thus engaged was Major Benjamin Tallmadge, who headed George Washington's phenomenally efficient intelligence service. The latest is Allen W. Dulles, who today directs the Central Intelligence Agency. Two other able Americans in the field are J. Edgar Hoover, whose personality is reflected in the competence of the Federal Bureau of Investigation, an agency dedicated primarily to counterespionage but producing good results in positive intelligence as well, and

General William J. Donovan, wartime chief of the Office of Strategic Services and later American Ambassador to Thailand.

"Donovan was born in a lace-curtain Irish home in Buffalo," two of his wartime agents wrote. "He won the Congressional Medal of Honor while leading the famous Fighting 69th in World War I, and afterwards rose to such prominence as a lawyer that he was the Republican nominee for Governor in New York in 1933. Throughout his career he had a shrewd penchant for first names, for meeting the right people, and for expanding generously in every direction. OSS was a direct reflection of Donovan's character. He was its spark plug, the moving force behind it. In a sense it can be said that Donovan *was* OSS."

Britain's Division of Naval Intelligence, founded in 1887, was a stuffy and backward organization in which clerks, standing before high desks, recorded the characteristics of foreign warships with quill pens in huge ledgers chained to the desks. But this dusty office suddenly blossomed into a den of perpetual adventure when, in 1914, Captain Reginald Hall was appointed its chief.

There were some who thought that Captain (later Admiral Sir) Reginald Hall was the greatest intelligence chief who ever lived. In a letter to President Woodrow Wilson, Ambassador Walter H. Page wrote: "Hall is one genius that the war has developed. Neither in fiction nor in fact can you find any such man to match him. Of the wonderful things that I know he has done, there are several that it would take an exciting volume to tell. The man is a genius—a clear case of genius. All other secret service men are amateurs by comparison."

Colonel Edward M. House, Wilson's confidant, wrote directly to Hall, "I cannot think at the moment of any man who has done more useful service in this war than you, and I salute you."

William Reginald Hall was the personification of intelligence. He was brilliant, curious, eager, and industrious. In him intelligence reached a climax unprecedented until then, and it has remained unparalleled till now.

Hall had a relatively large staff in D.N.I. but he worked personally with every one of his men. He invigorated them and drew from them loyalties and sacrificial work. He was usually all over the place, supervising the breaking of German codes here, the surveillance of Irish spies there, and extending his interest to the land war in Europe where one of his scoops enabled the French to win the decisive battle of Verdun.

The overwhelming influence of chiefs like Hall on the intelligence service was pointed up by Colonel Walther Nicolai, one of Hall's opposite numbers as chief of German Military Intelligence during World War I. When I met him in 1934, he was an aging and broken man. Yet in his own days, Nicolai, too, had the makings of a great secret service chief. If he was to gain nothing but the disappointments of an indifferent career, it was only because the importance of his work and his own personal brilliance were not recognized by his superiors.

Frustrated in his own ambitions, Nicolai wrote in a melancholy mood of the role a good intelligence chief is supposed to play within the organization. He regarded the chief as the fulcrum of the organization, the sole person who really matters. "The intelligence service is a service for gentlemen. It breaks down when it is entrusted to others. The chief must, in every respect, stand head and shoulders above his agents. Or else, it is not he who rules but his subordinates, with all their inferior characteristics."

A few words might be added about the special responsibilities of the ideal intelligence chief. Enormous power is concentrated in his hands, and he can use it for good or evil, against foreign adversaries or against his own government's leadership. The Soviet leaders realize this danger and do not allow an intelligence chief to stay at the helm for too long. This explains, too, why the life of every chief of the secret service ends by execution in the Soviet Union.

In France, secret service chiefs tried repeatedly to gain dominant influence on domestic affairs and shook the nation to its foundations with their interference. The famous Dreyfus case is the classical example of such mischief. In Germany, too, Admiral Canaris turned on Hitler and joined a conspiracy against the man he was expected to serve without qualification.

Rebellions and ambitions of this type are unthinkable in a democracy, yet even it must be on the guard against such possibilities. This is why Hanson W. Baldwin, military editor of the New York *Times*, suggested that the director of intelligence should be a civilian who could be trusted implicitly to recognize this basic responsibility of his position. "Military personnel," he wrote, "are rarely suited by training for the collection or evaluation of strategic or national intelligence; some will be needed, but they must be men of particular talents; and they must rid themselves of departmental, or

100

service, loyalties and acquire a higher loyalty to the national good. Above all, they ought to be strictly subordinate to the civilian director. The director should be a man of broad knowledge and intellectual attainments, thoroughly in accord with democracy."

The Rank and File

In the military branches, persons engaged in intelligence activity are usually called intelligence officers, and they are generally commissioned officers. Civilians of comparable position in the hierarchy are called intelligence specialists. Others constitute the rank and file of intelligence personnel: clerical staffs, security agents, and the various technicians needed in the trade for odd chores that range from safecracking to designing fountain-pen guns.

They are professionals who make a career of intelligence work, and amateurs who are used temporarily for *ad hoc* assignments. Whoever and whatever they are, they must possess certain personal characteristics to fit into the pattern. To excel in the war of wits, a man must combine in him such traits and qualifications as intellect and courage, percipience and enterprise, judgment and determination. He must love ideas as much as he loves adventure. He must be a man of erudition, with a good knowledge of history and geography. He must be thoughtful and articulate, with a philosophical turn of mind, a dash of cynicism. He must have technical competence and must be acutely conscious politically. He must be discreet.

He does not have to be physically powerful, and he need not have excelled in sports. Even a bookworm such as T. E. Lawrence, the fabulous Lawrence of Arabia, may surprise the professional in the field when he suddenly blossoms out as a buccaneer, leader of men, and guerrilla fighter. The rank-and-file intelligence officer or intelligence specialist is no adventurer. Above all, he is no spy. A majority of the personnel, even the officers, are chair-borne specialists who are never called upon to go on secret missions. Most of them acquire information simply by taking it from the "incoming" basket on their desks. Their most important assignments may send them no farther than the Library of Congress in Washington or the British Museum in London. Much of the information they are supposed to procure is accessible to anybody who has a library card.

Although the home office is usually their natural habitat, intelligence personnel may be sent into the field to serve as military, naval, and air attachés, or as "camouflaged" members of diplomatic missions. They may disguise their association with the secret service, but that is usually as far as disguise goes.

The function of the intelligence officer is the acquisition of information from legitimately accessible sources. Intelligence officers collate the reports that agents and informants send in and assign them to their appropriate dossiers. They write reports and so-called intelligence summaries, and they prepare position papers and estimates of situations under study, using files and libraries as the source of their information.

The intelligence specialist is essentially a bureaucrat who keeps office hours, attending to his duties during the working day and to his private affairs afterward. Once he is moved beyond this strictly circumscribed routine of activity and into the adventure of secret intelligence, he is no longer an intelligence officer or specialist but becomes a spy. This is an important distinction, but one that is not always recognized. In Britain, Reginald Hall was an intelligence officer, while Robert Baden-Powell, founder of the Boy Scout movement, was a professional spy. Both were among the greatest in their respective fields.

Women in Intelligence

Although intelligence is widely regarded as a man's world, there are many women engaged in its activities. They are employed as secretaries, occasionally as analysts, and more rarely as specialists, although there are fields in which a woman is superior to a man.

In Britain, two woman rose to the highest rank in intelligence—Gertrude Bell and Freya Stark. Miss Bell, a remarkable woman of considerable drive and enormous erudition, was responsible for the establishment of Iraq as an independent kingdom with the Hashemite prince Faisal as its head. Though she may not be as well known as T. E. Lawrence, she was equally as effective as Lawrence in the disintegration of Ottoman rule in Arabia. Miss Freya Stark also made Arabia her specialty and continued to work there after Gertrude Bell died.

We have already seen in the example of the brilliant Emmy Rado how effective women can be in American intelligence, and it may be said that, although women are numerically inferior to men in intelligence work, in every other respect they are their equals.

There is a tendency, however, to restrict women in intelligence activity and to confine them to the lower echelons. Hitler in particular had an extremely low opinion of women in intelligence and prevented their employment on higher echelons in his services. This was probably due to a painful experience he had with certain ladies, employed in the German High Comand, who were exposed one day as espionage agents for Poland. Because of the security risk, the German High Command made it a practice to employ as secretaries only the daughters of officers. However, in 1934, an intrepid and handsome Polish secret agent, Captain George Sosnovski, succeeded in enlisting two confidential secretaries working in the German High Command, both daughters of generals. He bribed them with his love in the old-fashioned romantic manner and got all the information he wanted from them.

In Washington, during the twenties, Japanese intelligence agents tried to obtain information by dating confidential secretaries of the U.S. Navy Department. However, experience shows that despite such incidents the great majority of women employed in intelligence work are as trustworthy and as security conscious as men. In fact, Colonel Nicolai expressed the view that they are, in the final analysis, even more discreet than men and pointed out that in the history of intelligence more men had been ensnarled by ladies than the other way round. Even fiction uses the beautiful woman to trap the male operator, but it ignores as unlikely the handsome male decoy.

Nicolai also held that the greatest German intelligence specialist of all time was a woman rather than a man. She was Elsbeth Schragmüller, a doctor of philosophy, a teacher in private life who attained fame in the lore of intelligence as the fabulous "Mademoiselle Docteur." Although she dealt with secret agents she was in fact an intelligence specialist who never worked in the field. Despite her achievements—and we shall see in due course that they were considerable —she was the exception to the rule that limits the employment of women in most of the intelligence services throughout the world.

The Intelligence Auxiliary

Aside from its professional practitioners, intelligence draws its personnel from the vast reservoir of the people at large. Among those who serve on an *ad hoc* basis journalists traditionally play an exceptional role, if only because they are themselves professional collectors of information. This is recognized by the Communists who suspect journalists as much if not more than they fear intelligence officers. In fact, Communist governments regard all Western newspapermen as *de facto* espionage agents.

Commenting on the arrest of Associated Press correspondent William N. Oatis in Prague in 1951, on charges of espionage, his colleague Dana Adams Schmidt of the New York *Times*, remarked: "Even though the prosecution disposed of every advantage and the defense of none, nothing was brought out at the trial that could, by Western standards, be called espionage. By those standards, Oatis was a perfectly legitimate, hard-working and enterprising reporter . . . But the Communists' conception of information and of the functions of newspapermen is different from ours. The idea that news might have value other than as propaganda is foreign to them. The only legitimately publishable information, so far as they are concerned, is that which comes from official sources. Anything else is espionage."

Frequently newsmen succeed better in procuring, evaluating, and transmitting information than professional intelligence people. A few days after Pearl Harbor, Raymond Clapper, the late columnist of the Scripps-Howard newspapers, commented with wry pride that a comparable debacle could not have happened in any self-respecting newspaper office in America. No newspaper, he said, could survive a similar blow to its prestige and certainly none could afford to be scooped on this scale by its competitors.

The occasional superiority of journalistic investigation over the largely bureaucratic methods of the intelligence services was demonstrated, for example, in 1912 when an enterprising Czech reporter named Egon Erwin Kisch discovered a major military secret which the intelligence services did not learn until it was too late. Kisch ascertained that the famous Skoda armament works in Pilsen had ordered hydraulic presses and tools of unusually large dimensions not justified by anything the plant appeared to be manufacturing at the time. Inquiry revealed that the Skoda target range was being enlarged. In the Hotel Waldek, Kisch encountered a group of artillery engineers. By talking to them and to a few workers, Kisch established that Skoda was making for Germany mobile howitzers of 30.5 mm. caliber. Kisch wrote up his discovery in a Prague newspaper, but his exposé failed to alert the interested intelligence services.

Then in the summer of 1914, these howitzers appeared suddenly in front of Belgium's "impregnable" system of fortifications and reduced them to rubble in no time. The Belgian High Command, as well as the Allied intelligence services, described these howitzers as Germany's new secret weapon "whose existence had been effectively concealed from the outside world."

The landing of the Anglo-French divisions in Salonika in October, 1915, came as a complete surprise to the Central powers. The move was described as "one of the best kept secrets of the [first] World War." Yet news of the impending landing was telegraphed by a Swiss newspaperman to his paper and the report was forwarded to Austrian intelligence headquarters in Vienna. What became of it when it reached the classified cemetery of intelligence nobody knows.

There is a great similarity between the work of intelligence services and newspaper offices, as was pointed out by General Donovan. There is, consequently, an inevitable relationship between bona fide working correspondents and diplomatic and intelligence personnel. The entries in Ambassador Dodd's diary show how close this relationship can be. It was a familiar sight during Hitler's occupation of the Rhineland, during the war in Ethiopia, and the Spanish civil war, as it is today, to see diplomats and intelligence officers frequenting the quarters of the press to "get the dope," although they have better facilities and the paraphernalia of "official espionage" for obtaining it themselves.

Even in the speed of transmission of information, newspapers frequently beat government agencies. The first report on Stalin's fatal illness, in March, 1953, did not go to the State Department. It went first to the Associated Press. It was from the AP's diplomatic correspondent in Washington that the responsible official in the State Department received the first news of this momentous event. The official asked, "How do you know it?"

"Our London monitor picked up the news from Radio Moscow," the correspondent answered.

"Then it must be the real McCoy," the diplomat said.

The news of the Communist invasion of South Korea, on June 25, 1950, reached the New York *Herald-Tribune* about an hour before it arrived at the State Department, and hours before it reached the Pentagon. This is remarkable, if only because the average editorial office operates with standard machinery that is inferior to the vast apparatus maintained by the intelligence services of the major powers. The ordinary foreign correspondent cannot, in his own interest, use some of the unusual gimmicks which should be normally available to good intelligence operatives.

Foreign correspondents have frequently served as unofficial intelligence agents, in the majority of cases for their own governments, but sometimes for alien regimes. Henri de Blowitz, fabulous correspondent of the London *Times,* provided much of the information Disraeli needed during the Congress of Berlin in 1878, and supplied the intelligence which enabled Britain to buy into the Suez Canal in 1875, a move that marked the beginning of British penetration of Egypt. But in 1935, a prominent British editor delivered classified information to the German Ambassador in London. It proved decisive in Hitler's efforts to forestall British opposition to the Nazis' occupation of the Rhineland. Documents which came to light after World War II revealed the existence of numerous such journalistic agents working for Germany, Italy, and Japan against their own countries, especially in Britain and France.

The extreme example of mixing journalism and intelligence is the Tass news agency of the Soviet Union, which is merely a branch of the Soviet intelligence service. If the value of a news agency is measured by the number of words printed from its correspondents' reports, then Tass is virtually useless. The total number of words which get into the Soviet press from dispatches cabled by a huge corps of Tass correspondents abroad is less in a whole month than the cables printed from a single special correspondent of the New York *Times* in one week. Yet if its value is measured in the number of words cabled to the home office, Tass is probably the most valuable news agency of them all.

In the United States, Tass maintains offices in New York and Washington. It has a number of editors and correspondents at both places, most of them Americans. While these men and women are recognized as functionaries of the greater Soviet intelligence apparatus, they have access nevertheless to the sessions of Congress, the press conferences of the White House, Congressional hearings, all the public functions of the American government. They are on the mailing lists of government agencies and private institutions, and receive releases on important developments which are actually confidential up to the release date. By cabling them to Moscow, Tass correspondents enable the Soviet government to find out about these events even before the American people learn of them.

When in 1945 the U.S. Government released the detailed Smyth Report on the development of the atomic bomb, every word of the lengthy report was cabled promptly by the Washington bureau of Tass to Moscow, but not a word of it appeared in the Soviet press. A Tass correspondent named Zheveynov was involved in the Canadian espionage ring, working under the cover name of "Martin." Tass correspondents in The Hague, Stockholm, and Canberra were found to be active operatives of the Soviet intelligence network.

It is important to distinguish between the bona fide newspaperman, who may perform occasional services to his country's intelligence organization as an *ad hoc* informant, and the intelligence agent who masquerades as a newspaperman. This distinction is acute in American minds, but it is somewhat hazy in the minds of Europeans and Asians. Americans, even those in the highest places, respect the basic integrity of the journalist and refrain from compromising or embarrassing him by drawing him into such extraneous functions. In Europe, however, newspapermen frequently double as full-time intelligence agents and sometimes operate as mercenary spies. British correspondents, for example, usually have a not too tenuous connection with the British secret service, or at least with the Political Intelligence Division of the Foreign Office. The journalistic front for intelligence work was used widely by Germany during the 1930's, by Italy and Japan, and by virtually every European country except the Scandinavian lands, which make the same distinction between journalism and intelligence work as do the Americans.

In addition to journalists, the auxiliary force of intelligence includes businessmen and industrialists, members of the academic professions, explorers and travelers, and engineers who may from time to time place information at the disposal of the intelligence services without actually belonging to any organization of this kind.

In times of emergency, such *ad hoc* informants are integrated into standing intelligence organizations whose wartime personnel is usually made up of "amateurs." An important secret branch of the U.S. Office of Naval Intelligence was thus headed by an officer who used to sell refrigerators abroad before the war. Most of his officers were newspapermen, college professors, and lawyers. The chief researcher of the branch was a stranger who used to make a living by selling stamps in a foreign country.

None of the British intelligence officers with whom I came into contact during World War II was a "professional." Some were former foreign correspondents, others were Oxford dons, still others were junior executives of various business enterprises. The exceptional effectiveness of American and British intelligence during World War II proves that rank amateurs can be as efficient in intelligence as the professional; it shows further that intelligence is by no means at its best when it is conducted by a cloistered caste—what General Smith called "a corps of professional intelligence officers"— but rather by a combination of highly trained professionals and enterprising and qualified amateurs.

The Education of Intelligence Operatives

The good intelligence officer, male or female, is not conjured up by any hocus pocus and is not molded by special calisthenics. He is the product of the educational system of his country. That Britain has produced some exceptional intelligence officers is probably a result of an educational system that stimulates the intellectual skills needed for this particular job. A young man who graduates from Cambridge or Oxford is almost ready to step immediately into an intelligence job, because of the emphasis those universities place on the humanities, on history, geography, and foreign languages.

This is why men like T. E. Lawrence or Peter Churchill or F. F. E. Yeo-Thomas were able to move directly from their peacetime specialties, in which they excelled, to wartime intelligence work in which they also excelled. There was a direct link between their education and the requirements of the secret service. Because of this, British intelligence has an atmosphere of culture and erudition, a civilized aura of intellectual accomplishment. I was frequently baffled by the style of British intelligence reports until I learned that they were composed by some of Britain's most gifted writers.

I recall in particular a magnificent report on Iran spiked with quotations from Homer, Sir H. M. Elliott, and Hamdallah Mustaufi, a noted Persian traveler who died in 1349.

Yet the report was as topical as that morning's newspaper and as informative as an intelligence report must be. It was written by a young man called Fitzroy Maclean, whose name I then heard for the first time, and who later became world-famous as the brigadier who represented Winston Churchill at Marshal Tito's headquarters in the mountains of Yugoslavia.

During the last war, in addition to writing such erudite reports, Maclean also organized the kidnaping of General Fazlallah Zahedi of Iran, who in 1953 became that country's premier, but who in 1943 had been conspiring to aid the Nazis. Before that Maclean had surveyed a good deal of the Soviet Union, covering a part of it on foot.

In the life of Fitzroy Maclean, as in the lives of Britain's most intrepid intelligence officers, there is that combination of Etonian erudition and the Cameron Highlander, of Cambridge and Oxford and the Coldstream Guard. Maclean was a graduate of Eton and Cambridge and had served in the Cameron Highlanders and in the Foreign Service. He learned the intelligence trade at first hand in Whitehall and Mayfair, Paris, and Moscow. Combining within himself elements of brain and brawn, he proved in the end to be good both as a writer of lucid intelligence reports and as a combatant on the secret front behind the enemy's lines.

By presenting these British examples, I do not mean to imply that only Britons excel in this field. The recent history of the French Secret Service shows that it had men who were the peers of Baden-Powell and Maclean, men like the late Jean Moulin, a provincial politician who commanded the French underground until his death at the Gestapo's hands in 1943, and the "Professor," Pierre Brossolette, and Colonel André Pierre Serot, a great intelligence officer who was killed by terrorists in Palestine at the side of Count Folke Bernadotte. I have known French intelligence officers of considerable stature, but I found that there was a wide gulf separating the "civilians" from the "military," and that the professionals were not particularly anxious to improve the efficiency of the brilliant amateurs.

Nor do I mean to say that Americans cannot graduate from their schools into intelligence work. However, in the United States it is often necessary to supplement formal education with some private extracurricular work. The American undergraduate must select a specialty that will come in handy later in an intelligence career, while such specialties are normally suggested by the special curricula of English institutions.

In intelligence work, on the level of the specialists, thorough familiarity with *specific* subjects is essential. It may be that a knowledge of a certain language is required. It may be archeology. It may be the geography of a foreign country, or some aspects of its culture. It may be the geology of remote regions. As we have noted, during the last war, an American intelligence agency was asked to supply information on the qualities of the soil of North Africa so that the boots of GI's could be adapted to that particular ground. This was one minute detail of the diverse information required of intelligence in the preparation for the North African landings in 1942.

Spectacular successes were scored by rank amateurs who served as intelligence officers during the Second World War. An American newspaper correspondent excelled in the interrogation of German U-boat men. A Wall Street banker charted the waters around the Pacific islands that were chosen as stepping stones in the slow conquest of Japan. They put to use skills and knowledge that they had acquired earlier in civilian pursuits. Intelligence often draws on the vast reservoir of a nation's civilian specialists, while it maintains only a relatively small corps of professional intelligence officers.

During World War II, the Office of Strategic Services included among the 12,000 people working for it a college president, presidents of large corporations, a gentleman jockey, a professional wrestler, an African big-game hunter, a missionary from Thailand, a Czarist general, and a Hollywood stunt man known as "the Human Fly."

The closest approach in the United States to a corps of professional intelligence officers was the small group of the Army General Staff assigned to military attaché duty abroad. A few of them achieved a modicum of fame, including Colonel Truman Smith, who became a highly respected, but by no means infallible, authority on Germany, and Colonel (later Brigadier General) Philip Faymonville, who came to be known widely as an equally controversial expert on the Soviet Union. There were a few such specialists in the U.S. Navy and the Marine Corps, including Ellis M. Zacharias, who began his distinguished career in intelligence as a language officer asigned to Japan.

According to General Walter Bedell Smith, a former director of the Central Intelligence Agency, the United States is now building its own corps of professional intelligence officers. I have known some of the officers and specialists who became the first members of the professional corps when it was decided that one be established at long last in the United

States. They are what the lingo of Sing Sing calls "lifers," in the service probably for the rest of their lives. They are without exception men of superior endowments. With them a new kind of "professional" was introduced into the field of intelligence—the specialist who combines all that is best in his British and French colleagues with the traits developed by the American brand of democracy, the enterprise, technological aptitude, adaptability, and ingenuity that is native to most Americans. There is still much of the old frontier spirit in these men. They combine a worldly informality with vast erudition and seem, indeed, to justify General Smith's opinion that Americans now make "the world's best professional intelligence officers."

"What enables the wise sovereign and the good general to strike and conquer, and achieve things beyond the reach of ordinary men, is foreknowledge." This dictum was expressed by Sun Tsŭ, a Chinese military scientist, in a textbook on tactics still highly regarded today. It was written five hundred years before Christ, and today, almost twenty-five hundred years later, the principle still can spell victory or defeat. In this atomic age it could mean the difference between survival and extinction.

Intelligence Service and the People at Large

Whenever power appears shrouded in secrecy we are inclined to view it with a certain amount of awe. The intelligence service is a mysterious power to the outsider, who is prepared to believe that its mystery conceals not so much national secrets and military strength as roguery, vice, and intrigue. A proper intelligence system, Hanson W. Baldwin wrote, is an institution with great potentialities for both good and evil. "It must utilize all men and all methods; it is amoral and cynical; it traffics with traitors and heroes; it bribes and corrupts; it kidnaps; sometimes, in war, it kills; it holds the power of life and death; it utilizes the grandest and the lowest passions; it harnesses in the same team the loftiest patriotism and the basest cupidity; it justifies the means by the ends."

He added: "Such an organization, of tremendous importance and terrible power, must obviously be blueprinted with care and maintained in a framework flexible enough to permit its efficient functioning, but not broad enough to develop as a danger to the democracy it must serve."

Those of us who have worked within an intelligence organization, and those who have participated in its clandestine work, can testify that this is the exact blueprint of the intelligence systems in countries like Britain and the United States. There is inevitably melodrama in the activity, because the very nature of secrecy breeds it; but the greater part of the activity is the uninspiring routine work that goes on behind the locked doors.

I recall my own first days in intelligence most vividly, since I approached my new profession with a great deal of romantic anticipation. I entered the inner sanctum with the melodramatic designation "Secret Agent." Even my hiring had elements of mystery. I had to use an alias during the negotiations, and my first meetings were arranged with circumspect secrecy.

My first day in intelligence served to develop in me a sense of mystery. I had no permanent pass as yet and was given a temporary slip that expired at 4:30 P.M. I had worked to a late hour, and when I was ready to leave my office building in Washington I was taken by a guard to the Provost Marshal to be checked out. A phone call was put through to my new chief to identify me, but, when my name was mentioned on the telephone, my chief said bluntly, "Never heard of the man!"

I was in a pickle. I was trying to explain my presence in the building in some excitement, when the door opened; my chief walked in and checked me out. "I'm sorry," he said. "Regulations! Your name is not supposed to be mentioned on the telephone."

Once I settled down to the routine, I still respected the importance of secrecy, but I no longer regarded my work as romantic or melodramatic. It was little different from work in a newspaper office where I had worked before, and where information is also collected for a purpose. There were the usual files and reference books, and there were the dispatches of the "correspondents" from their posts. My job was to collate them, to piece them together, to file them for future reference, and to prepare from them composite pictures which the policy makers, planners, and commanders could use when needed.

Once in a while a colleague from a neighboring office would come in to say good-by. He might be going on a secret mission—to the Philippines, then occupied by the Japanese; to Sicily, which was to be invaded; or to some European city, to contact a mysterious go-between. Such episodes never failed to bring home to me some special melodrama about the activity. These men had a job to do and they did it in the most impersonal fashion.

The Citizen's Role

In view of the important role the civilian specialist—indeed, the informed citizen—plays in the work of intelligence, the activity opens up and becomes of direct interest to persons in all walks of life. It is, therefore, important to desecretize the secret service and introduce it to the citizenry, somewhat in the manner in which warships are thrown open for public inspection on Navy Day.

In a democracy where the secret service has its basic roots in the people of the country, damage ensues from attempts to isolate the service, cloak it in impenetrable mystery, and thus separate it from the people on whom it depends in emergencies. In a country such as the United States there is a dual responsibility that converges in intelligence. Those attached to it should familiarize the people with the purposes, importance, and need for the secret service, and conversely the people should interest themselves in the work of their intelligence service, to be available when needed.

In the United States, neither responsibility is properly understood. The authorities do little to acquaint the people with the secret service, unlike J. Edgar Hoover whose policy is to establish the Federal Bureau of Investigation firmly in the popular imagination. The close relationship between the people at large and the FBI has yielded enormous dividends for both. But no such collaboration exists between the intelligence services of the government and the intelligent people of the nation.

The extreme of this attitude was expressed by General George C. Marshall during his appearance before a Congressional committee which, among other things, discussed intelligence. General Marshall bemoaned a tendency to discuss intelligence too widely in the United States and praised the secrecy that surrounds the activity in Britain where, he said not even the name of the organization is known to the public.

In may be true that the exact designation of the British secret service is concealed, even though Britain rarely hesitates to label intelligence services as such. I was frequently baffled when, while abroad, I encountered British officials

113

whose doorplates described them openly, in such sensitive areas as Egypt, Palestine, and the Sudan, as Intelligence Officers. And I was amazed by the frankness with which they discussed their jobs with me, a stranger and an outsider. "My dear fellow," an intelligence officer once told me in Khartoum, "if you don't know what I'm doing and don't know where to find me, how on earth can I expect you to come to me when you have a bit of information you think I ought to know about?" Obviously, however, no iceberg is wholly above water.

In Britain, MI, which is the Military Intelligence branch of the War Department, is as popular as the FBI in the United States, partly because the section called MI-5 is in charge of the romantic job of counterintelligence and counterespionage. But much is known about MI in general, and the director of MI-5, Sir Percy Sillitoe, even disclosed the exact location of his office in his biography in *Who's Who*. "War Office, Room 505," he wrote without undue security pangs, for "Room 505" is famous throughout Britain, a romantic synonym for excellent intelligence work.

Contrary to the impression that General Marshall tried to convey, it is the policy of the British government to publicize and popularize certain intelligence activities. This policy evolved from the realization that the government needs the close cooperation of the public to do a thorough and successful job of intelligence. A public kept in ignorance of the existence, methods, and needs of the intelligence service cannot be expected to provide the support it requires.

This deliberate effort to acquaint the people at large with the delicate work of intelligence extends to all of its branches, military as well as political, positive as well as negative. The British authorities not only encourage outstanding secret agents to publish their exploits for popular consumption, they not only collaborate with writers who prepare works on intelligence, they actually promote such books, including spy fiction. The outstanding example was that of the late Alfred Duff Cooper (Lord Norwich), who at one time served in high positions in the British secret service. He told about his career in a brilliant book of memoirs, later expanding the material into a novel.

Sir (later Lord) Robert Vansittart was often described as a former chief of Britain's top-echelon secret service, one of those glamorous and brilliant "chiefs" we have met before. He regarded it as a part of his job to educate the greatest possible number of people to the intricacies of intelligence work. He used a pseudonym in writing spy fiction and also

114

the scenario of a motion picture dealing with the adventures of certain spies. Motion-picture firms are encouraged by Britain's highest intelligence authorities to prepare such movies as will serve to help familiarize the public with one of their most essential government agencies.

If such a policy exists in the United States, or if anything is being done to educate the people on this score, I am not aware of it. On the contrary, I think there is a deliberate effort to mask the secret service and keep it cloaked from the public view. After the Second World War, two books appeared dealing with the theories of strategic intelligence and secret intelligence. They represented excellent beginnings of a high-level education program, but the practice was abandoned abruptly and completely. Mr. Allen W. Dulles, present head of CIA, permitted the publication of his remarkable exploits in Switzerland during the war, and since that time he has written a book on Germany's underground activities. He has also written a number of fascinating book reviews of other peoples' work, all revealing his exceptional skill in this field.

The efficiency of an intelligence service depends on a number of things: the government's attitude toward the activity and the service's place in the governmental table of organization, the so-called intelligence doctrine of the organization, the methods employed, and the tools used.

In the final analysis, however, its efficiency is dependent upon the men and women who make up the service. The secret service is a human organization; it represents a high form of intellectual activity. In the past society has been inclined to assign the solution of national problems to soldiers, a tendency prompting Georges Clemenceau to warn that war is too serious a matter to be entrusted to generals. And, probably, peace is far too precious to be entrusted to the diplomats and the politicians alone.

PART II

Espionage

The Art of Espionage

One spring day during the late war, a young officer came into my room in Tempo-L, the long temporary building that housed the secret branches of Naval Intelligence in Washington, to bid me good-by. He was a boisterous little Italian with enormous shoulders and bulging biceps, and a huge round head in which two laughing eyes flashed under bushy eyebrows. He often came over from his office a few doors away to discuss the war and tell stories whose punch lines, shouted in ribald Italian, brought forth the most appreciative guffaws.

Now he seemed solemn and, while his eyes still shone, they had a different luster. This office was hardly a place for histrionics. There was nothing romantic in our bare environment—the desks, the typewriters, the maps on the wall, and the huge safe with its combination locks. But as I stood up behind my desk to bid him good-by and bon voyage his solemnity impressed me deeply. He stretched out his hand, and I pressed it a bit more firmly and a little longer than usual.

For this man was about to go out into the field, to leave behind his desk job in intelligence, to become an espionage agent behind enemy lines. For a moment or two, I came to *feel* something of the great difference between intelligence work and espionage.

Intelligence on the whole, despite its elaborate secrecy and occasional drama, is transacted above ground. Espionage is carried out below ground, a clandestine operation. But behind the melodrama espionage has as exact a scientific and moral structure as intelligence. Moreover, it possesses its own dignity, often not apparent in the methods it is forced to employ, for espionage, like intelligence, is a legitimate and essential function of every government that is aware of its responsibilities. It is justified by the fact that all nations conceal important phases of their activities, and it is necessitated by their urgent need to acquire information about things concealed which may influence or threaten their peace and security.

Nations go to extreme lengths to conceal their affairs. They have made secrecy into a fetish and an institution and have set up elaborate machinery to protect their secrets. They have enacted severe laws to safeguard them. The United States has a complicated system of espionage laws and security regulations. Britain depends upon its Official Secrets Act of 1889, which punishes an official for communication of information concerning the military and naval affairs of Her Majesty to any unauthorized person. An article of the Soviet Constitution describes the keeping of secrets as "the fundamental duty" of every citizen, and calls the betrayal of secrets "one of the most heinous crimes." An American judge recently called the betrayal of our atomic secrets "worse than murder." Nations rate their secrets equivalent to human life and frequently punish the betrayers of highly classified information with death.

Different nations have different attitudes toward secrecy, the extreme viewpoint being that of the Soviet Union, where even production figures of industries manufacturing consumer goods are concealed. The Soviet Union regards concealment, as Andrei Y. Vishinsky stated in a speech before the United Nations, as her first line of defense.

Secrecy may conceal strength or weakness, the design of a new weapon or the location of the plant where it is manufactured. It may conceal the position of a single military unit in a tactical situation or the strategic plans of an entire army. Naturally, a potentially aggressive nation must obscure its intention of making war until it has marshaled its forces and is ready to strike.

There are today all kinds of secrets, little secrets and big secrets, state secrets and military secrets, official secrets and private secrets. Secrecy has always been recognized as one of the main conditions of success in war, as a highly effective form of diplomacy, as a necessary phase of private enterprise, and as an expedient even in simple, everyday human relations.

The very fact that concealment exists, and that it is maintained for the advantage of one side, makes it imperative that the opposition penetrate the secrets of other countries. This is the fundamental task of espionage.

Some years ago, in England, I discussed the moral aspect of espionage with Captain Franz von Rintelen, one of the most successful German spies of the First World War. Rintelen said: "Each country is entitled to its secrets and is at the same time duty bound to protect them. By the same token, each country is entitled to find out the secrets of other countries. You have to approach espionage in the spirit in which Darwin regarded vivisection. It is justifiable for real investigation, but not for mere damnable and detestable curiosity." He then added, "There is really nothing base about espionage. It is as much part of human nature as is the keeping of secrets."

This element of secrecy is responsible for the distinction we must make between intelligence proper and espionage. A clear understanding of this distinction is important for a proper appreciation of the activity that we are about to outline in detail.

What Is Espionage?

Espionage is that part of the total intelligence effort that is designed for the surreptitious inspection of the activities of foreign countries, to ascertain their strength and movements, and to communicate such intelligence to the proper authorities. It is the effort to discover by concealed methods the guarded secrets of others. Because of the circumstances and the difficulties of espionage, it is an autonomous function but, in the final analysis, still an integral part of the over-all scheme of intelligence.

Espionage, like intelligence, moves on different levels. We distinguish between strategic espionage, in which the surreptitious search is for important stakes, and tactical espionage, in which the objective is some secret of limited or localized importance.

In addition, there are political espionage and military espionage, whose respective designations indicate the nature of the activity. There is, too, industrial espionage, a widespread and highly developed activity practiced both in peace and war, by governments as well as by private enterprises.

At the top, there is a distinction between positive espionage, which is conducted aggressively to acquire the secrets of foreign countries, and negative espionage, or counterespionage, which is designed to protect one's own secrets and to apprehend those who try to penetrate them for the benefit of a foreign power.

Among the practitioners of espionage, operatives are usually grouped together under the generic and somewhat derogatory designation of spies. But there are all kinds of spies. Persons who are engaged in direct espionage, who go out under false pretense and disguise their identities in order to procure secret information, are called secret agents or operatives. In this category are so-called resident agents, who reside permanently in certain locations and operate on a permanent or long-range basis. Resident agents may be assigned to general espionage work, picking up whatever incidental information they can, or carrying out specific tasks such as watching trains, roads, or coasts. There are also so-called transient agents who go on *ad hoc* missions, hit or miss, hit and run.

In addition, there are couriers, whose job is the maintenance of liaison with agents in the field. They do not engage in espionage directly but merely relay the information procured by the operatives. Also there are a number of technicians and specialists essential to the system, such as clandestine radio operators, cryptographers, and secret-ink chemists. Another group of specialists comprises the authenticators, who forge documents and prepare or manufacture the other paraphernalia a spy needs in action. And there are the so-called double-agents, who work for two masters simultaneously, sometimes with the knowledge of at least one of the two employers. There are the agents provocateurs, whose job is to infiltrate the adversary's espionage organization, to compromise it or force it into the open, to expose its methods and personnel.

There are spies engaged solely in recruiting, who work like Hollywood talent scouts, trying to round up likely prospects for use in the net. There are the "cut-outs," or go-betweens, who, like couriers, do not engage in espionage themselves but form a link between two spies, or between a spy and a higher-up whose identity is usually concealed from the operative. In addition, there are so-called "mail-drops," or "letterboxes," who serve merely as relaying points in the communications system of espionage, often innocent-appearing persons not even remotely suspected of any illicit activity. They are usually located in neutral countries to receive communications from the operatives and in turn forward it to the headquarters of the espionage organization.

There are free-lance spies who work for the highest bidder on a professional and mercenary basis, and also "patriot" spies who engage in this dangerous pastime as a service to their countries, frequently without recompense, moral or material.

In negative espionage, operatives are called special agents

119

(as in the FBI) or investigators (as, for example, in Naval Intelligence). Popularly they are called "gumshoes" or "shoe-flies." Television and radio script-writers prefer to call them counterspies. Also in negative espionage there are the informers, whose job it is to supply information about their own fellow operatives, much in the manner in which stool-pigeons squeal on their fellow criminals.

Espionage has a more complex hierarchy than intelligence, chiefly because the activity is essentially more complex and its functions are more specialized. At the top is what may be called the spymaster, the head of the espionage organization or of that branch of an intelligence service that specializes in espionage. His proper title is usually director.

Under him are the resident directors, who conduct the business of the fixed, long-term, foreign branches of the espionage organization.

Then come the so-called collectors, who procure secret information from a great variety of sources.

Below them are the transmitters whose job is the forwarding of information acquired by the collectors.

Even lower in the hierarchy are the couriers who act as messengers. Then come the drops and cut-outs who relay information from collectors in the field to headquarters, maintain contact between the various echelons, and act as blinds for active agents.

And, by themselves in a separate category, are the specialists. They are the expert saboteurs, whose activities will be discussed in another section of this book.

What, then, is the difference between an intelligence specialist and an espionage agent?

The intelligence specialist is engaged comprehensively in the collection, evaluation, and dissemination of information—all kinds of information—most of which comes from overt and accessible sources. He performs a highly intellectual function in the integration of seemingly unrelated data. He is not required to masquerade, and although his activities are protected by considerable secrecy he is still able to retain his true identity.

The espionage agent is engaged exclusively in the procurement of secret information, performing a function that is but a part—often a small though extremely important part—of the total intelligence effort. Unlike the intelligence specialist, he is required to conceal his identity, the exact nature of his mission, and his lines of communications, by assuming a false identity and by applying airtight secrecy to his activities.

The Espionage Organization

In Britain, the most secret phase of the intelligence service, concerned with the procurement of secret information and clandestine operations, is called special intelligence, the word "special" being frequently employed to designate surreptitious intelligence. During the war, Britain called its major espionage organization "Special Operations Executive," and even this designation was further protected. It was housed in Baker Street, not far from Sherlock Holmes's mythical abode, in a building called Norgeby House. The plaque on the building identified the agency as "Inter-Services Research Bureau." Members of the organization referred to it as the "Old Firm."

In the United States, the most elaborate espionage organization maintained prior to the establishment of the Central Intelligence Agency was the Office of Strategic Services, the word "strategic" being used to camouflage the true activity of the agency. Its headquarters was openly designated, but it maintained a number of hide-outs for the pursuit of its secret business. Today, espionage activities are separated from the headquarters of CIA, whose address is available to all in the Washington telephone directory. But, while the location of its central headquarters is common knowledge, only the initiated know the location of its special branches.

Only a relatively small part of the espionage business is conducted at headquarters, most of it being transacted in the field. Headquarters personnel, in charge of preparing missions, selecting targets, and directing the activities of agents, represent a distinct minority, while the great majority of personnel consists of secret agents working in the field. These agents may never visit headquarters, may not even know where it is located. The only direct contact between headquarters and the field is maintained by resident directors and their aides, who in turn direct the network of agents in their respective areas.

The headquarters organization of espionage is usually split into a secret service section and an espionage subsection. The secret service section is largely a bureaucratic agency charged with the supervision of all offensive and defensive measures and with the administrative functions of this activity.

The duties of the espionage subsection embrace the selection, training, and indoctrination of personnel, and the assignment of missions to secret agents in the field. While it examines, analyzes, and verifies incoming reports, it does not usually evaluate them. It is primarily concerned with the forwarding of agent reports to a superior division where they are subsequently evaluated.

How an espionage organization functions in practice may be shown in a historic example—the procurement and transmission of information concerning Germany's impending invasion of the Soviet Union. Hitler had decided to attack the Soviet Union some time in 1940, but the detailed invasion plans were not drawn up until December of that year. Preparations for the execution of the plan, which was given the code name Barbarossa, began at once and, in May, 1941, a definite D-day for the commencement of operations was designated, June 22, 1941. Anti-Nazi elements within the German High Command, whose identity is still unknown, secured this information and decided to communicate it to Soviet authorities.

On June 2, the information was transmitted to a confidant of the anti-Nazi group in Switzerland, who then established contact with a go-between named Schneider, then working for the Soviet espionage apparatus in "Sicily," as Switzerland was called by Soviet agents. The confidant of the anti-Nazi group communicated his information to Schneider, alias Taylor, who in turn submitted it to a professional Soviet spymaster named Rado. The resident director, Rado, then drafted a report and gave it to his transmitter, a clandestine radio operator named Alexander Foote, for immediate transmission to Moscow. The radioman coded the report and radioed it at once. The code consisted of five-figure groups and read, in part: "85862 70113 48931 66167 34212 42883 76662 18984." In view of the extreme importance of the message, Rado instructed the radio operator to repeat the message for two full hours to alert the receivers in Moscow to the urgency of the report.

In Moscow the report was picked up and immediately forwarded to a Captain Ivanov who was in charge of the decoding section of the Soviet intelligence office. Ivanov recognized the urgency of the message and set out at once to decipher it. Within half an hour he had the first part of the message decoded. It read:

DORA TO DIRECTOR, VIA TAYLOR. HITLER DEFINITELY FIXED D-DAY OF ATTACK ON THE SOVIET UNION AS JUNE 22.

Ivanov called his superior at once and read to him the decoded part of the message. Then he deciphered the remainder of the report, which read:

HITLER REACHED DECISION TWO DAYS AGO. REPORT ARRIVED HERE VIA DIPLOMATIC COURIER OF SWISS GENERAL STAFF TODAY. WILL CONTINUE 0130. [*signed*] DORA

When the decoding of the message was concluded, Captain Ivanov's superior brought it at once to the attention of the "Director," General Golikov, who in June, 1941 was chief of the Soviet Intelligence Service. General Golikov was attending a meeting of the Red Army General Staff, but he left the conference room to receive the call from his subordinate. He gave instructions that a copy of the decoded signal be sent to the Kremlin and, when it arrived by special messenger, he immediately laid it before the chief of the General Staff.

Forty-eight hours later the same information was transmitted to Moscow by another agent, a high-ranking German official named Arvid Harnack, listed in the Soviet espionage network by the cover name of Coro. Despite this corroboration, and despite the Red Army General Staff's evaluation that the information was accurate, Stalin refused to accept it as bona fide. The machinery of Russia's espionage system had operated with perfection, justifying its existence by acting to preserve that nation in the face of military aggression through the penetration of the secret intentions of another nation. In this respect positive espionage constitutes a defensive action that vindicates its clandestine methods.

Prototype Organization

However specific information may finally be regarded in high quarters, the fact remains that in organization and efficiency the Soviet secret service towers over that of most other nations where espionage is concerned. There is a tendency to regard Soviet espionage as ruthless and sinister. To be sure, some of its activities may be so described. But it would be more profitable for the opponents of the Soviet Union to recognize its system as supremely efficient in organization, attainment, and amorality.

While Western countries like Great Britain, Germany,

France, and the United States place greater emphasis on the intelligence phase of the activity, Russia traditionally has emphasized espionage. In no other country's history has espionage played so dominant a role as in Russia's. No country's foreign policy has been as basically determined by its spy system as Russia's has. This was no accident. It was a deliberate design that began with Peter the Great in the seventeenth century and was continued without interruption by both czars and commissars.

During Czarist days, Russian spies succeeded in acquiring Napoleon's plans for the invasion of Russia, and, at the beginning of this century, they penetrated to the entire secret archives of the high Austro-Hungarian General Staff, including its campaign plans against Russia and against its own allies. This tradition was continued in 1941, when Russian spies managed to obtain Hitler's Russian invasion plans, complete to the exact date of his attack. As if to remind the world again of their efficiency, in 1945 Soviet spies procured the atomic secrets of the United States, Britain, and Canada.

There may be deep-seated psychological reasons for British preoccupation with intelligence and Russian preference for espionage. The Englishman's approach to the secret service has always been positive, influenced by his philosophy, character, and political tradition. There was sophistication, cynicism, and ruthlessness in the so-called empire builders, but there was also subtlety, elegance, and a sporting spirit. Frustrated critics of British imperialism from Bossuet to Goebbels, from Napoleon to Hitler, have called England perfidious for her devious ways in foreign affairs, but Tolstoy's characterization of the Englishman was far more accurate. "An Englishman," he made Baron Pfuel say in *War and Peace,* "is self-assured, as being a citizen of the best-organized state in the world, and therefore as an Englishman always knows what he should do and knows that all he does as an Englishman is undoubtedly correct."

Baron Pfuel regarded the Russians as nihilists at heart, but he found that they derived enormous self-assurance, drive, and an impetuous curiosity from this nihilism. Looking skeptically upon the world, Russians have always groped for knowledge, forever suspicious that part of it might escape them. They became insatiably curious and suspicious, and gravitated to espionage like ducks to water.

Virtually the first organization the Bolsheviks restored to the predominance it had attained under the czars was the espionage organization. At first it was tucked away in the military council, where it worked along conventional lines

124

inherited from the Czarist organization, to some extent with its old personnel. But it was soon established as the Fourth Bureau of the Red Army General Staff, where it was assigned new personnel of the generation that had grown up under the Soviet regime. Its methods were revamped and improved. It was lavishly endowed with funds and given a unique autonomy in a state where every function of government is strictly controlled and coordinated. Today, the Intelligence Bureau of the Red Army General Staff must be regarded as the perfect prototype of all agencies in the world dedicated to the conduct of espionage.

Formerly called Fourth Bureau, then renamed Main Intelligence Department, or RU for short, it is one of several agencies that the Soviet Union maintains to satisfy its insatiable curiosity. At the top is the Kremlin's own espionage bureau, called the Confidential Administration of the Communist Party's Central Committee. This is not a collection agency. It is rather the Soviet espionage network's highest organization for the evaluation of espionage reports pouring in from all quarters, the summarizing of their contents, and the delivery of the summaries to the few men in the Kremlin who control the Soviet Union. The agency is headed by a secretary general, who is aided by so-called "specs," or specialists, who possess specific knowledge or special qualifications for evaluation.

The direction of Communist espionage is in the hands of six separate agencies. As we have seen, one is the Fourth Bureau. Another is the Ministry of Foreign Affairs. Still another is the Foreign Department of the M.V.D., the Ministry of Internal Affairs. Fourth is the intelligence section of the Ministry of Foreign Trade. Fifth is the Tass News Agency. The sixth agency is the intelligence apparatus of the Communist Information Bureau, the Cominform, which continues the world-wide espionage activities of the defunct Comintern.

A German journalist named Richard Sorge, one of the foremost operatives of the Soviet network, who was hanged by the Japanese in 1944 for his espionage activities, had occasion to work with every one of these agencies. In his opinion, five of the six were not too efficient but were, as he put it, "somewhat one-sided, and therefore unable to meet the growing demand of the top leadership for comprehensive information."

Such comprehensive information is supplied by the General Staff's Intelligence Department. According to Sorge, it cannot be considered "a narrowly specialized organization

125

whose activities are restricted to military espionage, nor can it be equated with the *Abwehr* of Germany. Pure military espionage is only one of its activities," Sorge wrote. "It engages in the collection of intelligence in the spheres of military affairs in general, military administration, and economics. Reports accumulate there from military attachés serving with embassies overseas, military committees, wartime economic committees, secret intelligence groups, and spy rings. It also handles and studies a great deal of legitimate and semilegitimate material on the military governments, purely military problems, and wartime economies of other nations. Finally, there is a political section within the bureau where incoming information is fashioned into highly competent reports or summarized for top army and party leaders."

Sorge thought that "from the standpoint of technical level and seriousness of purpose, this agency was probably without equal." For all practical purposes, the Red Army's RU is the central intelligence agency of the Soviet Union, not in name, but in actual practice.

The RU is organized into three great strategic regional sections which comprise the entire world geographically, and into several functional sections for the execution of such technical tasks as communications, authentication, cartography, codes, and cipher work. Evaluation, according to Sorge, is the responsibility of the Political Section, while dissemination is handled by another branch.

At the apex of this Intelligence hierarchy is the Director. He is an old and trusted Communist Party member who knows all the top party leaders personally and shares their confidence. He is in close daily contact with them and reports to them weekly when the Kremlin leadership meets for its comprehensive conferences. The Director holds the rank of colonel general in the Red Army. At the time when the atomic secrets of America were procured Colonel General Fyedor Fyedorovich Kuznetsov was Director of Military Intelligence.

Second in command is a Deputy Director, with the rank of major general. He is to a large extent responsible for handling administrative problems. The various sections or desks are headed by Organizers, who hold the rank of major general or colonel in the Red Army. Under them are other members of the hierarchy, whose military ranks range from captain to colonel. Technical personnel and younger aides generally are lieutenants.

In the field, resident directors are in charge of what are called individual "rings." They are assisted by persons who take care of organizational matters and communications respectively. Networks of agents work for them, and a hierarchy exists even among the operatives. Each agent has his own "net," within which he is charged with the supervision of subagents, informants, and communications specialists, the latter called "musicians," since a radio is called a "music box" in Soviet espionage parlance.

Supplying a connection between the Moscow headquarters, called the "Center," and the rings and nets in the field are highly placed cut-outs or go-betweens. Only technical specialists are actually trained at the Center in Moscow, since agents are selected for their preeminence in certain special fields and therefore require no specific training. They are prepared for their missions in informal meetings with the Director and Deputy Director, and receive their assignments from the Organizer in whose area they are to operate.

The recruiting of agents is done primarily by the Cominform, while the selection of personnel for the Center is the task of a special "educational commission," which observes young students during their formative years or their term of compulsory military service and then transfers such men to work in the Center.

Soviet Agents in Action

In the field, the agent's first job is to establish his cover, set up his communications, and then organize his sources. The Soviet espionage organization operates in complete secrecy, far greater than is usual in intelligence proper. Cover names are assigned to all members of the espionage organization, a practice common to all espionage agencies of the world, but carried out to an extraordinary degree by the Soviet agency. Great care is taken that individuals are known only within a very limited circle. In Richard Sorge's Japanese ring, only Sorge knew all the subagents, including such important aides as Hozumi Ozaki, who was his link to Prince Konoye, the Prime Minister of Japan, and Yotoko Miyagi, his contact with General Ugoye. Most of the subagents of the Sorge group met for the first time, and found out about each other, only when they were brought together by the Japanese secret police after their arrest.

It then developed that the Sorge spy ring was organized into two echelons. One was Sorge's own, composed of himself, Max Klausen, who served as his radio operator, Ozaki, Miyaki, and a Yugoslav journalist named Branko de Voukelich. On the second level were twelve subagents, who were also in contact with a great number of informants. Most of the informants did not know that the data they had given, usually during casual or friendly conversations with acquaintances whom they trusted implicitly, actually wound up in the archives of the Fourth Bureau.

Soviet agents in the field are required to establish plausible covers for themselves. When in Japan, Sorge functioned as a foreign correspondent, which is one of the most effective covers. Klausen set himself up in business, and Ozaki worked as a respected journalist.

In Canada, the resident director was Colonel Zabutin, who had the legitimate cover of a military attaché. His Canadian agents used their real occupations as covers while they engaged in espionage on the side. In Switzerland during World War II, the resident director was a partner in a respected firm of cartographers.

Information is acquired through individuals who have either personal knowledge of certain secrets or access to them. The agent in the field begins his operations by gathering around himself a number of subagents from among clandestine party members or trustworthy sympathizers, men and women who in turn have good contacts with persons in government, the armed forces, the press, business, and elsewhere. Either directly or through subagents, the resident director, or the chief agent of a net, then exploits his sources for whatever information can be acquired.

Such sources usually are drawn from eight major groups whose members are in a position to supply valuable information: 1. politicians; 2. diplomats; 3. military, naval, and air personnel; 4. journalists and foreign correspondents; 5. scientists; 6. businessmen; 7. engineers and chemists; and 8. professionals such as writers and artists.

The exploitation of these sources is rarely left to the scouts who discovered them. In 1936, for example, a Soviet agent named Hede Massing appeared in Washington, where she collected a number of informants among the younger government officials. She posed as a German refugee from Nazi persecution and frequented various Washington parties where many young but influential officials congregated. She began by striking up seemingly innocent friendships with some of them. She continued by slowly drawing certain ones of them into the net. Once a prospect was thus caught, Miss Massing handed him over to the agent whose job it was to develop him as a source.

The development of sources is a tedious process that follows a circuitous but carefully plotted route. How sources of vital information are developed was demonstrated in a dramatic fashion in the great Canadian atomic espionage case, which broke in 1945. The most important single source of Colonel Zabutin, the Soviet military attaché, was the informant who gave one of the first tips that the Anglo-American-Canadian combine was building an A-bomb.

When Colonel Zabutin arrived in Ottawa in 1943 to take up his post as the Soviet Union's fully accredited military attaché, he brought along a list of prospective contacts to assist him in the establishment of his spy ring. This list had been prepared for him by the *cadre apparat* of the Comintern espionage organization, that section which keeps, in a central section in Moscow, the roster of all Communists and sympathizers.

Among the suggested contacts was a man named Fred Rose, a member of the Canadian Parliament and of the Labor Progressive Party. Rose was among the first Canadians enlisted by Zabutin to serve as a scout, to develop and recommend individuals who could themselves supply information or who had access to other possible informants.

During a train trip, Rose met an old acquaintance named David Gordon Lunan, a Scotsman by birth, working in the Canada Wartime Information Board.

During the trip, Rose discovered that while Lunan himself had no information of any real value he did have a number of acquaintances who had access to enormously valuable scientific data.

Rose reported Lunan to Zabutin as a promising prospect, and Zabutin in turn assigned Colonel Rogov, one of his aides, to recruit Lunan for the ring.

Shortly after, in March, 1945, Lunan found an unsigned note on his desk in his office inviting him to meet someone at a certain time on a street corner in Ottawa. Lunan kept the appointment and was accosted by a man who introduced himself as "Jan," in fact Colonel Rogov. The colonel openly invited Lunan to join the ring and form a net consisting of himself, as go-between, and three of his acquaintances, Isidor Halperin, Ned Mazerall, and Durnford Smith, all scientists employed by the National Research Council and the research division of the Department of National Defense. They were known to be sympathetic to the U.S.S.R. and to possess much valuable information that the Fourth Bureau was most anxious to acquire.

When Lunan agreed, Rogov assigned to him the cover name "Black," and told him to proceed with the organization of his net and with the subsequent exploitation of his sources.

Lunan began by inviting Smith to lunch in order to sound him out. The two met in a downtown restaurant where, after some preliminary sparring, Lunan broached the question: Would Smith be willing to supply information for the Soviet Union? Smith asked for time to think it over, but at their next meeting agreed to the proposition. After their second meeting Lunan wrote to Rogov: "Badeau [Smith's cover name in the ring] warmed up slowly to my request and remained non-committal until he had checked independently on my *bona fides*. Once satisfied, he promised to cooperate." Durnford Smith, a scientist of impeccable reputation who had access to some of his country's most sensitive information, was in the Soviet net.

Durnford Smith proved to be a most valuable informant, and on March 28, 1945, Lunan reported to Rogov: "Discussing the work of the National Defense Council in general, Badeau informs me that the most secret work at present is on nuclear physics (bombardment of radioactive substances to produce energy). This is more hush-hush than radar and is being carried on at the University of Montreal and at McMaster University at Hamilton. Badeau thinks that government purchase of a radium-producing plant is connected with this research."

This was momentous information, the first the Soviet espionage organization had received about atomic developments in the Western sphere. The information reached Soviet intelligence three months before the first experimental A-bomb was exploded at Alamogordo. But from the time Lunan's report reached Zabutin the Canadian spy ring concentrated on the acquisition of additional information about the A-bomb.

Scattered data was then received from a number of other sources that Zabutin had succeeded in developing in Canada and the United States, and, in time, a major scoop was scored when samples of the uranium used in the A-bomb were acquired through another source.

A British scientist named Allan Nunn May was listed in the Comintern files as a clandestine sympathizer, willing to cooperate. Contacts in London reported to Zabutin that Dr. May was working in Canada on the same project Smith had mentioned to Lunan. May was already in the net, but he was not yet active. Zabutin then instructed another one of his aides, Lieutenant Angelov of the Fourth Bureau, to call on Dr. May at his apartment in Montreal and ask him to obtain samples of uranium 235. A few days later, May again met with Angelov and handed over samples of both uranium 235 and uranium 233, thus making what was probably the greatest single contribution to the Soviet Union's own atomic energy project, equal in importance to the contribution of Dr. Klaus Fuchs, another source, who had been developed in the United States.

This is the most common method of developing and exploiting informants (sources), and it is followed by espionage organizations everywhere. Yet while the methods may be the same everywhere, the results are not. Neither is the zeal, skill, and pitiless efficiency with which they are applied. Where both quantity and quality are concerned, Soviet espionage is far superior to any other in the world. Of the 1,902 espionage cases reported by the New York *Times* between 1917 (when the Bolsheviks came into power in Russia) and 1939 (when the Second World War broke out and espionage became a wide-spread activity practiced extensively by all belligerents), the Soviet apparatus was aggressively involved in more than 1,500 cases, while only about a dozen cases involving spies working against the Soviet Union were reported.

Although the number of Soviet spies caught by the counter-espionage agencies of the world is enormous, this does not mean that Soviet spy rings are inefficient or insecure, or that Soviet spies are easily trapped. The vast majority of Soviet agents were caught only *after* the completion of their missions, when they had already delivered the information they were sent out to acquire. The atom spies, for example, were not arrested in Britain and the United States until 1950, a full five years after the completion of their missions, and many of them were not caught at all. The British branch of the atomic espionage ring, for example, was never fully exposed.

The numbers cited above merely indicate the extent to which the Soviet Union engages in espionage throughout the world. It is generally figured that only about ten percent of all spy cases are exposed, and that not more than one out of ten operational spies is ever caught. If this calculation is correct, the Soviet intelligence service may have had approximately 15,000 espionage missions in operation in just twenty-two years. If only ten agents were engaged, on an average, in each operation, there were then some 150,000 persons working for Soviet intelligence service during those years. Actually, I am inclined to place the number of Soviet spies even higher—as many as 250,000 to 400,000 men and women working in all echelons and all capacities for the acquisition and transmission of information by surreptitious means.

The efficiency of Soviet espionage is reflected in its results. In the United States alone Soviet spies succeeded in procuring information on the following highly classified subjects:

Details of the hydrogen bomb; the theories and plans of the atomic bomb; the defense details of the Panama Canal; blueprints of the proximity fuse; data on the gaseous diffusion plant at Oak Ridge; American cosmic ray research; details on the Hanford atomic plant; samples of U-233 and U-235; the experimental layout of Los Alamos; the identity of America's atomic scientists; the designs for atomic aircraft; the dates of atomic tests; plans for the so-called Earth Satellite, a project involving the construction of a "space fortress"; the formula of RDX high explosive; data on American turbo-prop aircraft; jeep plans; blueprints of the research equipment of Edgewood Arsenal, test center of American chemical warfare; details of experimental bacterial warfare; radiation data; blueprints of the B-29; aircraft production data; techniques in breaking codes; the formula of the Dina explosive; sonar antisubmarine devices; the formula of the Torpex explosive; details of radar and scanning radar; progress in guided missile research; data about air-borne distance indicators; waterproof maps.

Between 1947 and 1953, a single Soviet spy stationed in Switzerland supplied the following information:

The location of RAF airports in Germany; a roster of all American officers stationed in Germany; the battle order of American troops in Germany; a critique of the various maneuvers and exercises staged by Allied troops in Europe; the organization of the U.S. Air Force in the United Kingdom; Allied military installations and constructions in Germany; the battle order of the French Army in France and in Indochina.

Between 1930 and 1945, the Soviet espionage organization reputedly had agents, some of them very highly placed, in the following key posts of foreign countries:

THE UNITED STATES. In the office of Naval Intelligence, the State Department, the Department of Justice, the Counter Intelligence Corps in Germany, the Manhattan Project, and thirty-nine other government departments.

FRANCE. In the Ministry of Foreign Affairs, the high command of the resistance movement during the war, the cipher department of the French Admiralty, the scientific department of the French War Ministry, the minister's cabinet in the Air Ministry, the Sûreté Nationale, and at least fifty other sensitive government departments.

THE UNITED KINGDOM. In the code rooms of the Foreign Office at London and the British Embassy at Moscow, the American division of the Foreign Office, the Admiralty; the Harwell center of atomic developments, and many more government agencies and departments.

CANADA. In the cipher department and passport division of the Ministry of External Affairs, all branches of atomic research and other scientific developments, the Bank of Canada, the Canadian Wartime Information Board, and numerous other key departments.

GERMANY. In the highest command of the Wehrmacht, the Reichs Ministry of Air, the Ministry of Construction and Supplies, the Propaganda Ministry, and at least sixteen other sensitive government departments where Soviet spies were identified but not necessarily caught.

JAPAN. In the private cabinet of Prime Minister Konoye, the confidential office of General Ugoye, the House of Representatives, the Foreign Ministry, the headquarters of the South Manchurian Railroad, various government research departments, Japan's so-called China Research Institute (itself an intelligence organization), various Manchurian administrations in Tokyo, and many other sensitive agencies.

The highest tribute to the efficiency of Soviet espionage was paid by Adolf Hitler, who attributed his own setbacks in Russia not to the superiority of Soviet arms but to the superiority of the Soviet intelligence system. On May 17, 1942, he hold his intimates, "If we don't know what to do with the armored divisions of the Russians, this is because the Soviets are so highly superior to us in just one field—espionage." In praising the supreme efficiency of Soviet espionage, he bemoaned the apparent inferiority of his own espionage system. He overlooked the fact, however, that in espionage technical efficiency is no more essential than the zeal and determination with which a country pursues it, or the mental and physical aptitude that the people of different nations bring to the task. In the highly civilized countries of Europe, where Christian ethics influence the thinking processes and instincts of the individual, espionage cannot be developed to the high level of efficiency that it attains in countries where no equally limiting influences affect this particular phase of intelligence.

133

The Scheme of Espionage

An espionage organization is by far the most delicate precision instrument operated by a government, and it is also the most unethical and lawless activity in which a nation may engage, apart from final unwarranted military aggression. Partly because of the amoral and immoral aspect of espionage agencies, governments painstakingly camouflage them or deny that they exist at all.

In general, spies are regarded as expendable, and they are aware that they must be regarded, even by their own governments, as criminals and outcasts. When the English writer W. Somerset Maugham was recruited in World War I to serve as a British agent in Switzerland, he was told by a superior: "There's just one thing I think you ought to know before you take on this job. And don't forget it. If you do well you'll get no thanks, and if you get into trouble you'll get no help."

When caught, spies are disavowed by the governments for which they have worked, and any association with them is emphatically denied. While governments publicly and brazenly disavow their espionage agents when they are exposed, they do everything possible behind the scenes to aid and protect them, to facilitate their work, and to make their survival possible. The basic protection of a secret agent is the over-all efficiency of his organization, its secrecy, and the efficacy and practicability of the entire espionage plan.

Espionage services are so organized as to provide for a maximum of efficiency while keeping the danger of compromise at an absolute minimum. Within the organization everything is arranged and planned with clocklike precision. The organization is kept tightly knit and as small as possible. It is maintained at a permanently high level of efficiency with every person assigned to a specific detail, the nature of which is meticulously defined.

The work of the organization in general, and of the agents in particular, is further protected and facilitated by a basic operations order, called the "espionage plan." It is patterned after the operations plans of armies in action. The "general espionage plan" involves the current needs of a government concerning information that can be procured only by surreptitious means. It includes the table of organization of the espionage service, the principles of recruitment, and personnel policies. The plan also outlines the methods of operations, the system of concealment, and the rules of internal security. Such a general espionage plan is outlined at the inception of the service, and changes are afterward made in it only when circumstances make them advisable or necessary.

For individual missions or special operations, directives or field orders are issued. In the British secret service such orders are called "Operations Instructions." They prepare each mission with meticulous care and outline every maneuver in advance, always trying to anticipate every possible exigency.

In view of the complexity of espionage, the difficulties involved in spying, the difficulty of securing reliable agents, and the complications of maintaining agents at large and keeping contact with them, even countries which engage in the activity on a substantial scale employ only a relatively small number of operational agents or full-time professional spies. The great majority of the people who procure information are not full-time or professional spies but *ad hoc*, part-time informants.

Espionage is an expensive and extremely difficult activity, often producing no return whatever for an enormous investment. Much of the information needed, even that of great strategic value and immediate importance, can be obtained from open sources by the simpler methods of intelligence proper. Experience shows that spies in general produce insignificant results and add little to the information obtained by conventional intelligence. An agent-at-large sent to a foreign country with instructions to obtain whatever he can, with no mission specified, is unlikely to produce data justifying the investment in time, money, and effort. Occasionally such an agent will pick up information of real value, but this is the exception rather than the rule.

Agents on special missions produce better results and are sent out to procure information about specific subjects. A great number of spies were sent from Britain to the Continent to obtain detailed information about the "V" weapons of the Germans after the existence of the Peenemünde project had been established through the examination of aerial photographs. Although most of these agents returned empty-handed, when they returned at all, one of them did bring back a blueprint of the V-1. She was a small, raven-haired Frenchwoman who is still known today only by her cover name, *La Souris*, The Mouse. She got the name from her secret recognition signal, a delicate scratching on a windowpane, like a mouse. She managed to obtain the blueprint from a Vichy French engineer who had spent some time working in Germany and who helped reconstruct the design of the V-1 from memory. The assignment of *La Souris* was a specific mission. Recalling the days of these missions, Winston Churchill wrote: "Every known means of getting information was employed, and it was pieced together with great skill. To all sources, many of whom worked amid deadly danger, and some of whom will be forever unknown to us, I pay my tribute."

Instead of using secret agents sent out from headquarters on special missions, espionage services often utilize inhabitants of foreign countries to obtain whatever information is needed, whether general or specific. To this end, a clandestine network of local residents must be established within foreign countries, the members of the network acting as spies and agents on a free-lance, part-time basis, usually for monetary rewards. This network then feeds the information to full-time representatives of the espionage organization who pass through the target countries at irregular intervals or reside there for longer periods, and who confine their own activities to relaying the information instead of going out and acquiring it themselves.

In this way, an espionage organization needs to maintain only a limited number of full-time, professional spies, even while it has a very large number of part-time spies on its roster. This is the method now used by most espionage agencies, in particular by the Soviet intelligence service. The Soviet system has the advantage of drawing on local Communist parties in foreign countries to produce the spies and informants it needs. These agents are then used either directly by themselves in supplying the information to which they have immediate access, or indirectly by acquiring information from contacts who may not actually be in the net.

The establishment of a network of local spies is not as difficult as it may seem. When Colonel Zabutin arrived in Canada in June, 1943, for example, he found only a skeleton ring which had been functioning since October, 1942. It consisted of a total of sixteen persons, of whom five are still unknown. Of the remaining eleven individuals, three were Soviet nationals serving as organizers and eight were Canadians serving as spies.

Colonel Zabutin arrived in Canada with a substantial staff. It consisted of eleven members of the Fourth Bureau, all officers, and even such assistants as door guards and chauffeurs were actually lieutenants in the Red Army. In addition, he had three civilian aides who were on diplomatic assignments to camouflage their real activities. Zabutin's inner staff did not engage in direct espionage action but served merely to establish the network of Canadian spies, direct and supervise their activities, handle administrative matters and disbursements, and maintain the line of communications both within Canada and to the Center in Moscow.

Zabutin's ring of active spies consisted of one Englishman, two Americans, and twenty-four Canadian subjects. Among them were scientists with direct access to Canada's most carefully guarded secrets, a registrar in the office of the United Kingdom High Commissioner, an official of the Bank of Canada, officials of the Department of Munitions and Supply, a cipher clerk in the Department of External Affairs, and a member of the Canadian Parliament.

This phenomenal network was established within six months of Zabutin's arrival in Canada and functioned without interruption until September, 1945, a total of twenty-six months. It is significant that the ring was exposed, not by any of its Canadian members, but by Igor Gouzenko, a Soviet national, Zabutin's own cipher clerk, who deserted to the Canadian authorities with a great number of documents, thereby exposing the activities of the entire network. Gouzenko proved the only weak link in the Russian chain, while the local agents of the ring, those who owed their allegiance to Canada, proved to be loyal and reliable Soviet instruments. This Canadian example serves to show that a local network, composed of citizens who are willing to spy on their own country for a foreign power, is usually trustworthy and dependable when properly organized.

Another ring of comparable efficiency operated in Switzerland between 1937 and 1943. Unlike the Zabutin ring, it was not connected with the Soviet diplomatic mission but operated independently under a resident director whose "roof"—as a respectable or plausible cover is called in the Soviet espionage lingo—was established in advance. The ring consisted of the resident director, three cut-outs, three wireless operators, and one courier, altogether only eight persons serving as the ring's inner administrative and communications staff. These eight then tapped a local network of sixty sources who supplied the information. Among these sources were officials of the League of Nations and the International Labor Office, members of the French, Chinese, and Yugoslav military attaché staffs, officers of the Swiss general staff, an official of the Swiss Passport Office, and several clandestine members of the Swiss Communist Party under a man named Leon Nicole, who was the Swiss representative of the Comintern's espionage bureau. Not a single member of the Swiss ring was a Soviet national.

The main Japanese ring of Soviet espionage under Richard Sorge consisted of thirty-five members, but only two of them, Sorge himself and a radio operator, were full-time agents of the Fourth Bureau. All others were local residents and, with the exception of one Yugoslav, all of them were native Japanese. Two of them were women. The average age of these people was 40 years, the youngest member of the ring being 21, the oldest 61 years old. Among them were editors and journalists, researchers, manufacturers, businessmen, brokers, government officials, railroad officials, a member of the Japanese House of Representatives, and a physician. The thirty-three local members of the Sorge ring had access to a network of 160 informants, among them the Prime Minister of Japan and an influential general, neither of whom, of course, suspected that data supplied by them was going to the Fourth Bureau. None of the members of this entire ring was a Soviet national.

The Germans and Japanese operated similar rings in the United States before World War II. They sent to America only a few trained professional spies, Japan only a handful attached to the Japanese Embassy, and Germany only two or three agents to organize the networks of local residents. The active members of the ring were all Americans, both native-born and naturalized, including a former officer and a former petty officer of the U.S. Navy and a number of businessmen, all working as part-time spies through cut-outs.

Before the outbreak of World War II, Britain made an effort to establish such a network of local agents inside Germany, operating from headquarters in the Netherlands. This ring was infiltrated and exposed on November 9, 1939, when its two British directors were lured into a trap and kidnaped by counterintelligence agents of the Gestapo. After the ring was smashed, Britain apparently never succeeded in establishing a substitute network in Germany during the war. The main Soviet network within Germany was smashed by the Gestapo in 1942. The elimination of the British and Soviet networks left only one such network at large in Germany, the one established by the Office of Strategic Services from its headquarters in Switzerland.

The establishment of this network of agents working for the United States, none of whom was an American citizen, represented a new departure in the traditional attitude of the United States toward espionage. As late as 1924, Colonel Walter C. Sweeney, a former chief in the Military Intelligence Division of the U.S. Army's General Staff, described the method of procuring information through the establishment of a network of local resident agents in foreign countries as "a system whose use would not even be considered by the United States." The idea of using foreign nationals as spies was repugnant to the American government, even when the need of the information they could have supplied became increasingly pressing.

Several recommendations were submitted to the authorities in Washington urging that a network of resident agents be set up inside Japan to supply information concerning her plans of aggression and military organization. One plan of this kind, known as the M-plan, was prepared and submitted by Colonel Sidney Mashbir but it was rejected without ever being considered seriously. The result was that the United States had no network of agents inside Japan on the eve of Pearl Harbor and obtained no direct information from spies on impending events. The military and naval attachés, whose job it was to collect such information, were deceived both by an efficient camouflaging of Japan's actual war preparations and by their acceptance at face value of information deliberately planted by the Japanese High Command to mislead them. On the very eve of the attack on Pearl Harbor, the American naval attaché in Tokyo expressed the opinion that a surprise attack was unlikely, convinced that the fleet was still at its main base at Yokosuka simply because of the great number of sailors who could be seen crowding the streets of Tokyo. In acual fact, the fleet was at sea, on its way to its wartime destination. The sailors so much in evidence were soldiers dressed in naval uniforms and sent into the streets of Tokyo for the sole purpose of misleading people such as the American service attaché.

Had the United States maintained an espionage network in Japan as proposed by Colonel Mashbir, it would have been possible to anticipate Japanese intentions. This was proved by the fact that the Soviet network of Dr. Sorge did actually acquire the information that Japan would commence operations against Britain and the United States on December 7, 1941, and that it would not attack the Soviet Union as was expected. This information proved to be of extreme value to the U.S.S.R., since it enabled the Soviet leaders to demilitarize their Far Eastern provinces and transfer their garrisons to fronts in Europe where they were urgently needed. We may perceive on the basis of this strategic example how essential the maintenance of an espionage network in sensitive areas of the world can be, and how disadvantageous the absence of such a network can be to the intended victim of an aggressor. This is no longer solely a matter of international ethics or moral scruples. In our competitive human society it is a matter of survival.

During the war the United States made no serious effort to establish a network of spies within Japan, since the difficulties of such an effort were far too great in proportion to its possible value. It is virtually impossible to set up a local network in an enemy country under wartime conditions; it has to be established prior to the outbreak of hostilities. Even the Russians failed to reestablish one within Germany when their original network, known as the *Rote Kapelle* or Red Orchestra, was smashed. They managed to create such networks only in the countries of their wartime allies, Canada, the United Kingdom, and the United States, and in neutral Switzerland, traditional battleground of international espionage.

But where the Russians failed and the experienced British dared not tread, the United States succeeded, largely because of the exceptional skill, ingenuity, and tenacity of the American intelligence genius, Allen W. Dulles. Mr. Dulles arrived in Berne, capital of Switzerland, in the fall of 1942, a few months after the establishment of the Office of Strategic Services. He was to set up a Swiss branch of the OSS for the purpose of procuring information about neighboring Germany. In a brownstone house in Berne's quiet Herren Street, Dulles devised a new operation to which the whole underworld of espionage was soon beating a path. "My first and most important task," Mr. Dulles later recalled, "was to find out what was going on in Germany. Among other things, Washington wanted to know who in Germany were really opposed to the Hitler regime and whether they were actively at work to overthrow it. As far as the outside world could see, it often seemed as though Hitler had succeeded in winning over, hypnotizing, or terrorizing the entire German nation.

"From Switzerland I was able to establish contact with the German underground and for many months before the culmination of the plot on July 20 I had kept in touch with those who were conspiring to rid Germany of the Nazis and the Nazi state. Couriers, risking their lives, went back and forth between Switzerland and Germany with reports. . . ."

The network Mr. Dulles succeeded in establishing within Germany was large in numbers and exceptionally high in quality. In all the history of espionage there had been no precedent for this achievement. While this type of network usually is maintained only to procure tactical information of a specialized or localized nature, the high quality of the Dulles system produced at least one strategic result of the greatest significance. Through this network Mr. Dulles managed to start a conspiracy within the high command of the German armies in the south and to bring about the surrender of the very army on which Hitler was dependent for the prolonging of the war from behind the legendary "Alpine Redoubt."

The grand scheme of espionage is all-embracing. It is world-wide in scale, and so detailed as to be concerned with every phase and aspect of life in individual countries. The most important job of all is the infiltration of the opponent's armed forces. Yet here, just where spies are needed most, the difficulties of planting them appear to be greatest. All civilians are automatically suspect in combat zones. Passing from one front line to another presents great and often insurmountable difficulties. Espionage agents have to be dropped behind the lines of the enemy and then, disguised as soldiers, approach the front from the rear areas.

Contrary to common belief, spies are rarely used in this manner in the combat zone since conventional methods of intelligence, aided by the practical exigencies of war itself, are capable of supplying most of the information that commanders need. Whatever additional or specific information is required may be obtained from local residents or *ad hoc* agents recruited on the spot. Often such information may be procured from a few scattered espionage agents established at fixed positions before the commencement of hostilities and activated during the war when needed.

One of the outstanding cases of such wartime espionage involved an elderly couple in Germany, named Müller, and a British agent sent specially to assist them. The Müllers owned an inn on Brunsbüttelkoog, the southern terminus of the Kiel Canal that connects the Baltic with the North Sea. The Müllers were great favorites with the German submariners who passed through the canal on their way to operational cruises in the Atlantic. As a matter of fact, it became their custom to visit the Müllers' inn for a last glass of German beer in the Fatherland, donated as a patriotic gesture by the friendly innkeepers.

A little ritual developed around these calls. At the end of each farewell celebration, old man Müller would produce a guest register and invite his guests to sign their names as a memento of their visit. Then, as soon as the men had departed and the coast was clear, Müller would descend to his

141

cellar and, through an underground passage, make his way to a neighboring house and hand the guest register to a friend awaiting him there. This friend was the British agent. He would copy off the names and radio them to England from a transmitter operated by the radioman of his team.

In this manner, Naval Intelligence in the Admiralty was promptly informed whenever a U-boat departed on an operational cruise. From the name of the U-boat's commanding officer, Naval Intelligence determined the number of the submarine and thus established her class and tonnage, her cruising range, and occasionally even the nature of her mission.

The case of the Müllers illustrates several points in the grand scheme of espionage. First of all, it demonstrates the complex nature of organization and the need for establishing such nests long in advance of war. The Müllers were recruited by a full-time itinerant professional agent of British intelligence when he became aware of their anti-Nazi sentiments during a trip to Brunsbüttelkoog before the war. He realized the strategic location of their inn and accordingly planned the whole scheme, including the parting glass of beer "on the house" and the guest register.

Another important point that the case of the Müllers demonstrates is the difficulty of keeping secret even such an isolated military move as the passage of a single submarine in home waters. Also, the case shows the personal danger inherent in this kind of operation and the high price spies must often pay for their part in it. The Müllers paid with their lives.

The Ideal Spy

Whatever contributions good organization, iron-clad secrecy, and meticulous planning might make, the success and survival of the individual spy will ultimately depend on factors within himself, whether innate or acquired. It is often assumed that men must possess certain specific character traits to qualify as effective spies, and that many of these traits are morbid or else a man would not select such an odd vocation. It is true that the secret agent must live by a special code, in which conventional morality is of necessity secondary to more immediate and less ethical motivations. Since elaborate deceit is the essence of espionage, it is often believed that if the spy is not an unprincipled scoundrel to begin with, his character inevitably disintegrates during his life as a spy.

Undoubtedly there have been psychopaths among the spies of history. Some of them were show-offs, egotists, what William Bolitho called truants from obligation. Others were sheer adventurers who sought and found satisfaction, not in the aims, but in the thrills of espionage. Still others were driven into espionage by jealousies, persecution and inferiority complexes, overweening ambitions, deep hatred, and violent prejudices—or simply by the love of money or the urgent need for it.

It has been gossiped that some of the famous spies of recent history were notorious homosexuals. Actually, in the entire history of espionage, there are only two renowned spies who were proven homosexuals, and only one whose homosexuality caused him to engage in espionage. The legend is that sexual deviates are vulnerable to blackmail and so forced into spying activity. In point of fact, very few homosexuals have been trapped by their sexual aberrations compared with the great number of normal men who have succumbed to the charms of the opposite sex acting as decoys.

Scientific studies of the psychology of espionage show that psychopaths and freaks do not make good spies. On the contrary, such studies prove that the effective spy is neither a freak nor a psychopath. He is rather the "citizen spy," who acts upon the incentive of enlightened patriotism and to whom deceit and intrigue are only temporary expedients that he knows how to keep under strict control.

The personality problem has long baffled all organizations engaged in espionage. They have tried by all kinds of methods to establish the pattern of what is called the "ideal spy," although this is admittedly a futile quest for unattainable perfection.

Different countries have different concepts of the perfect spy. The British, for example, visualize the ideal spy as a sporting young man of excellent birth and independent means, with a better than average education, inconspicuously handsome, rationally courageous, tenacious, and mildly philosophical. He feigns snobbishness, dullness, cynicism, disinterest, and a tendency to swagger, while in reality he is sensitive, alert, poised, erudite, and inquisitive. The personalities of British spies I have known were made up of all those traits, both natural and pretended.

The Russian approach to the personality problem of espionage is at once pragmatic and dogmatic. The Russians envisage their spies as eager and practical intellectuals with enormous book knowledge, serious, industrious, with an unquestioning respect for rules and regulations and an unshakable reserve, to whom all action is a conditioned response. The actual Russian agent, on the whole, is a kind of polished automaton who does everything exceedingly well as long as the sailing is smooth, but who is immediately lost in a crisis since he does not know how to deal with problems not treated in his textbooks.

In the United States the spy is popularly thought of as an easy-going rugged individualist, not necessarily brilliant in all fields, but a wizard at his own specialty, ingenious, instinctive, and intuitive, with little liking for pure reason, adventurous and brave, adaptable, friendly, dexterous, a quick improviser in tight situations, somewhat indiscreet, and a daredevil. In actual fact, successful spies possess all of these traits to some degree.

Several scientific efforts were made, especially in the United States where psychological prognostication is a fad, to establish the personality structure of the ideal spy. On the basis of these studies, there was drawn up a catalogue of ten major groups of traits which the good spy is supposed to possess in order to qualify.

First of all, his morale must be high and he must be genuinely interested in the job ahead.

Second, he must be energetic, zealous, and enterprising.

Third, he must be resourceful, a quick and practical thinker. He must have good judgment and know how to deal with things, people, and ideas. He must be proficient in some occupational skill.

Fourth, he must be emotionally stable, capable of great endurance under stress. He must be calm and quiet, tolerant and healthy.

Fifth, he must have the ability to get along with other people, to work as a member of a team, to understand the foibles of others while being reasonably free of the same foibles himself.

Sixth, he must know how to inspire collaboration, to organize, administer, and lead others. He must be willing to accept responsibility.

Seventh, he must be discreet, have a passion for anonymity, and know how to keep his mouth shut and preserve a secret.

Eighth, he must be able to bluff and mislead, but only when bluffing and misleading become necessary.

Ninth, he must be agile, rugged, and daring.

Tenth, he must have the ability to observe everything, to memorize details accurately. He must be able to report on his observations lucidly, to evaluate his observations and relate them to the greater complex of things.

Naturally, it is the rare individual who combines all of these traits in his personality. Men who were highly intelligent were found to be strong in leadership, excellent observers and reporters, and good salesmen. But their emotional stability was often low, their discretion left something to be desired, their sociability was deficient, and they generally lacked a physical skill.

Emotionally stable persons were found to be sociable and good leaders, adequately discreet and fairly skilled, but their intelligence was somewhat lower. They were also poor observers, inaccurate reporters, and not good salesmen.

It was found that the ideal spy was not so often the brilliant spy but the average spy. This averageness extended even to his personal appearance.

Spies in Action

Now that we have seen how espionage is organized and have examined the basic qualifications for an effective spy, let us see in some detail how espionage operates. For the individual drawn into this activity, service begins on the day of his recruitment and ends with the termination of his mission. A mission may terminate either with the man's arrest or with his return to his base. Naturally most of the best known espionage cases had unhappy endings, although once in a while a spy returns from his mission to tell his own story when circumstances or security no longer impose silence on him. Often the agents who return come back from the shadow of death. However melodramatic this may sound, it is a grim reality in the espionage business.

The narrative of the famous *White Rabbit*—F.F.E. Yeo-Thomas, one of the foremost British agents of World War II and Mr. Churchill's personal liaison with the underground in France—demonstrates most dramatically the odyssey of even the best spy. The story of his adventure, as told by Bruce Marshall, covers 256 pages. But his mission ends on page 99 with a breathtaking description of his arrest by the Gestapo in Paris, after he violated a cardinal rule of the trade and waited a few minutes for a tardy contact. The rest of the narrative describes his interrogation and torture, his anguished

145

years in German concentration camps, his every minute awaiting the seemingly inevitable end.

Another great British agent, a woman named Odette Sansom, the only living female spy to wear the George Cross, was also caught, as were about ninety percent of her colleagues in the field. Life expectation is low in wartime espionage; the mortality rate is high. The balance sheet of espionage shows that despite the enormous investment of money and effort expended on this most complex and difficult of human activities, failure is far more frequent than success. Some of the world's best spies did not live to tell their own stories, even though most of them managed to send back invaluable information before their untimely death.

Agents in the field may operate as lone wolves, going out by themselves and carrying through their missions without outside aid. But missions of this kind are rare and very seldom successful. They are mounted when a man or woman is planted permanently in an opponent's organization.

More often spies are sent out in teams, usually in pairs, one man to procure information, another to transmit it. Even the smallest team needs a communications apparatus to back it up. It needs a contact in the home office, one who conceived and organized the mission and remains essentially in charge of it by remote control.

Spies in the field obviously cannot go to banks and withdraw the funds they need, for a bank account may eventually betray even the long-term resident agent. He cannot account for the source of his funds, or be expected to pay taxes on his espionage income in the normal manner of the wage-earner. Most of the monetary transactions in espionage are handled on a cash-and-carry basis, the cash ordinarily being supplied in the currency of the country in which the spy operates and brought in by special couriers.

Nor can the espionage agent buy his supplies in the country where he operates. If he buys the chemicals he needs to mix his secret ink, or the film on which he photographs his documents, his periodic purchases may trap him. Virtually all the supplies a spy needs in the field—the chemicals, the films, the tubes for his radio set, the bullets for his gun—have to be smuggled in from headquarters.

Even in the field the spy is rarely left to himself. Small though the operating circle may be, there are always a few people at the point of his assignment who work with him and on whom he depends. He has an *agent-de-liaison*, a kind of espionage apprentice who performs his errands, usually a native of the country in which he is working. He often has a host assigned to provide a roof over his head, a trusted but peripheral member of the organization. He is given the names of contacts and guides, and supplied with accommodation addresses where he may hide out in emergencies, operate his radio transmitter, or remain for a while to camouflage his movements. Despite this circle of aides, contacts, and associates, the spy is a lonely man, necessarily keeping to himself as much as possible, since any association may compromise his security.

Espionage organizations strive to anticipate every possibility and eventuality that will confront an agent in the field. Among other things, they try to warn him of the possible ways in which he may be trapped, and suggest alternate means of evasion and escape. They try to prepare him for every possible emergency, and to arrange everything in advance so as to reduce his chances of exposure or arrest. Espionage organizations are perforce eminently practical and ingenious. They conduct their operations in the field in ten different stages, each stage having exact rules painstakingly outlined in manuals and operations orders.

These ten stages are: 1. recruiting and selection; 2. training and indoctrination; 3. establishment of cover and authentication; 4. routing, or the agent's journey to his place of assignment; 5. the establishment of his cover on the spot; 6. development of local sources of information; 7. the surreptitious procurement of confidential information; 8. meetings with contacts, subagents, cut-outs, and couriers; 9. communications and transportation; and 10. safety and security, often the most difficult part of the operation. We may now examine these various stages one by one.

Recruiting and Selection

Because agents usually operate in alien lands whose language and customs are different from their own, persons who speak the language and know the customs of the countries to which they are assigned are preferred. This is a primary consideration in recruiting. Agents are sought who fit this basic condition by virtue of an exceptional linguistic ability or by long previous residence in the foreign country of assignment. In other instances, agents may establish a temporary nationality as a cover. A British agent, for example, may be sent to work in Rumania posing as a German, provided he speaks German fluently and without a detectable accent and is thoroughly familiar with at least certain parts of Germany. At any rate, fluency in some foreign language and familiarity with a foreign country is an essential prerequisite in recruiting.

Recruiting poses no problem to the Soviet espionage organization, which draws its agents from the vast reservoir of international Communist parties. Nor is it too great a problem in the United States, which can draw its agents from its foreign-born population, or from among refugees, escapees, and political exiles.

It is not so simple in Britain or France. To overcome this obstacle, Britain selects prospective spies at an early and impressionable age. Very young men are encouraged to take up residence abroad and fade into their environment, become bilingual, and prepare themselves for whatever mission might at one time or another be assigned to them, either in the countries where they have grown up, or in countries to which they might be sent, pretending to be nationals of the country of their long residence. This may seem a tedious process in the breeding of spies, but it is actually followed.

The Japanese had an even greater problem to overcome in the selection of their agents, since their physical features automatically set them apart from much of the rest of the world. They solved the problem by using their own trained agents only as administrators, organizers, and supervisors, and hiring Caucasians to act as operational spies. The Germans prefer their own nationals, or recruit their agents among German residents abroad. The Italians do the same, often using agents who are absorbed into the large Italian populations of the countries where they operate.

Actual recruiting is usually done by specialists assigned to that sole function. They are the "talent scouts" who bring likely prospects to the attention of the special branch of the espionage organization which is in charge of undercover personnel. The candidate is gradually introduced into the organization, invited to become a spy in due course, and initiated only when he passes severe tests.

In the Soviet Union, a man's competence in certain special fields is the decisive factor in his selection. His aptitude for a job is assessed subjectively through personal observation and interview.

The United States is the only country in the world that selects its secret agents on the basis of scientific tests. These tests were developed during World War II by the assessment staff of the OSS, operating at a secluded estate in Virginia. Here candidates were required to spend three days, during which they underwent a number of ingeniously devised psychological and aptitude tests, under conditions simulating those met in the field. They were given cover names and bogus identities. During their tests they were exposed to strange situations and required to participate in hazardous procedures.

One such procedure was, for example, the "Belonging Test," designed to test a candidate's ability to observe a situation and draw the correct conclusions from his observations. He was taken into a bedroom which, the candidate was told, had been occupied several days earlier by a transient. On his departure, the transient had left behind a number of his belongings, twenty-six items in all, including articles of clothing, written material, newspapers, clippings, and a timetable. The candidate was told to examine them carefully and, from the clues these objects offered, to make a try at sizing up the guest in exactly four minutes.

The three-day trial period ended with a test designed to measure the candidate's ability to endure stress and strain. An arrest was simulated and the candidate taken to a small room in the basement where he was placed in the glare of a blinding spotlight. The room was otherwise dark, but from the darkness came harsh, relentless voices which tried to confuse and unnerve the candidate, to make him betray his original cover story. The test was a good imitation of interrogation by the secret police of a totalitarian state.

Men who passed these tests were then assigned to that branch of the OSS which seemed best suited to the candidates' particular talents revealed by the examination. Similar methods are used today in the selection of agents for the CIA.

I think the United States is probably the only country in the world that goes to so much trouble and expense to select its secret agents. But the investment has paid off in the field. The record of the Medical Branch of the OSS showed that men and women passed by the Assessment Staff had fewer neuro-psychiatric symptoms—and fewer breakdowns in the field than those who obtained assignments without this screening.

Training and Indoctrination

Indoctrination of prospective secret agents is an abstract educational process. It is designed to cultivate inner strength in an agent's personality, to impress him with the basic nobility of his effort, and to develop in him loyalty, responsibility, and reliability. It is undertaken in the form of lectures that possess a high degree of emotional appeal but have little

149

bearing on the actual work for which the candidate is being prepared.

Training, on the other hand, is a concrete and functional exercise or practice to teach the agent all the practical aspects of his trade. It is designed to equip him with certain skills that he will need in the execution of his missions, and to prepare him for all eventualities and emergencies. An agent's training is less concerned with the teaching of specialties, since it is assumed that anyone slated for the job already possesses certain fundamental knowledge or experience in the field to which he will eventually be assigned.

Secret agents are trained in special espionage schools. During World War II, the Allies maintained sixty of these schools, since many agents were required in meeting the exigencies of war, and many more to work with the various underground organizations. The present-day number and location of existing schools is, of course, classified information, as are some of the details of the curricula. Even so, it is possible to describe the training of secret agents in general terms, or on the basis of past or foreign examples.

The primary training of all personnel follows certain uniform lines and later branches into the various specialized fields, somewhat in the manner of teaching at medical schools, which require the mastery of fundamentals before allowing the student to specialize. In intelligence and espionage there is a distinction between basic and advanced training. Basic training covers all the subjects every agent needs to know. Advanced training is designed for developing specialists with individual skills.

In the training of secret agents the so-called "applicatory system of instruction" is used. In this method, theory plays only a minor role, whereas the heaviest stress is placed on practical factors. Candidates are given problems in which all possible situations are assumed, and they are required to solve these problems under simulated field conditions.

Since the agent's primary purpose is the procurement of information, his training is primarily concerned with this phase of activity. First of all, the meaning, nature, and value of every type of information is explained generally, after which its collection is taught in detail. It is ordinarily emphasized that any information at all is important, although it may not seem at a given moment to be of immediate or actual value. Agents are thus conditioned to recognize information in general, then to recognize that of some specific value, and finally to recognize the value of specific information to individual branches of government.

The next step is the development through training of the candidate's ability to observe and to record his observations. Obviously, the candidate must bring to the job some natural aptitude and ability. His training is then designed to sharpen and channel this ability. Students are taught to read maps quickly and accurately, to interpret aerial and ground photographs, to examine and study documents, to identify military and civil installations, and to identify airplanes and naval vessels by silhouette, to recognize machines, devices, and the equipment, uniforms, and insignia of the various branches of armed forces.

They are taught methods of recognition, identification, and location. They are instructed in the proper and efficient use of compass, telescope, and field glasses. They are told how to make observations and what to look for during apparently routine train trips, hikes, and journeys in airplanes and on ships.

Instruction is given in the recording of observations, the making of notes, maps, and sketches, and the taking of photographs both openly and surreptitiously. Candidates are taught how to write reports in which information is properly coordinated and focused, and in which observations are described in a concise and graphic manner. During this phase of the training, in addition to the art of interrogation, languages are improved and candidates are acquainted with the national characteristics of the peoples they will later work among.

The Russian system makes a sharp distinction between the training of secret agents or spies, and of conspirators, who may be agitators, propagandists, or revolutionary agents. The training of secret agents is short and to the point, and stresses such technical matters as the arranging of meetings, microphotography, the use of radio, coding and decoding, and the various methods of establishing and maintaining covers. This training is conducted within the Fourth Bureau, which has a special division for the training of its own agents and technicians. Some are trained by the MVD, and others by the foremost college of conspiracy maintained anywhere in the Communist world, the Lenin Academy in Moscow.

In the Lenin Academy students from all countries are taught: how to handle light arms of their own and of other countries; how to use the weapons at the disposal of the police abroad, and how to defend themselves against such weapons; how to break codes; how to enter offices and plants surreptitiously, how to search files, pilfer documents, make photostats of microphotographs; how to assemble and operate

151

radio transmitters; how to wage what is called conspiratorial warfare—street fighting, action behind barricades, partisan operations, civil war; how to ascertain the location of food stores, armament dumps, warehouses, public utilities, communications nerve centers, railway stations, junctions and marshaling yards, telephone exchanges; how to wreck trains, sabotage ships, slow down or stop production, destroy installations in key factories, demolish centers of resistance such as hostile newspaper plants, police stations, etc; how to publish clandestine newspapers and operate secret radio stations; how to print leaflets; how to induce labor disputes and organize strikes; how to propagandize members of the armed forces; how to organize meetings and raise the "mob spirit"; how to infiltrate governmental apparatuses and sensitive private institutions, such as public utilities plants, newspaper offices, banks; how to conduct counterespionage and maintain the security of their own espionage organization and of individual agents.

The German system of training was originally developed by a great intelligence specialist who became famous in the literature of espionage under the pseudonym "Mademoiselle Docteur." She was Elsbeth Schragmüller, a graduate of Freiburg University and a teacher by profession. At the outbreak of the First World War, Dr. Schragmüller volunteered her services to Colonel Nicolai of the High Command's intelligence bureau. She impressed Nicolai with her ideas about the training of spies and was allowed to organize a spy school of her own. Her pioneering methods have since been adopted by most of the modern espionage schools, not only in Germany, but in Britain and the United States as well.

Dr. Schragmüller's school was in Antwerp, at 10, rue de la Pepinière. She chose the house because it was inconspicuous and because it had a rear entrance on rue de l'Harmonie. Her students were brought to the school in curtained cars which stopped at the Harmony Street entrance. As soon as a car arrived the back gate was opened from the inside, and the student was whisked into the house. Inside he was received by Dr. Schragmüller, who showed the newcomer to his quarters. This was always a large and well-furnished room. It was equipped with a small library, manuals and maps, a phonograph, and games that a person could play alone. From then on the student was kept to himself. His door was locked from the outside and opened only when his meals were brought to him.

On the door was the given name by which the student was known in the school, common and impersonal, such as Hans or Karl or Willy. For the first few days, the new man was observed closely although never given a chance to see his observers. Every room had a mirror on the wall that was actually a screen, authentic in appearance from within the room but transparent from the opposite side. In this way Dr. Schragmüller could observe certain personal characteristics of her pupils, especially their ability to endure solitude.

After a week instructors began coming to the room one by one. Language experts came to teach the dialects and idiomatic speech of the country to which the man was to be assigned. Cipher experts taught cryptography, and communications specialists the use of secret inks, radio, and telegraphy. In time, all of the many arts in which the accomplished spy is adept were introduced and mastered, and for his final examination the student was taken to demonstration rooms where he proved his aptitude for the manifold requirements of espionage work.

Dr. Schragmüller herself wrote the manuals used in her school as texts, which today still serve as standards in the most modern espionage organizations. There was a basic manual in the Schragmüller school that is regarded as the best document of its kind ever produced for the instruction of secret agents. Here are a few items from it, as valid today as they were four decades ago:

1. Conceal whatever linguistic gifts you may have, to encourage others to talk freely in your hearing.

2. Never write or speak a word of your native tongue while on duty in a foreign country.

3. When procuring information, make your informant travel as far as possible from his place of residence and away from your immediate field of operations. Make him go to the meeting by a devious route, preferably at night. A tired informant is less cautious or suspicious, more relaxed and expansive, less disposed to lie or to bargain shrewdly—all advantages in the transaction which you should reserve to yourself.

4. Collect every available bit of information without indicating undue interest in any of it. Never fasten upon some item of intelligence you think you can or *must* acquire. By pursuing a single item, by making inquiries conspicuously, you expose your determination to learn a particular thing.

5. Always disguise newly acquired data with some apparently innocent cover. Figures or dimensions that have to be recorded may best be put down as items of personal expenditure.

6. When burning a letter or other papers, do not forget that their charred or ashen remnants are readable. Microscopic examination can do a great deal with paper ash. Tearing up papers and throwing them away does not mean that they are destroyed effectively. Paper scraps are never disposed of with absolute security, even in lavatories.

7. Never talk or behave mysteriously, except when trying to make a talkative person talk to you about things he knows.

8. Avoid every temptation to show off, to be too smart or too original or inventive. Remember what Talleyrand told his young diplomats: "Above all, no zeal!" You will certainly get farther by moving slowly. The best genius in espionage is the one who is never conspicuous. Remember, too, what Henry Austin said: "Genius, that power which dazzles mortal eyes, is oft but perseverance in disguise."

9. When securing a lodging, try to obtain a room or apartment that has more than a single entrance and exit. Plan and rehearse your escape in advance.

10. Always make sure that you are not being trailed, and learn the technique of eluding your follower.

11. Do not drink to excess. Cultivate the company of only those women you know and can trust.

12. Never take anything for granted, neither proffered friendship nor apparent hostility, neither the reliability of a report nor the seeming uselessness of some bit of information.

The ideas and methods of Dr. Schragmüller were studied in the United States when the OSS established its espionage schools during World War II. These American schools incorporated many of the methods of foreign institutions in their own curricula and, as a result, turned out some excellently trained personnel. One such OSS training station was established at the Congressional Country Club in Washington, where students were taught an amazing variety of subjects. Among its courses were cryptography, clandestine meeting, tailing, interrogation, residence searching, mine laying, arson, the handling of explosives, the use and maintenance of firearms, judo and other forms of self-defense. Students learned to read maps and to draw them, to make a lethal weapon from a folded newspaper, to immobilize automobiles by pouring sugar into their gasoline tanks, and to duplicate the imprint of rubber stamps with half a potato.

The British secret service operated a great number of schools of this type. At one of them, located at the municipal airport in Manchester, agents were trained in the art of parachuting from planes into hostile areas. Probably the best Allied espionage school of World War II was in Canada, an institute for advanced studies where instructors went to be taught.

Establishment of Cover and Authentication

When the training and indoctrination of a candidate is concluded and he is initiated into the organization as a secret agent, he is required to give up his former identity and assume an entirely new one called a cover, under which he then operates in the field. This metamorphosis is accomplished through a carefully plotted procedure in which nothing is left to chance. It begins with the preparation of a "legend," or "cover story," which is the bogus biography of the agent.

The construction of a cover story requires considerable effort. In the legend, the agent's knowledge of trades, peoples, and places is taken into consideration. It changes his birthplace, his educational background; it conceals his real work, his actual place of residence, all that is real about him. However, it must be plausible and easy to remember in the most specific detail, since a man is supposed to be able to maintain and defend his legend under exhaustive grilling and even torture.

I once saw a bogus biography that covered eighteen closely typed pages. Before it was finished, the agent not only had a new name, a new set of parents and grandparents, and a new birthplace, but also new hobbies and a new name for his pet dog.

In the Soviet Union every official of the Fourth Bureau is required to prepare a legend before going abroad. Igor Gouzenko, the Russian who exposed the atom spy ring, described the meticulous care with which his legend was prepared before his assignment to Canada. The compilation of his cover story took several days. "The idea behind these 'legends' is rather curious," Gouzenko wrote. "In case the authorities of a country, to which the subject of a 'legend' is assigned, wished to check on him, they would communicate with their embassy in Moscow. The embassy, however, would find itself incapable of attempting a private investigation, for the simple reason that practically all such 'legends' give phony home addresses outside Moscow, and even an embassy representative would hardly be permitted to conduct enquiries in towns and cities beyond Moscow." Gouzenko's legend, submitted to the Canadian authorities when the passport visa was issued, was accordingly completely false.

After the completion of the cover story, the agent is given an alias for administrative purposes within the organization. In internal communications and in his relations with other agents, he is referred to by this alias, which is really a code concealing the identity of the person in the event that the communications network is tapped or decoded. While generally any code name that comes to his superior's mind might be assigned to an agent, sometimes a system is employed in its selection. During World War II, for example, the French secret service picked aliases for its agents to indicate their specific assignments. Military delegates used geometric nomenclature, officers in charge of aerial operations utilized titles such as Count or Archduke, while saboteurs were given cover names from maritime lingo.

The melodramatic designations of spies, such as "Q-43" or "Z-8," which occur in thrillers or motion pictures, are seldom used in practice. If used at all, they are bureaucratic designations, indicating the agent's number in the personnel index file.

The cover story of the secret agent usually determines the disguise he will use. Contrary to common belief, secret agents rarely use elaborate disguises on their missions but conduct their secret activities under the cover of a legitimate profession or blind. Once I heard it said of a not-too-popular individual that he went to a costume ball in the disguise of a gentleman. This quip tells a lot. The guise of gentleman is an excellent one in the espionage business.

"The spy requires not merely an appropriate disguise," Winfried Lüdecke wrote, "but the skill to play the part he undertakes. He must be a good actor, and especially a first-rate quick-change artist, capable of meeting with boldness and presence of mind even the most perilous situations." Generally, a secret agent will require only temporary disguises for brief tactical missions. He may have to pose as a waiter, barber, telephone repairman, or night watchman in order to enter a hotel room, office, or plant. In other instances, spies may pose as priests, monks, hospital attendants, tourists, workers, farmhands, businessmen, traveling salesmen, or writers. Secret agents are sometimes obliged to pose as members of the foreign armies against which they operate. Ordinarily, the illegal donning of a foreign uniform is resorted to in only the most stringent cases, although instances have been recorded in which an agent was thus disguised for many years.

British agents are past masters in the art of disguise and have worn the uniforms of many foreign countries. One of the best of their practitioners of the art of disguise was Baden-Powell, the officer-spy, who was blessed with an exceptional gift for altering his appearance. In these transformations he rarely changed his costume. He merely assumed the personality of someone else. Once, when he had been assigned to establish the caliber of the guns in the Dalmatian fortress of Cataro, Baden-Powell decided to go as an entomologist. In preparation for the mission, he not only studied entomology but also the personal habits of the professors who instructed him, copying their ways of carrying the butterfly net and of keeping notes in the field book.

He embarked on this particular mission carrying a box of paints and brushes and a sketch book that contained a number of completed drawings of butterflies done by him beforehand. His pursuit of lepidoptera brought him close to the fortress of Cattaro, and into his sketch book went the outlines of the fortification intricately woven into the details of a beautiful butterfly.

At another time, in an attempt to get close enough to a secret German military installation to study its armaments, Baden-Powell stuck a bottle of brandy in his coat pocket and approached his target. He had almost completed his mission when he was discovered by sentries who had been ordered to arrest any intruder, but, finding the stranger badly intoxicated and his clothes soaked with the liquor, they ordered him away from the fort, too certain of his condition to bother with a staggering drunk.

To be effective a disguise should be inconspicuous and commonplace. The less it entails in the way of costume and gimmicks the better it is. Disguise by costume should be the exception rather than the rule. Outside of such changes as can be accomplished with the hair and eyebrows, and a beard or mustache, there is little that can be done to disguise the facial characteristics without resorting to plastic surgery, which, incidentally, has often been done. The ability to change one's bearing and gait is invaluable. The spy is served well by a spare necktie, different in color and shape from the one previously worn. Experience has shown that, in a brief encounter, the color and shape of a tie leaves a greater impression than features of the face or the color of the eyes. A spare hat may also be kept handy, since a Homburg or a bowler will change a man's appearance more effectively, and with less danger of detection, than false eyebrows or a wig, whereas sunglasses make a man immediately conspicuous.

The making over of an agent is completed with his "documentation," the false papers he is given to provide his new identity. Among them may be his passport, identity card, registration of residence, trade-union card, and such papers as are carried by the people of the country where he is to operate, including ration cards, draft board registration, and driver's license. To make his new identity even more convincing, the agent may be issued season tickets for certain commuter lines, correspondence with friends, stubs of used theater tickets, and such scraps and papers as might be found in the pockets of a person anywhere.

His passport is the agent's most important document. Frequently the passport he carries may be genuine. The espionage organizations of all countries have on hand an assortment of foreign passports for use by their spies. The only change made in them is the substitution of the spy's photograph for that of the legitimate owner. A Russian agent assigned to the United States was provided with a Canadian passport made out to a certain Ignacy Witczak. This Witczak fought on the Republican side in the Spanish civil war, and his passport was taken from him by the political commissar of his battalion and never returned. The document later turned up in the possession of the Soviet agent, who was operating in California.

Routing

The agent is now ready to depart on his mission. All that is left to do is to prepare him for his specific assignment. He is required to rehearse his mission at headquarters, to participate in "dry runs," to exercise on mockups. In the United States, during the last war, agents who were to be sent out to obtain information about factories abroad were first sent into factories here to secure similar information, never knowing when the FBI or plant security forces might expose them. German saboteurs sent to the United States in 1942 were similarly prepared for their mission. Since their targets were the aluminum plants of the United States, they were planted in aluminum factories in the Reich and there went through all the motions of their mission, short of actually blowing up the factories.

Agents are given operations instructions in which every phase of their assignment is outlined in detail. A typical document states the nature of the mission, enumerates the specific information sought and what part of it is already available, states the cover name of the operation and the alias assigned to the agent, reiterates his cover story, and lists the code names of all those who participate in the mission. In addition, it outlines all the information and so-called assumptions on file about the target, lists the names and locations of contacts in the field, in particular the spy's *agent-de-liaison*, his route, alternate routes, and hide-outs, his accommodation addresses, means of evasion, his lines of communication, transportation and supply, and his code—everything to the smallest detail. Such operations instructions are memorized before the agent's departure on the mission, since he obviously cannot carry a document of this nature with him.

The agent is now completely prepared for his mission. Although he may have a base on which to fall back and at least some connection with his headquarters, he is by and large left to shift for himself.

The agent's trip to the place of his assignment is a delicate operation within itself. It is planned with painstaking attention to every detail by his home organization, where special traffic managers plot every stage of his journey from departure to arrival. Occasionally, his cover enables him to travel directly and more or less openly to his destination. In other cases, an agent may have to be smuggled into a country by being dropped from a plane, landed from a submarine, or put across a frontier at night by surreptitious means. Frequently, agents approach their places of assignment by circuitous routes, especially when they assume a false nationality as a part of the cover. In such cases, the agent will first go to the country whose citizen he later pretends to be and settle there for a few months before approaching his final destination.

Upon arrival, the agent will notify his organization, by radio signal, postal card, or possibly the insertion of a fictitious ad in a newspaper's classified section, that he is ready to begin his work. He then contacts any other persons slated to work with him. Frequently, his mission is well prepared in advance on the spot, where he is awaited by contacts, and his lodgings are provided for him so that he may begin the mission at once. Timing is important in espionage, for time lost may be a life lost, or it may result in the failure of a mission.

Establishment of Cover on the Spot: Local Contacts

Earlier in the chapter we have seen how a plausible cover is established upon arrival and, secondly, how the agent will go about developing his ring or net, his circle of informants, his sources. The next stage, of course, is the mission itself: the acquisition of information.

Surreptitious Acquisition of Information

Such information is obtained either directly or through informants and go-betweens, but espionage organizations are like courts of law. They are impressed only with hard facts supported by convincing documentation. Information based on hearsay is rarely accepted by the agent's organization, nor is data accepted if it is submitted without an exact description of its source. The need for exactness and documentation makes the work of an agent tedious and difficult, and it keeps him extremely busy. In addition to all of the effort of preserving his identity, and to the work of the mission itself, the agent must attend to the job assigned to him as a cover.

An agent always strives to obtain actual documents or blueprints from his sources, either in their original forms or as photographed copies. There are manifold problems involved in the acquisition, copying, and transmission of documents, and everything must be accomplished with the greatest possible speed, since most documents cannot remain long in the possession of the agent but must be returned to their legitimate sources.

In order to obtain such documents, the agent develops contacts within the agencies of the foreign government, people who will "borrow" them temporarily for his use. In the early thirties, Soviet intelligence was eager to obtain the blueprints of a new American tank developed by the inventor Walter Christie. Contact was established with a high-ranking American officer, who lifted the documents from the War Department files at the end of the office week on Friday and delivered them to a go-between, who in turn transmitted them to the agent. They were returned to the officer in time for him to replace them in the files early on Monday morning.

Photographed copies of original documents represent the best possible intelligence material any espionage organization can acquire. This type of information is ordinarily obtained only from persons who have immediate access to it, and, of course, surreptitiously. In handling the documents, the agent acts as a trustee or clearing-house. His chief problem is to develop sources who have access to such materials, and then to receive the documents without attracting attention. In order to camouflage this part of the activity, personal contacts are arranged with extreme circumspection and, therefore, meetings with contacts are regulated on the basis of the espionage plan of all such organizations.

Meetings with Informants and Couriers

There are three major groups of espionage personnel with whom an agent may engage while on a mission. In the first group are routine social contacts; in the second are contacts with informants and cut-outs who supply or relay the information; and in the third are meetings with couriers who carry the information back to headquarters.

General social contacts are made and pursued overtly. They

do not differ from those made by the average person within his own circle of friends and acquaintances.

Contacts with informants and cut-outs, and meetings with couriers, are in a different category and constitute some of the most melodramatic aspects of a secret agent's work. It is in these contacts that the often routine business of espionage approaches most closely the Hollywood version of the activity.

An agent may use a number of different ways and means to keep in touch with his informants. A very simple way was described by Whittaker Chambers. Mr. Chambers was not a spy, inasmuch as it was not his function to acquire information at the source. He was a cut-out or courier. His function was to pick up information from the source and relay it to the collector. Chambers would simply go to the house of an informant, pick up a number of documents, and take them to a drugstore in downtown Washington where he would meet the technician of the net whose job it was to photograph them. This technician then would take the material to his home in Baltimore, photograph the documents, return with them to Washington, meet Chambers again, and return the material to him.

While such straightforward traffic is simple enough, it is actually a perilous phase of espionage work. First of all, if a cut-out or courier makes numerous visits at regular intervals to the home of an informant, he will invariably attract attention in any country where counterespionage is alert. If the cut-out is under surveillance he is certain to lead the counterespionage agent to the informant, thereby destroying this vital source and compromising the whole operation. Secondly, documents should not be in transit for too long a time or over great distances. Their security might be easily compromised en route, they could be lost, or something could happen to the person who carries them. If Chambers actually used such a procedure to relay documents from their source to the collector, he not only employed the most primitive and precarious method, but he also violated a very important rule in the Soviet spy book. The Soviet espionage organization prescribes special procedures for the meeting of informants and the transmission of documents. These procedures specify that the Center in Moscow must make all arrangements for meetings, some of which might take place thousands of miles away.

In Soviet espionage, meetings are arranged by go-betweens. Informants rarely meet with collectors or even with couriers. They are contacted by cut-outs to whom they hand the information. The cut-out then relays the information to the collector by the shortest possible route in the least possible time. It is a strict rule in Soviet espionage, for example, that all meetings in the course of which documents are transferred from one person to another must take place on a street or in a public place. A Soviet instruction sheet prepared for the orientation of cut-outs stipulates:

"Any meetings [with informants] must take place outdoors, on the street and, moreover, separately with each, and only once a month . . . The material they supply must be received the same day on which you must meet me in the evening. The material must not be kept by you even for a single night . . . Wives of informants must not know that you work with and meet their husbands."

The lengths to which espionage organizations go in arranging meetings of cut-outs and informants was shown in the contact that a Soviet go-between was supposed to make with Dr. Allan Nunn May in London in the fall of 1945. This meeting was originally prepared by the Soviet military attaché in Canada. He had to submit his plan for approval to Moscow, where it was completely revised. When the final arrangements were made, they were spelled out in an operations order that is reproduced here as a typical sample of such arrangements. The order was signed by the "Director" personally and sent to the military attaché on August 22, 1945, almost two months before the meeting was to take place.

The document read as follows:

1. Place: In front of the British Museum in London, on Great Russell Street, at the opposite side of the street, about Museum Street, from the side of Tottenham Court Road repeat Tottenham Court Road, Alek [May's cover name] walks from Tottenham Court Road, the contact man from the opposite side—Southampton Row.

2. Time: As indicated by you, however, it would be more expedient to carry out the meeting at 20 o'clock, if it should be convenient to Alek, as at 23 o'clock it is too dark. As for the time, agree about it with Alek and communicate the decision to me. In case the meeting should not take place in October, the time and day will be repeated in the following months.

3. Identification signs: Alek will have under his left arm the newspaper *Times*, the contact man will have in his left hand the magazine *Picture Post*.

4. The Password: The contact man: 'What is the shortest way to the Strand?' Alek: 'Well, come along. I am going that way.' In the beginning of the business conversation Alek says: 'Best regards from Mikel.'

Meetings with couriers are invariably arranged by the

headquarters of the espionage organization. Before a courier is sent out, the place and time of the meeting and the signals of identification are communicated to the agent by the best available means, frequently by radio. Richard Sorge emphasized in his testimony the circumspect care with which the Soviet espionage organization arranges meetings with couriers. Similar procedure is practiced by all espionage organizations.

For example, Sorge once received instructions from Moscow to go to a certain restaurant in Hong Kong where he was to meet a courier. Sorge was to be seated at a table at a certain time, and the courier was to enter the restaurant a few minutes past 3 P.M., take from his pocket a long Manila cigar, and hold it in his hand without lighting it. As soon as Sorge saw the signal, he was to approach the counter of the restaurant, take a pipe from his pocket, and hold it in his hand without lighting it. When this signal was recognized by the courier, he was to light his cigar and Sorge his pipe.

The courier was then to leave the restaurant and Sorge was to follow him to a park. There the courier would approach Sorge with the words, "Greetings from Katcha." Sorge was to answer, "Greetings from Gustav." This was the exact procedure the two men followed. Sorge had to go all the way to Hong Kong from Tokyo for the meeting, an added precautionary measure to avoid detection by the Japanese secret police. It was assumed that two total strangers would not attract the attention of the authorities in Hong Kong.

The manner in which documents are actually handed over is very strictly outlined to avoid attention. The document is often concealed inside a folded newspaper, which the agent places on the bench beside him, and, at the end of what appears to be an innocent, and often chance conversation, the newspaper is picked up, not by the agent, but by the courier.

Such precautions are essential for the security of all personnel involved in espionage, their organizations proceeding from the assumption that their agents are known to the counterespionage authorities of the countries in which they operate, or at least that they are under surveillance. It is, therefore, essential to perform all functions connected with the mission only when it is absolutely certain that nobody observes the operation, or when it is painstakingly camouflaged. Even so, secret agents are in the greatest danger of being trapped when meeting with others, whoever they may be. Judith Coplon was arrested on the street during a meeting with her Soviet go-between, as was British agent Yeo-Thomas while awaiting the arrival of his *agent-de-liaison*. Such meetings are unavoidable, but they are kept at a minimum.

163

No matter how isolated a secret agent is, he must maintain a line of communications with his headquarters, to which he must forward whatever information he collects—unless his instructions are to bring back personally. The latter instance is extremely rare, since there is an important time element in espionage. The value of an item of information is computed on the basis of its significance and the speed with which it comes into the hands of the organization. Any item, even of the greatest intrinsic value, is obviously useless if it reaches the organization too late to be used. Therefore, espionage services do their utmost to expedite the transmission of information, at the same time maintaining iron-clad safety and security. In this phase of the activity, which often involves a great number of people, all moves involving collector and transmitter, sender and receiver, are coordinated and synchronized. Every member of the team must attend to his own duties on the split second and in the exact manner prescribed in the operations plan.

In addition to word of mouth, there are fifteen means of transmission used by espionage agents. In the order of frequency with which they are used, they are: the mail, couriers, radio, underground telephones, telephone, telegraph, carrier pigeons, airplanes, runners, dogs, hand flags, signal fires, heliograph, rockets, and flares. Also, freak methods may be used when circumstances compel them. Messages have been transmitted by lighting bonfires on hilltops, or by turning lights on and off in the windows of houses to spell out words in Morse code. Even smoke has been used, as in September, 1914, in Poland when, according to a communiqué of the Austro-Hungarian command, "the troops suffered great losses owing to the espionage and treachery of the natives who indicated the positions of artillery and infantry by employing columns of white and gray smoke by day, and light signals by night." In the Boer War, native spies working for the British would mark out a trail by cutting the bark of trees, and indicated a direction by inclining treetops or laying bundles of grass. Cases are on record in which the hands of clocks in church steeples were so set as to indicate the location of enemy troops, or in which the movement of the sails of windmills communicated a specific message in a complex and unsuspected code.

Of all the means of communication, the mail is still used most often, not only in times of peace, when censorship is relaxed or non-existent, but also in wartime when every single letter, postal card, telegram, or cable must pass the scrutiny of censors. Espionage agents use ingenious methods to outwit or evade the censor, often writing their letters in code or with secret ink. The progress of microphotography makes it possible to reduce even the longest espionage reports to the size of a dot over a typewritten "i." Even when no censorship is feared the agent must disguise his communications, partly to protect his own cover and security, and partly to conceal the contents of his message. Letters are never mailed directly to an espionage service, but instead to cover addresses, the so-called letterboxes or mail-drops. These drops then forward the mail to the home office of the secret agent, sometimes via several intermediary drops.

Frequently, agents are instructed to send in their messages in duplicate or triplicate through several drops located in two or three different countries. If all letters arrive safely at their destination, it is assumed that all is well. If, however, one or two of the letters fail to show up it is assumed that certain drops have been found out, and they are then promptly abandoned and new ones are set up.

Espionage reports may be sent in letters whose real contents are camouflaged by the use of a code. This method was used by a German agent operating in the United States in 1941 who sent his reports to Berlin via drops in Spain and Portugal. He would write an ordinary business letter in which every sentence had a dual meaning. This same agent used secret ink and chemicals which made writing invisible but which could be made visible at the receiving end. The message was written in secret ink and inserted between the lines of the ordinary letter. In this manner, in the spring of 1941, the German agent reported on the ships loading at New York piers ready to depart in convoys with war material consigned for Britain. It so happened that his letters were intercepted by British censorship in Bermuda, which also exposed the writing in secret ink.

Despite the elaborate organization and efficiency of modern censorship, the mail still continues to deliver innumerable communications sent by spies. One of the great secret agents of our times was a self-effacing, industrious little man named Jules Crawford Silber. He actually operated under the cover of British censorship in which he had a modest job on the German desk. There he made good use of the suspect list, composed of persons suspected of espionage and for whose correspondence the censors were constantly on the alert.

Silber culled information from the very mail he examined. He then wrote out his own reports, placed them in envelopes, stamped them "Examined by Censor," and posted them to addresses in neutral countries picked at random from the suspect list, which listed them as possible drops. Every one of his unsolicited but extremely valuable reports reached the German secret service in Berlin.

The preparation of an agent's report for mailing follows a set routine. Whenever information is received, the agent will write it up and encipher it. The message is divided into portions of about 500 cipher groups each. These portions are then individually microphotographed until they produce a negative about the size of the head of a pin. This tiny negative is pasted on a postcard in a predetermined position and sent to a drop, who either sends it to still another drop or to the diplomatic mission of the country for which the spy works.

A special corps of couriers is maintained by all espionage services, men and women who maintain personal contacts with agents in the field. They carry to the agent the funds and supplies he needs and pick up whatever information or documents he may have for transmission. This is an unexciting but extremely important phase of espionage work, and, although couriers never do actual spying themselves, they run as great a risk as any spy engaged in the collection of information.

There is a great variety of methods employed by couriers to disguise the messages they carry. Messages have been found in soles and heels of shoes, in buttons and linings of clothing, in sweatbands of hats, in false bottoms of suitcases and food cans, in toothpaste and cakes of soap, in cigarettes and cigars. They have been tattooed on the body of the courier, or written in secret ink on his skin. Once the label of an overcoat was found to contain a coded message. A pretty espionage courier plying between Hungary and Turkey during World War II carried microfilmed messages in the glass eye of her silver-fox scarf.

Although radio does not play so dominant a role in the transmission of information as is commonly believed, it is nevertheless widely used, especially in wartime when the mail is slowed down by censorship and when the traffic of couriers is complicated. The development of radio as a tool of spies has changed the complexion of the battle of espionage. It has broadened the field of secret war enormously. In the Second World War, in particular, constant liaison could be maintained between headquarters and spies in the field, and between groups of resistance fighters, by the use of clandestine radios. Every espionage service maintained extensive networks and hook-ups of clandestine transmitters, especially the Soviet Union, whose espionage service operated several hundred secret radio stations in German-occupied Europe.

The radio operator is responsible for the setting up of his technical installations, and, since he obviously cannot establish himself in a hotel or a boarding house where he might be surprised in the midst of transmission, he must find a suitable apartment from which he can operate. The top floor of an apartment house is desirable, if only to make detection by counterespionage agents somewhat more difficult. The apartment should be self-contained and situated so that the operator may hear anybody approaching and thereby gain time to conceal his transmitter before having to answer the doorbell.

Radio sets used in clandestine operations are small and handy instruments about the size of portable typewriters. They can be assembled easily and just as easily concealed. Radio operators usually set up their instruments in kitchens, bathrooms, or closets. Unexpected visitors are not likely to penetrate to such places immediately, and the operator often has time to conceal his set.

Naturally, all messages go out in cipher. Usually the operator of the radio will encipher messages handed him *en clair* by the agent, but once in a while the agent takes care of enciphering. The purpose of ciphers and codes is to prevent the enemy from reading the messages, while the constant changing of wavelengths, transmitting times, and call signals confuses the enemy's listening posts. To avoid detection, several transmitters are used to service the same ring or net.

Generally, radiotelegraphy is used, since it is more reliable than radiotelephone, and because Morse signals are more difficult to intercept. Telegraphy uses a very narrow band of only one kilocycle, while radiotelephony needs a band of six to seven kilocycles. A radiotelephone message can be easily overheard and the voice recognized, often leading to the identification of the transmitter. As a matter of fact, the radio operator of an espionage team is its most vulnerable member and yet, without him, the operational spy would lose his voice.

When putting his message on the air, or when he entrusts it to the mails, the spy gives up a bit of his cover. He not only reveals himself to a certain extent, but in fact runs the risk of exposing his mission.

We have already seen in general terms what security means and how it is maintained. Now we may examine the problem more specifically on the basis of actual examples.

By security, espionage services mean the sum total of all measures designed to preserve the secrecy of the central organization and its branches and agents operating in the field, the concealment of methods used in the collection, transmission, evaluation, and dissemination of information, the concealment of all individual items in which the service may either be interested or actually already possesses, the concealment of individual missions, codes, and ciphers, and the protection of personnel from exposure.

To insure the safety and security of agents operating in the field, a broad foundation is laid during the agent's indoctrination and training, when the importance of security is impressed on him and when he is acquainted with all the possible pitfalls of his profession. He is then taught in great detail how to avoid them. The counterespionage methods and institutions of foreign countries are studied, and precautionary measures based on these investigations are devised.

But, however efficient an agent's preliminary indoctrination may be, it may still prove insufficient to protect him in practice. The agent in the field is secure only as long as absolutely nothing is known to the opponent about his clandestine activities. Once even the slenderest lead points to him the counterespionage agents of the country where he operates will inevitably develop that lead and expose him. One arrested agent can unwittingly lead the authorities to others, and in due time the whole ring or net will be exposed.

If the security of agents seemed far greater during the 1930's, this was a result chiefly of the laxity of counterespionage measures which, in most countries of the West, were almost non-existent. In countries where counterespionage was pursued effectively, agents were insecure.

The precautionary measures used by the Sorge ring in Japan were unusually excellent. They were all described during the interrogation of Sorge, Klausen, and Miyagi, and became known when the transcripts of their interrogation fell into American hands at the end of World War II.

Sorge himself went to extreme lengths to camouflage his espionage activities. He was painstaking in establishing his legitimate cover as a foreign correspondent and sought continuously to maintain it. He did not engage in any espionage activities for several months after his arrival in Japan because he knew that in most countries foreigners were watched by the local police authorities. He examined carefully every sign that indicated such surveillance. In order to avoid suspicion, he made his movements widely known and advertised his legitimate activities to direct attention away from those of his mission. He employed only one housemaid, a dull old woman, and made her live away from his quarters so that she could not identify visitors who called on him late at night, after her departure.

Max Klausen listed the precautionary measures he considered essential for agents in the field, as follows:

All members of the ring must have rational, legitimate, occupational covers. The radio cipher must be altered by the use of different scramble numbers at each transmission. The transmitter must be dismantled, packed in a case, and moved after each operation. Messages must be sent from different locations, never from a single house over long periods. Liaison with couriers must be carried out in the utmost secrecy, never mentioning real names on either side. Each member must have a cover name. Real names must never be mentioned either in messages or in conversations. Place names must be disguised in code. Documents must be destroyed immediately after they have served their purpose.

How precarious the security of any espionage ring may be in the field was shown dramatically in the exposure of the Sorge organization, which was discovered despite the most scientific measures of protection and the high internal security of its top echelon. Sorge followed his instructions from Moscow never to have any contacts with the Communist Party in Japan, a standing rule prescribed for most Soviet spy rings. Their sole contact with the "corporations," as regional Communist parties are called in Soviet espionage parlance, is with those "corporants," or party members, who have already gone underground and are enlisted in the espionage apparatus of the Cominform.

This is usually resented by local Communists, who are left outside the rings. Just such a frustrated Communist was Ito Ritsu. He suspected that a Soviet espionage ring was working in Japan and became jealous when he was not allowed to have any connection with it. He suspected that one of his acquaintances, a woman named Tomo Kitabayashi, was a member of the Sorge ring and shared this suspicion with the Japanese authorities when he himself was picked up in a raid against Communists in general.

It so happened that Mrs. Kitabayashi was a minor member

of the Sorge ring. She was a dressmaker by profession and managed to secure some information from her customers. She then transmitted these items to her own contact within the Sorge ring, the artist Yotoko Miyagi.

Working on the tip they received from Ito Ritsu, the Japanese police arrested Mrs. Kitabayashi and forced her to confess her relationship with Miyagi. Then Miyagi was picked up and tortured. A frail consumptive man, he broke under torture and revealed his contacts, including Hozumi Ozaki, who then disclosed his association with Sorge and Klausen before succumbing to the brutal tortures of his Japanese interrogators.

Ito Ritsu was first picked up in June, 1941. He tipped off the Japanese police to Mrs. Kitabayashi in early September, and she was arrested on September 28, 1941. Following that it did not take long for the police to blow up the whole ring. Sorge himself was arrested on October 18, 1941, and within a few months no member of his ring was at large.

In those rare cases when an agent succeeds in preserving his security to the very end, he will leave his assignment and return to headquarters, often by simply purchasing a steamship ticket or a place on a plane and leaving the country. Occasionally, the termination of a mission requires as circumspect preparations as its establishment, especially when an agent is required to hand over his ring to a successor.

Once in a while, completion of a mission means the end of a man's connection with espionage. There are hundreds of former secret agents living among us to whom espionage is only the memory of past adventures. Others, however, are destined to stay in the business for good, not necessarily because they choose to, but because they are considered indispensable. Others are forced to remain active because their organizations feel that they know too much to risk letting them go.

Cryptography and Cryptanalysis

In conclusion, there remains to be reviewed just one other form of what may be called "applied espionage": cryptography in its various manifestations. In John Eglinton Bailey's classic definition, "Cryptography is the art of writing in such a way as to be incomprehensible except to those who possess the key to the system employed." Cryptanalysis is the organized effort to translate such writing into its original meaning and to make it again comprehensible.

Cryptography is properly placed under the heading of espionage, since it plays an important role as a major tool of concealment. Cryptanalysis is itself a form of espionage. Every major government utilizes it today in an elaborate and complex effort to penetrate the most closely guarded secrets of other nations by breaking their codes and solving their ciphers.

In cryptography we distinguish between codes and ciphers. A code is a system of words or groups of letters or symbols, selected arbitrarily to represent other words. Under this system a single word may have several meanings, it may represent several words combined, or it may be the equivalent of an entire predetermined sentence or paragraph.

An Austrian code of World War I, for example, used the word "Mama" to mean "three torpedo boats of the *Avanti* class"; the word "Easter" to mean "in the direction of Cattaro"; the word "doctor" to mean "depart" in its various tenses; the word "sun" for "heavy cruiser *Italia*"; the word "apartment" to mean "launching"; and "garden" for the month of August. A message an agent sent in this code read: "Three torpedo boats of the *Avanti* class departed in the direction of Cattaro; heavy cruiser *Italia* will be launched in August," actually read when it was encoded: "We expect Mama to move after Easter. She went to see the doctor yesterday, since the pain in her shoulder was getting worse. He suggested that she spend a lot of time in the sun and this will be no problem, since her new apartment has a lovely garden of its own."

A cipher may use any letter of the alphabet as a substitute for another, it may transpose them, spell words backward when enciphered, make arbitrary divisions between words, or substitute numerals or certain characters for letters. Ciphers are made increasingly complicated by the multiple use of transpositions or substitutions and the scrambling of numerals, and by the insertion of dummy letters.

The cipher is a very ancient form of concealment. The prophet Jeremiah, for example, wrote (xxv, 26) *Sheshach* for "Babel" (Babylon) to conceal the meaning of his prophecy. Jeremiah made up this cipher by transposing the letters of the Hebrew alphabet. Instead of using the second and twelfth letters from the beginning, Jeremiah wrote the second and twelfth from the end. Julius Caesar devised a special cipher for his own secret correspondence. He wrote *d* for *a, e* for *b, f* for *c,* and so on, using the third letter after the one standing in the original text. This particular system is still called "the Caesar." There are other more modern systems, including the "Beaufort," named after the famous British cryptographer Admiral Sir Francis Beaufort, the Sliding Alphabet Cipher, and various French systems called "St. Cyr," after the famous military academy. They represent considerable improvement over the primitive Caesar, but employ the same basic principle.

The fundamentals of cryptography are also ancient and unchanged. They were first enumerated by Bacon centuries ago when he stipulated that "a cipher must be simple to write and read; it must be impossible to decipher; and it must not arouse suspicion." These are perfectionist rules. If they appear to be unheeded it is not because cryptographers do not try to live up to them. But the art of cryptography is so complex and exacting that it is humanly impossible to devise the perfect cipher or code.

Individuals engaged in this activity are called cryptographers. They may be encoders or decoders, encipherers or decipherers, or cryptanalysts, according to the nature of their functions. Code and cipher experts specialize in encoding or decoding, enciphering and deciphering messages, that is, in translating a plain or *en clair* message into code or cipher and then retranslating incoming messages into clear. Cryptanalysts are the actual "spies" of this traffic. Their job is to break the codes and ciphers of others, to find a key to their solution, and then to expose the contents of the concealed message.

This is an exact science involving mathematics and statistics, as well as the ingenuity of the specialist. Cryptanalysts base their operations on the fact that in each language certain letters occur more frequently than others. In the English language, the letters *e, t, a, o, i,* and *r* occur most frequently, and *v, k, x, j, q,* and *z* most rarely. In French, the letters *e, a, i, s, t,* and *n,* and in German, the letters *e, n, i, s, r, a, d,* and *t,* are the most frequent. The first thing a cryptanalyst does is to look for such "frequencies" in the text. He will then prepare a "frequency table," in which all letters of the text are catalogued according to their frequency. After that, a number of complicated methods are used, and really skilled and imaginative cryptanalysts usually succeed in breaking even the most complicated cipher.

Ciphers are often as treacherous as any other type of security leak. While every country hopes and trusts that its systems are the best and safest, the history of cryptography shows that there have been very few ciphers in the world which survived the ingenious assaults of expert cryptanalysts.

The same is true of codes. Codes are specially prepared in the form of books, or "dictionaries," in which each word means a different word, sentence, or phrase. Although codes are more difficult to break than ciphers, they are still vulnerable, especially when code books fall into unauthorized hands. As a result, coded books are among the favorite targets of spies. Divers have actually been sent into the hulls of sunken ships to recover whatever code books they might find in them. And agents are used to entrap individuals engaged in the code rooms of government agencies and diplomatic missions, to acquire through them the secret code books entrusted to their care. The Soviet Union once gained access to the diplomatic code of the British Foreign Office by luring a code clerk into espionage. In an almost identical manner, the Germans and Italians acquired American diplomatic codes by persuading an American code clerk named Tyler Kent, working in the Embassy in London, to spy for them. The outstanding espionage case of our times, which resulted in the smashing of the Soviet spy ring in Canada, had a code clerk, Igor Gouzenko, as its pivot.

Every intelligence service has its own cryptographic department to handle the codes and ciphers used by its agents, and some of them maintain cryptanalytic branches to break the codes and translate the ciphers of others. However, some governments keep this function separate from the intelligence service and maintain it under the signal corps of their armies or the communication branches of their navies. These departments are usually shrouded in supersecrecy, and their methods are protected as carefully as the personnel working in them.

While every country in the world has practiced cryptography and cryptanalysis, England and the United States have made the greatest contributions to the science. Britain, in particular, pioneered the art in modern times. The great Reginald Hall, director of Britain's Division of Naval Intelligence, first recognized the overwhelming importance of cryptography as a source of information, and he made elaborate arrangements immediately after the outbreak of the First World War to monitor German radio communications and break the codes and translate the ciphers of the enemy. With the help of Sir Alfred Ewing, a professor whose hobby was the solving of intricate puzzles, he set up a cryptanalysis branch of Naval Intelligence in the famous 40 O.B. and broke virtually every code the Germans used during the war. Among his great achievements was the reading of telegrams which the German Foreign Office sent to its envoy in Mexico, urging him to bring Mexico into the war against the United States. His unusual ability to break operations orders sent to fleet units of the German Navy on the seven seas enabled the British Admiralty to make its own arrangements in the fullest knowledge of the enemy's plans, intentions, and strength. Thanks to the information Admiral Hall culled from coded German signals, the Royal Navy triumphed in the battle of Dogger Bank and in the battle of the Falkland Islands.

On September 16, 1945, Hanson W. Baldwin, military editor of the New York *Times*, wrote in a column: "It is not, has not been, and since the Battle of Midway never could be a secret that the [United States] Navy broke the Japanese code fairly early in the war and, by interception of Japanese radio messages and other means, learned in advance of many Japanese operations." John A. Beasley, Australian Minister of Defense, came out with the flat statement that "U.S. Naval Intelligence Officers had cracked Japanese naval codes even before the Battle of the Coral Sea" in 1942.

Admiral Chester W. Nimitz, commander in chief of the U.S. Pacific Fleet, was later asked in a press conference, "How were we able to shoot down Admiral Yamamoto, commander in chief of the Japanese fleet?" He answered with a frankness that is quite rare when discussing these matters, "We had broken the latest Japanese codes and ciphers and knew where Admiral Yamamoto would be at a certain fatal minute of a certain fatal day."

In April, 1943, the cryptanalysts of the U.S. Navy's Communication Intelligence intercepted a top secret signal sent from Japan's naval high command to its China stations and units in the South Pacific. When the signal was translated, it was found to contain a message of enormous immediate importance. It advised the various commanders of the Japanese fleet that Admiral Isoroku Yamamoto, their commander in chief, would make an inspection of their units. The intercept included an exact itinerary of the admiral's trip. It revealed that he would go to China, then to Truk, and then to Bougainville. Every stop-over was listed, as were the exact date and time of his arrivals and departures.

The information was relayed immediately to Frank Knox, then Secretary of the Navy, who rushed it to President Roosevelt. The American leaders were confronted with a grave dilemma. The question before them was: Shall we attempt to intercept Yamamoto's plane and destroy him, and thus deprive Japan of the guiding genius of its war effort, or shall we let him pass despite our knowledge of his itinerary?

During the more chivalrous days of warfare there used to

be an unwritten code that somehow protected the lives of leaders in war. Kings and generals were frequently killed in battle, and Napoleon III was captured by the Prussians, as was Leopold III of the Belgians in World War II. In World War II, however, several deliberate efforts were made to destroy the leaders of the enemy. A German U-boat tried to torpedo the ship on which President Roosevelt was sailing to one of his wartime conferences. During the Battle of the Bulge, the Germans devised a plan to assassinate General Eisenhower. An attempt was made to shoot down Prime Minister Winston Churchill as he was flying back to London from a vacation in the Mediterranean, but the Germans blundered and shot down the plane in which the famous actor Leslie Howard was traveling, mistaking it for Churchill's plane. The secret war book of the Germans did, in fact, advocate "the assassination of war leaders" as a legitimate and justifiable method "if it led to the prejudice of the enemy."

The United States normally deplored such practices. There were several opportunities to participate in attempts made to assassinate Hitler and Mussolini, but the United States refrained even from lending a helping hand. The case of Yamamoto was different. He had outlawed himself on "the day of infamy" and had forfeited the protection of the articles of war when he himself violated them with the sneak attack on Pearl Harbor. Moreover, he was traveling in a combat zone, where a top admiral is as fair a target as any sailor manning a gun.

The issue was decided by President Roosevelt. He ordered that an attempt be made to intercept Yamamoto's plane and shoot it down. An operations plan was drafted under the personal supervision of Secretary Knox and the decision reached to ambush Yamamoto's plane as it was approaching Bougainville.

The order and the plan were then sent to the operations officer of a Marine unit in the South Pacific, directing him to make a "maximum effort" to intercept Yamamoto's flight. "Destroy the target at any cost," the order read, "then break off and return to base, evading all further action." Utmost secrecy before and after the operation was enjoined.

At exactly 4 P.M. on April 17, 1943, two Army Air Force pilots were summoned secretly to a dank, musty room on Guadalcanal, the office of the Marine operations officer. They were Major John W. Mitchell and Major Thomas J. Lanphier, Jr. They were shown the Navy's signal and told that they had been chosen to carry out this supersecret mission. Various plans were discussed at length. The Marine officer

175

suggested that Yamamoto be attacked in Kahilli harbor where he was expected to conduct his inspection aboard a sub-chaser. But the pilots said, "How do you expect us to pick out that particular craft with all those ships in the harbor?"

They suggested that Yamamoto's plane be intercepted in midair while flying from Truk to Kahilli. Yamamoto was known to Naval Intelligence for extreme punctuality in his schedules. The decoded itinerary said that he would reach Kahilli at exactly 9:45 A.M. on April 18, in a flight of two Mitsubishi bombers escorted by six Zeros. He was to be ac-companied by his entire staff. "I'll bet my last silver dime," Major Lanphier said, "that he will be on time!"

A map was produced and the very spot chosen where Admiral Yamamoto was to be intercepted. It was fixed at a point thirty-five miles from Kahilli, just eleven minutes flying time from the airport where he was scheduled to land. Then the detailed arrangements for the interception were made. Two groups of Lightnings would fly out from Guadalcanal to ambush him. One group, commanded by Major Mitchell, would fly high as a decoy to draw off Yamamoto's escorts. The other group, commanded by Lanphier, would then at-tend to the destruction of the Mitsubishis.

The planes were chosen and their crews picked. On the morning of April 18, the men received their last briefing from two intelligence officers, Lieutenant Joe McGuigan of the Navy and Captain Bill Morrison of the Army. At exactly 7:35 A.M. the Lightnings took off. They flew in a 435-mile semicircle to avoid all known Japanese positions. They kept radio silence all the way. Using only compass and air-speed indicator to navigate, they reached the chosen spot at the prearranged time, only fifty seconds before the expected arrival of Yamamoto's flight. Then at 9:34 A.M., Lieutenant Doug Canning called out on the intercom, "Bogey! Ten o'clock high!"

Exactly as predicted by the original intercept was Yama-moto's unsuspecting convoy, the two bombers and six Zeros. Major Mitchell's group climbed to 20,000 feet to draw off the Zeros, whose pilots immediately left the bombers un-protected to attack the American fighters. Below, and un-seen, Major Lanphier climbed straight into Yamamoto's course. He had his engines wide open as he tried to cross ahead of the Mitsubishi. He was followed closely by his wing man, Lieutenant Rex Barber, and by Lieutenant Joe Moore, leader of the second element, and his wing man, Lieutenant Jim McLanahan.

At last Lanphier and Barber were even with the two

Mitsubishis. Too late, the protecting Zeros noticed them for the first time and wheeled into power dives in an attempt to cover their admiral's unprotected bomber. Lanphier opened up with a long steady burst, and in a moment the right engine and then the right wing of Yamamoto's Mitsubishi burst into flames. As the bomber fell away towards Kahilli, Lanphier poured another burst into it. The wing of the bomber flew off and the big plane plummeted earthward. Its fuselage exploded among the trees of the jungle, only a few miles from its destination at Kahilli.

In spite of the desperate efforts of the returning Zeros diving to the rescue, Rex Barber shot down the second bomber, which carried members of Yamamoto's staff. The mission was accomplished.

An operation that had begun in the secret offices where the Navy housed its Communications Intelligence in Washington was completed in Bougainville as planned.

Although the importance of secrecy had been enjoined upon the personnel engaged in the operation, news somehow leaked out that Yamamoto had been shot down. Except for the alertness of the naval censor at Pearl Harbor, who was able to intercept the news reports, this unique incident in the history of espionage would have been broadcast right then to the world—and, more important, to the Japanese. Fortunately, the secret was preserved. Stunned by the disaster, the Japanese tried to find out what had happened, but their intelligence services could never supply a single clue. Unaware that their code had been broken, they believed that Yamamoto's death was a freak accident, and left it at that. Their ignorance of the actual facts prevented them from taking precautions against the repetition of such leaks.

Agents at Large

For every espionage exploit that becomes known, there must be dozens of cases which will remain secret forever. Among these, indeed, are the true epics of espionage, in which the identity of the agent is never exposed, not even deduced from the sometimes monumental clues he leaves behind in the frequently historic consequences of his successful mission. Before World War I, the French General Staff obtained an authentic copy of the famous Schlieffen Plan from a mysterious man who traveled to Paris disguised as a seriously injured patient in the care of a nurse, his whole face and part of his body covered with bandages. The document was concealed in the bandages. But although the case became known after the war, no one actually knows who the agent was.

Throughout both world wars, the British had a high-ranking officer of their secret service planted within the German General Staff. But only a handful of initiated persons knew the identity of the spy. During the Second World War, scores of Italian submarines were lured to their destruction by using the top-secret code of the submarine service. It was stolen by a British spy. But only the initiated knew the identity of this agent, and the counterespionage organs of Italy were never able to identify or catch him.

While Britain succeeded in unmasking most of the German agents of World War II, one truly effective German spy managed to evade the net. This man succeeded in outwitting Britain's entire counterespionage machinery for seven years, from 1937, when he entered Britain allegedly from Canada, to 1944, when his trail eventually vanished. During those seven years, this phantom spy supplied the German secret service with a remarkable collection of intelligence. Among his deliveries were:

1. A top-secret report prepared by Sir Alexander Cadogan, then British Permanent Under-Secretary of Foreign Affairs, representing the Foreign Office's estimate of Anglo-German relations. This document existed in only four copies, one each for the Cabinet, the War Office, the Admiralty, and President Roosevelt.

2. A dossier of maps showing the emergency system of food and fuel distribution in the United Kingdom.

3. Information about the deficient defenses of the great Scapa Flow naval base in the north and the delay in the arrival of submarine nets and booms. This enabled German Lieutenant Commander Gunther Prien in submarine *U-47* to penetrate to the heart of the "impenetrable" base and, on October 14, 1939, to sink the battleship *Royal Oak* with a loss of more than 800 lives.

4. Blueprints of the docks of London and Hull, as well as detailed maps of both key ports.

5. Maps of the system of airfields in Kent built to protect London from attack by the Lutwaffe. Later, this phantom spy was said to have directed the Lufwaffe raids on these airfields in preparation for the Battle of Britain.

6. A complete report on the dispersal of British industries and on the organization of so-called shadow industries concentrated around Birmingham and Coventry. The spy was

later credited with the guiding of the German bombers to these crucial targets.

This is only a partial list of the man's achievements. His activities still baffle British counterespionage and even such a taciturn spy-catcher as Colonel Hinchley Cook of MI-5 pays an unstinted tribute, if not to the efficiency of the German secret service, then to the competence of this one agent. Who was this formidable adversary? How could he remain undetected? How could he escape?

Even today, no one professes to know the answers to these questions. Some say that all these scoops were scored by a single operative, probably one of the greatest spies who ever lived. Others presume that there were, in fact, three different men behind those coups, none of whom was ever caught. Still others insist that they were the work of a brilliant network of Germany's ace operatives led by a single genius who not only understood how to direct his men but also how to protect them from the spy-catchers.

Whoever he was, this phantom was still going strong in the fifth year of the war, on the very eve of the Normandy invasion. When, in March, 1944, General Eisenhower moved his headquarters from London to Busy Park to evade German spies, the phantom reported the transfer to Berlin within 72 hours. Later, he reported the exact date of D-Day, but Hitler trusted his intuition more than a report from his master spy. He simply refused to believe that the Allies would have the audacity to invade his continent.

It may be that this elusive Scarlet Pimpernel was someone whom MI-5 and Scotland Yard did meet, but only as a corpse, in a deserted air-raid shelter in Cambridge, with a bullet in his head and a German revolver at his side, apparently a suicide. From the papers in his pocket he was identified as a native of Holland, Jan Willem Ter Braak, but it was obvious that this was an alias. Later the body was recognized by a landlady who reported one of her boarders missing. In Ter Braak's abandoned room, the spy-catchers found forged documents and a powerful German-made radio transmitter.

However, it is more likely that the phantom spy was a German-Canadian who called himself Karl Dickenhoff. He lived quietly in a villa in Edgbaston. His real name was Hans Caesar. His is a weird story, somewhat in the Conan Doyle tradition. Caesar is said to be still alive and in England, the demented, amnesia-stricken inmate of an insane asylum. Nobody will say whether he is really unbalanced or merely simulates insanity to escape the consequences of his wartime activities.

Sometimes not even the boldest spy is caught, even though his escape may be due more to luck than anything else. During the war, one of the most successful Allied spy rings operated in neutral Sweden. It was a ring of amateur spies composed of German anti-Nazi refugees, led by an intrepid agent named Kurt Englich. He discovered that the center of German espionage in Sweden—a kind of clearing house of all incoming secrets—was in a vaultlike room of the German air attaché's office in Stockholm. Englich found out, too, that the room was always abandoned at night, left in the custody of a single guard.

Englich got a lead to this guard and established that the man was not too well disposed toward the Nazis. The adroit refugee went to work on him, and the guard was soon convinced that Germany would lose the war. So he joined the anti-Nazis and permitted Englich to enter the air attaché's office every night to copy important documents that were left lying on the desks in the locked room.

Kurt Englich worked in the room night after night, and, only once, for a few tense moments, did he nearly get caught. That was the time an aide of the air attaché suddenly showed up in the office. At first, Englich was undecided as to how to meet the emergency, but then he decided to go on copying the document on which he was working as if he belonged to the place. The young Luftwaffe captain walked straight to one of the safes, opened it, and removed from it a bottle of Scotch whisky. Then he locked the safe again and left.

"There is no end to espionage," Alan Moorehead wrote in his account of the Klaus Fuchs case, "it flows on, in a private world of its own, through wars and centuries." As it flows on, it increases in cunning and violence, until it overflows the banks of espionage to leave physical destruction in its wake.

PART III

Sabotage

What Is Sabotage?

The term sabotage is derived from the French word *sabot*, a kind of wooden shoe worn by the lower classes in some European countries. The *sabot* came to be regarded as the symbol of rebellious farm laborers or revolutionary workers who trampled the properties of squires or threw their wooden shoes into machines in the factories during the periodic unrest of the eighteenth and nineteenth centuries. When later a word was needed to describe the act of wanton, deliberate destruction of property to further one's own ends, the act was called sabotage, and the perpetrators of such acts became known as "saboteurs."

In the official language of the secret service, sabotage is usually called "special operations." The saboteur is listed merely as a secret agent, or as a "specialist."

Sabotage is a form of subversive warfare. It is usually physical action designed to damage the enemy's military or economic machinery. It is action against an enemy's administration, industrial production, food and commodities production, armed forces, lines of communication—everything, in fact, that aids his war effort.

Sabotage takes different forms, not all of them necessarily physical or violent. There is direct action, or active sabotage, sudden violent actions against key targets. There is indirect action, or passive sabotage, directed at an opponent's morale or his material resources by non-violent means. There is an intangible form called psychological sabotage, whose purpose is the manipulation of crowd psychology to cause strikes, panic, or riots.

Direct action is carried out in a number of ways and on various scales. It may be aimed at major targets, such as factories or entire regions in which the enemy may have important installations. Such operations are usually performed by scores, sometimes hundreds, of men. They are called sabotage troops: in Britain, Commandos; in the United States, Rangers; in Germany, the Brandenburg Divisions; in the Soviet Union, partisans. Sabotage may also be directed at smaller, pinpointed targets, such as boiler rooms in factories or single railroad switches. These operations are carried out by small sabotage crews of two or three men, and often by only one man.

Arson, explosions, and mechanical interference are the most common forms of sabotage by direct action. Fires may be started either by conventional methods or by such ingenious means as substituting incendiary solutions for non-volatile fuels, or deliberately overloading machines in essential industries. Explosives, including bombs and infernal machines, are used against the enemy's system of communications and his military and economic installations, such as command posts, government offices, ammunition dumps, telegraph lines, radar stations, and the like. Other forms of direct action are the damaging of machinery by placing emery dust in delicate bearings, tossing bolts into dynamos and turbines, jamming steel waste into machine works, or simply dropping keys into the mechanisms of conveyor belts. Direct action may also involve anti-personnel operations, in which sentries and guards are killed, key personnel kidnaped, or important personages assassinated.

Indirect action, or passive sabotage, aims to achieve similar ends without open violence. Encouragement of absenteeism or deliberate slowdowns in industry are common forms of passive sabotage. By feigning a cold and having to leave his job periodically, a worker may effectively interfere with production. Failure to lubricate machines will inevitably lead to breakdowns. Spare parts are often deliberately mislaid. A worker may pretend to need a wrench to tighten a loose bolt, using this excuse to effect sabotage. The cumulative effect of even scattered passive sabotage is enormous. In the spring of 1949, a quarter of a million workers used such methods in the metallurgical industries of Italy, causing a sixteen percent reduction in output. Periodic and systematic looting of enemy stores is another form of sabotage, designed to withhold from the enemy raw materials, fuel, and spare parts which he needs for uninterrupted production.

Psychological sabotage is designed to cause strikes, panic, or riots, and to harass an opponent in his own country or in those that his forces occupy. When small boys in China during the Second World War sprayed Japanese officers with evil-smelling liquids, they were conducting a form of psychological sabotage. At one point during the German occupation of Czechoslovakia the public was persuaded by the underground not to buy newspapers on certain days. In satellite countries of the Soviet Union audiences watching Russian movies sometimes laugh at the wrong time or break out into exaggerated applause at the performance of a collaborationist or a Russian actor.

Psychological sabotage may have serious physical consequences when, for example, a saboteur calls a factory to tell the switchboard operator that a bomb is about to go off in the plant. This method was used repeatedly by German saboteurs in the United States during the Second World War. When such a call is received production is usually stopped and the plant evacuated while guards and police search for the bomb, and without using violence or resorting to any direct physical harm, the saboteur causes the loss of innumerable man-hours and reduces the output of equipment that might be urgently needed.

Maritime sabotage is a very special branch of clandestine warfare, designed to interfere with ships, maritime installations, and navigable waterways. Aboard ships compasses are disturbed by tampering with the magnets. Fires are started in ships, especially in hot weather, by pouring gasoline on the coal. Cargoes of meat and other perishable goods are drenched with kerosene. Ships are occasionally sunk by opening the sea cocks and flooding the holds with water. A very common form of sabotage aboard vessels, both at sea and in port, involves the cutting of electrical cables where the repair of such damage is extremely costly and delays the ship's departure.

In port the saboteur will often interfere with the operations of cranes, thereby delaying loading and unloading, or he may alter the shipping marks on cases containing essential goods to delay their delivery, often by months. Saboteurs working as agitators may induce certain key personnel of ports to go on strike. Even if only the crane operators walk out, the whole port comes to a standstill.

Navigable inland waterways may be sabotaged by destroying locks, bridges, and reservoirs. In this manner saboteurs succeeded in delaying for three months the supply of Ruhr coal to the industrial regions of Lorraine during the Second World War.

Effectiveness of Sabotage

Sabotage, or the calculated destruction of an opponent's vital material resources and installations, is relatively recent as a means of warfare. It may be that American recognition of its value was the result of an unstaged disaster that befell the Germans in 1916. In a munitions dump near Spincourt in France the Germans had stored 450,000 fully fused heavy shells. It is not known how or why, but the dump blew up and all the shells were exploded. With their heavy shells gone, the Germans were unable to supply their artillery with adequate ammunition during the battle of Verdun. This "accident" helped save Verdun.

In the Allied camp, a French general named Palat was the first to recognize the value of such "accidents" and urged that the deliberate use of sabotage be considered. But the Allies felt uneasy about it, largely on the same ethical grounds that prevented the use of poison gas and that retards the employment of atomic weapons.

The Germans, on the other hand, had no such qualms. As early as 1915, their military attaché in Switzerland suggested that Russian communications be sabotaged by blowing up the bridges of the Yenisei River on the Trans-Siberian Railway. At about the same time, the German high command decided to conduct history's first organized campaign of sabotage and picked a neutral country, the United States, as its target.

On the night of July 29, 1916 the Germans blew up the freight terminal of the Lehigh Valley Railroad in lower New York Harbor, opposite the Statue of Liberty. Thirty-seven carloads of high explosives, several large warehouses filled with sugar and food, a dozen barges and ships, and a complete railway yard went up in the explosion. Then on January 11, 1917, the Kingsland Assembling Plant in Kingsland, New Jersey, was blown up by German saboteurs. The plant, "Black Tom," was extremely important since American supplies were finally crated there for shipment to Russia.

If sabotage was but a minor phase of World War I, it became a large-scale operation in World War II. The Germans regarded it as a definite weapon and prepared for it long in advance by training saboteurs in great numbers. Adolf Hitler actually initiated his aggression in the Second World War with a most cynical sabotage operation. It was a staged attack against a German radio station on German soil by six German saboteurs disguised as Polish irregulars. Behind this strange operation was Hitler's desire for "justification" for his unprovoked attack on Poland. With one eye on history, Hitler tried to preserve decorum by putting the onus of aggression on the attacked. Once before, on April 18, 1938, he had seriously considered the assassination of the German envoy in Prague by one of his own strong-arm men to "justify" a strategic attack on Czechoslovakia.

The Czech coup was abandoned, but an SS man named Alfred Helmut Naujocks, according to his own account, was ordered "to simulate an attack on the radio station near Gleiwitz near the Polish border and to make it appear that the attacking force consisted of Poles." The operation was given the code name Canned Goods. The idea was to seize the Gleiwitz radio station and hold it long enough to enable a Polish-speaking German to make an incendiary speech against Germany. The operation was to be carried out by five SD men, terrorists of the Secret State Police, headed by Naujocks. A prisoner taken from a German concentration camp and carrying forged Polish credentials was to be left dead on the ground to "prove" that the attack was mounted by Poles.

The sabotage operation was executed, exactly as planned, at 8 P.M. on August 31, 1939, about nine hours before German troops crossed into Poland. The Gestapo delivered their human prop directly to the radio station. He was unconscious and dying from a fatal injection administered by a Gestapo doctor. The six German saboteurs seized the station, held it for four minutes while the prearranged speech was broadcast in Polish, fired a few shots, and departed, leaving the dead "Pole" at the entrance of the station. Hitler had his justification for starting World War II with what he then called "counterattack with pursuit."

German sabotage never succeeded in interfering seriously with the Allies, partly because the Nazi leaders of the military intelligence service, which was responsible for sabotage operations, opposed such action on the grounds that it was ineffectual. When these opponents of sabotage were removed and the job was assigned to a fanatical Nazi, an Austrian soldier of fortune named Otto Skorzeny, there was insufficient time to cause serious damage before the war ended.

But where the Germans failed the Allies succeeded brilliantly. Sabotage became accepted as a legitimate means of war chiefly because its value and effectiveness were recognized in the type of war the Allies were compelled to wage in Europe and Asia between 1940 and 1944. Whatever qualms might have existed before were overcome. "This form of warfare," Bruce Marshall wrote in his account of the exploits of Yeo-Thomas, "was both more accurate and benign than aerial bombardment. An agent insinuated into a factory could sabotage effectively and without loss of human life a piece of essential machinery which a squadron of bombers would be lucky to hit by chance."

Sabotage expectations were fully borne out by achievement

in World War II. It required more than 175,000 incendiary bombs dropped from squadrons of Royal Air Force planes to create damage equal to that caused by German saboteurs in 1916 in New York harbor alone. In one instance, seven separate air raids failed to destroy a bridge in France which later fell after a single charge was laid surreptitiously by only two saboteurs. In twenty-six months of the Second World War, a single group of Soviet saboteurs destroyed 52 railway trains, 256 bridges, 96 munition dumps, 2 oil refineries, 150 miles of track, and 20 tanks, and killed over 1,000 German soldiers. Sabotage groups operated as far as 600 miles behind the German lines.

After the war, sabotage was the chief weapon of the Communist guerrilla forces in Greece. In August, 1948, for example, when sabotage operations were at their peak, they wrecked 91 trains, destroyed 153 railroad stations, and sabotaged 21 factories.

We may witness the truly decisive effectiveness of sabotage with an example from the Israeli-Arab war in which a combined operation actually saved the Israelis from defeat.

Israel was proclaimed an independent state in May, 1948. The young state was then promptly attacked by an alliance of Arab countries. An Egyptian army, led by a tank division, crossed into Palestine, overcame feeble military resistance, and rolled along the coastal road toward Tel-Aviv, the temporary capital of the new state.

The danger to Israel was extreme. The fall of Tel-Aviv would have ended the war and established Egypt as the virtual ruler of Palestine. At that stage, the Israelis drafted a plan in which they assigned a major role to a single and seemingly minor sabotage operation. The Israeli Air Force had a total of four planes, smuggled in from Czechoslovakia, antiquated German Messerschmitt fighters. Their purchase and arrival in Israel had been kept secret. Maintenance crews went to work behind the locked doors of the hangars at an airport that appeared deserted to Egyptian reconnaissance planes. The grass was allowed to grow high over the runways. Spare parts, left behind by the Royal Air Force, lay rusting in the sun.

While the Israeli mechanics worked frantically in the hangars to assemble the four planes, the Israeli intelligence service managed to obtain the operations plan of the Egyptian tank division. The division was to reach the outskirts of Tel-Aviv on June 10, 1948. The tanks were to halt there and then move on next day, the schedule calling for them to arrive in Tel-Aviv on the 12th.

Just outside of Tel-Aviv the Egyptian column had to cross a bridge, which immediately became the focal point of the Israeli counterplan. A team consisting of four saboteurs was chosen as a suicide squad. Their job was to wait under the bridge for the approach of the Egyptian tanks, and to blow it up just as the first tank reached it.

At dawn of June 12, the Egyptians rolled toward the bridge. There was no resistance and consequently no reason for them to disperse their tanks. They moved along the excellent highway, tank following tank, armored car after armored car, forming a column several miles long. The rear was brought up by huge army trucks carrying Egyptian infantrymen to serve as occupation troops in Tel-Aviv.

The first tank was sighted by the four saboteurs, waiting with their charges already laid. When the tank was within a few yards of them, the saboteurs blew up the bridge with tremendous force, throwing debris on the approaching tanks. The driver of the lead tank brought his vehicle to an abrupt stop. The second tank halted instantly, and so on, until the whole column was stalled on the open road, stretched out for five miles.

At that moment, the closed doors of the hangars on the airfield were pushed open and the Israeli "air force" rushed out for the take-off. The newly assembled planes were not even flight-tested. Although built to take off from hard runways, they now had to use the strips on the neglected field overgrown with high grass. As if by sheer will power of the pilots they were pulled into the air and headed for the immobilized Egyptian tanks. They swooped low over them, raked them with round after round from their machine guns, and dropped bombs on them.

As the planes appeared overhead, coming so unexpectedly from nowhere, the Egyptians were seized with panic. The orderly column of the Egyptians was thrown into confusion. At headquarters, Israeli military intelligence listened on monitoring sets to the excited chatter of the tank radios and shortly afterwards picked up a signal issued by the commanding general of the Egyptians ordering the tanks to disperse and await further instructions. Later that day came the decisive signal from the Egyptian general. It ordered the tanks to reform and retire. And so, at 9 A.M. on June 12, 1948, Israel was saved by the suicidal daring of four saboteurs.

Sabotage is a major weapon in a cold war. Today it is conducted by the various resistance forces in eastern Europe and Asia, and within the Soviet Union, especially in the Ukraine.

It is part of a greater operations plan, about which more will be said later.

Due to the physical aspects of sabotage, it becomes a complex operation even when only a single agent is involved. Sabotage, like intelligence, is an exact science, which demands exceptional military, economic, technical, and psychological preparation. It must have a general or strategic plan for campaigns, and tactical directives for individual operations. It requires large standing organizations both at headquarters and in the field, both at home and abroad. It must have its own lines of supplies and communications, and it uses personnel especially chosen and trained for the job.

The combination of these major elements represents the over-all scheme of sabotage. Now let us survey them one by one.

The Sabotage Plan

Even though in the final analysis everything will depend on the courage, inventiveness, and initiative of the individual saboteur in action, sabotage operations evolve from a general plan drawn up originally on the strategic level and then broken down into tactical directives for individual operations.

The sabotage plan is prepared at headquarters on the basis of general military requirements and detailed intelligence. It considers and evaluates the total potential of an opponent's resources accessible to sabotage. This potential includes raw materials, power sources, basic industries, military strength, food and water resources, auxiliary industries, and lines of transportation and communication. Information about all the resources is obtained by what is called general reconnaissance. It is designed to establish the military and economic importance of a country's industrial regions and to locate the various installations within them. After that, so-called special reconnaissance is used to supply data for the technical and tactical details of individual operations.

These are intelligence functions which must precede all sabotage operations and, indeed, must supply any information needed in the drafting of the basic sabotage plan. When such a plan is organized it follows logical lines which promise maximum effectiveness with a minimum of compromise. A logical plan, based on proper strategic considerations and exact information, will not ordinarily destroy assembly plants that produce finished products. Instead, it will attack the sources of raw materials needed by a great number of factories, or it will strike at auxiliary plants manufacturing special parts and accessories upon which final production is dependent.

The basic sabotage plan must determine in advance the extent to which a country is to be sabotaged. All such plans must be prepared on a long-range basis, the planners bearing in mind that indiscriminate destruction is bound to interfere seriously with postwar reconstruction and, during the war, with one's own operations in sabotaged areas. A wise military commander does not conduct wholesale sabotage operations against regions that he expects to occupy within a short time. He may find that indiscriminate sabotage, which often leaves bridges blown and rail lines cut in its wake, will hinder his own advance or retreat far more than it interferes with the enemy's operations.

In a blind fury of destruction, Hitler ordered large-scale attacks against Warsaw, capital of Poland, even though it was obvious that the city would fall to him within a few days. The destruction his own forces wrought eventually proved detrimental to the Germans, and Warsaw, instead of being an asset to Hitler, became a liability.

Within a sabotage plan, each target is treated separately, much in the manner in which an air force treats its aerial targets. Individual objectives are chosen in advance and all information concerning them is placed in separate "objective folders." These folders contain the operations instructions, evaluated intelligence reports and maps, information about protective measures, all worked out to the most minute detail. The objective folder also contains an estimate of the over-all situation, an evaluation of the target, and an assessment of its relative value to one's own plans, to the military organization of the enemy, and to his national economy.

The Sabotage Organization

Sabotage operations are generally conducted, first, by citizens against their own government or industries; second, against the occupation forces in a defeated country; third, by one country against another, either in the latter's own territory or in territories occupied by its forces; and fourth, in support of over-all military operations or as an independent effort to take the place of conventional military operations.

Despite the special nature of individual operations, sabotage is regarded as an intelligence function and is placed or-

189

ganizationally within the intelligence service, where it represents the brawn in a brainy function. This activity is included under intelligence chiefly for two reasons: because it requires the most detailed advance information to be effective, and because it has to be conducted in the deepest secrecy, which can only be achieved within intelligence services.

During the late war, sabotage operations represented one of the main functions of the OSS. There they were conducted by an autonomous branch called Special Operations. German sabotage was handled by a division of military intelligence, with saboteurs directed by what was called the Brandenburg Division for Special Operations. In Britain, sabotage was used as a major weapon between 1940 and 1944 to harass the Germans on the continent and prevent them from consolidating their victories.

The Italians and Japanese made very limited use of sabotage. The Russians, on the other hand, practiced sabotage on a truly gigantic scale. For domestic reasons, this activity was separated from the Fourth Bureau and established within the Ministry of Interior, and also in a special organization which served as headquarters for all partisan forces. This separation is explained by the fact that members of the Communist Party of the Soviet Union were traditionally experts in sabotage, having used it extensively in their struggle for power. Today it is further motivated by the Kremlin's fear of domestic saboteurs who might, if not closely controlled, use it as a weapon against their rulers. As long as all sabotage activities are controlled by the party, the men in the Kremlin feel secure against being sabotaged themselves.

Within underground movements, sabotage is usually one of three major "networks," the other two being intelligence and propaganda. Sabotage is sometimes called "action network," and is organized into regional, departmental, and local committees which conduct sabotage operations with crews, and guerrilla warfare with *francs-tireurs,* or partisans. Usually a separate network is maintained for the reception of material smuggled into the country. This network is also organized along regional lines, each sabotage region handling separately its own problems of supply from reception to distribution.

Sabotage organizations now generally maintain their own means of transportation and systems of communication. The former is often composed of speed-boats, submarines, and small planes for landing in hostile territory, and larger planes from which agents can be parachuted. Early in the war, sabotage organizations were dependent on regular navies and air forces to provide the means of transportation, but they since have developed their own means, since it was found that because of interdepartmental bureaucracy transportation from the other services could not be depended upon.

The communications net consists of couriers, wireless operators, and any of the other means of transmission used in intelligence operations. The communications center at headquarters is the nerve center of a sabotage organization. In addition, field transmission centers act as a kind of switchboard to maintain liaison between various communications posts on a regional basis. In sabotage operations, radio is considered the best medium of liaison. However, other media are also used to maintain personal contacts and to transmit messages by less direct means.

Permanent sabotage organizations are rarely maintained in times of peace, outside the Soviet Union. Whatever sabotage operations are conducted in peacetime are handled by small special teams detached from the intelligence service for such special missions on an *ad hoc* basis.

When employed on a nation-wide scale, in an armed conflict or in a cold war, sabotage organizations cannot subsist in the field as totally independent and self-contained units. Even though composed entirely of citizens of the country being thus attacked, organizations cannot survive when left to themselves. In order to be effective, they have to be organized, directed, and supplied from abroad. Material aid is of prime importance, but political and diplomatic direction is also necessary. Consequently, liaison is a vital function of all sabotage organizations, not merely to sustain sabotage groups in the field and to supply them with whatever equipment and tools are needed, but also to provide them with policies, strategic directives, and tactical guidance. This is necessary in order to integrate them into the greater strategic aim which sabotage, on whatever scale it may be conducted, must ultimately serve.

The Perfect Saboteur

Like an intelligence service, a sabotage organization stands or falls on its personnel. If possible, the question of personnel is even more important in sabotage than in espionage. In view of the complex nature of these operations, and the fact that far more persons have to be employed in them than in espionage, sabotage organizations usually involve the greatest personnel problems of intelligence services. The membership of such an organization is classified according to the specific functions they are supposed to perform. There are directors and planners, agents, couriers, guides, weapons instructors, and specialists. There are also the various technicians, including radio operators, pilots, naval personnel, signalmen, and many more. While each man is assigned to a highly specialized function, he must know something about the functions of others and be capable of coordinating his work with the whole. In the field, the distribution of labor so neatly drawn in tables of organization is seldom apparent. A man who starts out as a follower may suddenly find himself in the position of leader. Or a specialist may go on a mission to operate a clandestine radio and wind up mixing explosives or laying charges.

Like the "ideal spy," the "perfect saboteur" is actually only a figment of the imagination. Yet all sabotage organizations go to great lengths to select men best qualified for a perilous job, and to train them scrupulously for special missions of all types.

Let us see, then, who the men are who go out to create destruction. Are they unbalanced persons whose urge to destroy is morbidly overdeveloped? Are they depraved, incapable of recognizing the traditional limitations that humanity has imposed on the means of conflict? Are they low-class, low-intelligence brutes whose personal background predestines them to such deceit and violence? By no means. As a matter of fact, history's best known saboteurs have been men of superior background and standing in their own societies. The chief of German sabotage in the United States in 1916 was Captain Franz von Rintelen, a member of the old Reich's historic nobility. Italy's most effective sabotage expert, a naval officer who infiltrated British ports in tiny underwater craft and single-handed attacked battleships and carriers, was a prince, a descendant of the Borgias. The leader of the British Commandos was Lord Louis Mountbatten, a great-grandson of Queen Victoria, and his most efficient lieutenant was Simon Christopher Joseph Fraser, 15th Lord Lovat, whose barony was created in 1485. The "brain" behind most of Britain's wartime sabotage actions was Nathaniel Meyer Victor, 3rd Baron Rothschild, a member of the famous family of bankers and a brilliant scientist in his own right.

According to Colonel F. O. Miksche, who was chief of operations in General de Gaulle's secret service during World War II, "it is not altogether a question of military ability, for the technical knowledge required is of a relatively simple nature." It calls more for psychological instinct and political skill. "They are less chiefs in the military sense than they are

192

chiefs of popular tribes," Miksche wrote. "They must be men who have risen from the people, and are accustomed to a simple life. By achieving distinction among their fellows, they gain the individual confidence of their followers. The best training for guerrilla chiefs (or, for that matter, for leaders of sabotage teams) is a hard life."

The sabotage leader must be a born conspirator. He must be able to deceive not only the enemy but his own comrades, since in sabotage operations one of the cardinal rules is that each man should know only what is essential to his own task. In addition, he must have quick judgment and appreciation, an alert and inventive mind. He must possess the moral courage to assume responsibilities and the will to accomplish what often may seem impossible. He must be physically vigorous, ascetic and austere, capable of adjusting to the strangest environment.

The sabotage chief must be deeply devoted to his cause and imbued with strong political convictions. Otherwise he is no better than the mere *sabot*, a man driven by impulses of senseless destruction too difficult to control. In practice, organizations strive to indoctrinate their personnel along ideological and political lines, and to impress upon them the nobler motives of their destructive occupations. Responsible nations approach sabotage with certain fundamental misgivings, and they try to impress at least a basic self-restraint upon their operatives. Sabotage, when engaged in over long periods of time on an active scale, tends to destroy the conscience of a man, to lull him into a false sense of justification of its methods. Men long accustomed to the violent struggle are inclined to believe too readily that any end justifies the means, and without a proper balance between the conscience and the evils of destruction may find it difficult to readjust to a normal positive life.

"Was it a wise policy on a long-term reckoning," Captain Liddell Hart, the British military writer, asked when assessing the implications of secret warfare, "taking account not only of winning the war but of securing the peace that should follow victory? Was its contribution to victory outweighed by its legacy of disorder?" He answered his own questions in a dubious mood. "The habit of violence," he wrote, "takes much deeper root in irregular than it does in regular warfare. In the latter it is connected by the habit of obedience to constituted authority, whereas the former makes a virtue of defying authority and violating rules."

Gunnerside: The Mission That Succeeded

One of the historic feats in the annals of sabotage is an operation identified by the code name Gunnerside. This was the fantastic mission of a small group of Norwegians during World War II who proved conclusively that, unlike crime, sabotage does pay. When the United States decided to develop the atomic bomb, plans were made simultaneously to prevent the Nazis from acquiring one first. Special intelligence groups were formed in Britain and the United States. Their mission was to find out where the Nazis had their own atomic plants and laboratories.

Such a plant was discovered in the Norsk Hydro factory in Vemork, in the Norwegian province of Telemark, known the world over for its fine skiing. Norsk Hydro was the world's largest producer of heavy water, a substance needed in the construction of the atomic pile. The possession of the plant, and the heavy water it produced and stored, gave the Germans an enormous potential advantage in the development of atomic weapons.

It was decided, therefore, in the highest councils of the Allies, to sabotage Norsk Hydro at any cost. On March 28, 1942, a Norwegian agent whom I will call Einar was parachuted into Telemark province to pave the way for a sabotage party to follow. He worked alone for months in this enemy-infested land, gathering invaluable data essential for the drafting of the eventual operations plan. From his observations on the spot, and the observations of others, the plan was evolved. Since this became the greatest single operation in the entire history of sabotage, and since this operations plan has become the classic type for all such directives, I will reprint here its salient features, to show the care and detail that go into the drafting of such directives.

INTELLIGENCE

Fifteen Germans in the hut-barracks between the machine room and the electrolysis plant. Change of guard at 1800, 2000 hours, etc. Normally two Germans on the bridge. During an alarm: three patrols inside the factory area and floodlighting on the road between Vemork and Vaaer. Normally only two Norwegian guards inside the factory area at night, plus one at the main gates and one at the penstocks. All doors into the electrolysis factory locked except one that opens into the yard.

From the advance position at the power-line cutting, the following will be brought up: arms, explosives, a little food. No camouflage suits to be worn over uniforms. Claus to lead the way down to the river and up to the railway track. Advance to the position of attack some 500 meters from the fence. The covering party, led by the second in command, to advance along the track, followed close behind by the demolition party, which the Gunnerside leader will lead himself. The position for attack will be occupied before midnight in order to be able to see when the relieved guards return to the barracks. According to information received from sketches and photographs, we have chosen the gate by the store-shed, some 10 meters lower than the railway gates, as being best suited for the withdrawal and as providing best cover for the advance. The attack will start at 0030 hours.

COVERING PARTY

Duty: To cut an opening in the fence. To get into position so that any interference by the German guards, in the event of an alarm, is totally suppressed. If all remains quiet, to stay in position until the explosion is heard or until other orders are received from the demolition-party leader. The commander of the covering party to use his own judgment if necessary. If the alarm is sounded during the advance into the factory grounds, the covering party to attack the guard immediately. When the explosion is heard, it may be assumed that the demolition party is already outside the factory grounds, and the order is to be given for withdrawal; the password is, "Piccadilly? Leicester Square!"

After that, the operational order reached its own climax, the detailed instructions for the sabotage action proper:

DEMOLITION PARTY

Duty: To destroy the high-concentration plant in the cellar of the electrolysis factory. At the exact moment when the covering party either take up their position or go into action, the demolition party will advance to the cellar door. One man, armed with a tommy-gun, takes up position covering the main entrance. Those carrying out the actual demolition are covered by one man with a tommy-gun and one man with a .45 pistol. An attempt will first be made to force the cellar door; failing that, the door to the ground floor. As a last resort, the cable tunnel is to be used. If fighting starts before the H.C. plant is reached, the covering party will, if necessary, take over the placing of the explosives. If anything should happen to the leader, or anything upsets the plans, all are to act on their own initiative in order to carry out the operation. Any workmen or guards found will be treated in such manner as the situation may demand. If possible, no reserve charges will be left behind in the factory.

It is forbidden for the members of either party to use torches or other lights during the advance or withdrawal. Arms are to be carried ready for use but are not to be loaded until necessary, so that no accidental shot raises the alarm.

The order concluded on a highly melodramatic note, spelled out in the matter-of-fact language of such an operations plan: *"If any man is about to be taken prisoner, he undertakes to end his own life."* These were the only lines underscored in the whole document.

Planning required eleven months. Then on February 27, 1943, two teams composed of gentlemen saboteurs stood ready to execute the plan. One group went by the code name Swallow. The other was called Gunnerside. Here, in the very words of their own log, is the story of this part of the operation.

FEBRUARY 27

. . . left our advance base, a hut in Fjosbudalen, about 8 P.M. We started on skis, but were later forced to continue on foot. . . . At Vaaer Bridge we had to take cover, as two buses were coming up the road with night shift from Rjukan. . . . We advanced to within about 500 meters of the factory's railway gate. Carried on a strong westerly wind came the faint humming note of the factory's machinery. We had a fine view of the road and the factory itself.

FEBRUARY 28

. . . once more I checked up to make sure that every man was certain about his part in the operation and understood his orders.

Cautiously we advanced to some store-sheds about 100 meters from the gates. Here one man was sent forward with a pair of armorer's shears to open the gates, with the rest of the covering party in support. The demolition party stood by to follow up immediately.

The factory gates, secured with padlock and chain, were easily opened. . . . At a given sign the covering party advanced toward the German guard-hut. At the same moment the demolition party moved toward the door of the factory cellar, through which it was hoped to gain entry. The cellar door was locked. We were unable to force it, nor did we have any success with the door of the floor above. Through a window of the high-concentration plant, where our target lay, a man could be seen.

During our search for the cable tunnel, which was our only remaining method of entry, we became separated from one another. Finally I found the opening and, followed by only one of my men, crept in over a maze of tangled pipes and leads. Through an opening under the tunnel's ceiling we could see our target.

Every minute was now valuable. As there was no sign of the

other two demolition party members, we two decided to carry out the demolition alone. We entered a room adjacent to the target, found the door into the high-concentration plant open, went in, and took the guard completely by surprise. We locked the double doors between the heavy-water storage tanks and the adjacent room, so that we could work in peace.

My colleague kept watch over the guard, who seemed frightened but was otherwise quiet and obedient.

I began to place the charges. This went quickly and easily. The models on which we had practiced in England were exact duplicates of the real plant. I had placed half the charges in position when there was a crash of broken glass behind me. I looked up. Someone had smashed the window opening on to the back yard. A man's head stood framed in the broken glass. It was one of my two colleagues who, having failed to find the cable tunnel, had decided to act on their own initiative. One climbed through the window, helped me place the remaining charges, and checked them twice while I coupled the fuses. We checked the entire charge once more, before ignition. There was still no sign of alarm from the yard.

We lit both fuses. I ordered the captive Norwegian guard to run for safety to the floor above. We left the room.

Twenty yards outside the cellar door, we heard the explosion. The sentry at the main entrance was recalled from his post. We passed through the gate and climbed up the railway track.

For a moment I looked back down the line and listened. Except for the faint hum of machinery that we had heard when we arrived, everything in the factory was quiet.

It was calculated that 3,000 pounds of heavy water were destroyed, together with key parts of the high-concentration plant. Five men of the Gunnerside team skied 250 miles to safety. They were flown out of Norway and back to England shortly afterwards. The sixth man, Knut, stayed behind for another mission, together with the entire Swallow team. Only one member of the two teams ever encountered the enemy, so well was the operation planned and staged.

He was Claus Helberg, a member of one of the advance parties who did most of the original intelligence work for the operation. On March 25, 1943, on the high, snow-covered Hardanger Vidda plateau, Helberg was ambushed by a German patrol of three soldiers. He turned around and skied away from the spot, but was pursued by one of the Germans, himself a master on skis.

Claus stopped and turned, then drew his pistol and fired one shot from his Colt .32. The German had a Luger. Helberg knew that the man who emptied his magazine first would be the loser, so he held his fire but exposed himself as a target at a range of fifty-five yards. The German fell into the trap and emptied his magazine at Claus. Then he turned and started back.

Helberg was unscarred. And now it was his turn. He fired a single shot at the retreating German and saw him stagger, then stop, hanging over his ski poles. Claus raced away, apprehensive that the two other Germans, attracted by the gunfire, might join the fracas after all. By then the countryside was enshrouded in darkness, but Helberg kept going for two more hours, groping his way as he went, until the inevitable happened. He stumbled on a protruding rock and fell over a cliff. He dropped forty-four yards, but escaped with a broken arm and a bruised shoulder. But he was safe—and a few days later he, too, was flown back to England.

By November, 1943, spies in Norway reported to London that, despite the initial success of the operation, Norsk Hydro was back in production. This was bad news, since no more teams were available then to repeat the coup of Swallow and Gunnerside. It was decided, therefore, to bomb the plant from the air. On November 16th, strong formations of the 8th United States Bomber Command attacked the Vemork power station and electrolysis plant. But where the handful of saboteurs had managed to blow up 3,000 pounds of heavy water, the costly air attack destroyed only 120 pounds. Even so, the Germans had had enough. They resolved to dismantle the plant and ship it to Germany.

Then on February 7, 1944, another agent report reached London from Norway. It announced that the transportation of the plant would take place on February 20, in the Lake Tinnsjøe ferry boat *Hydro*. Her orders showed that she would be going to Hamburg.

The new situation was discussed by the British War Cabinet, and orders went out to destroy the *Hydro* by sabotage. The operation was extremely hazardous, if only because it had to be carried out under the noses of an alerted enemy. Special SS detachments were assigned to the whole area. Each day, German planes patrolled the mountains in that vicinity, and security guards were stationed along the railway line from Vemork to the *Hydro's* pier. Yet not a single guard was posted on the *Hydro* herself.

February 20, 1944, was a Sunday. At one o'clock in the morning, four saboteurs led by Knut, the member of the Gunnerside team who had remained behind after the first operation against the factory, left by car specially requisitioned for the purpose. They drove up to the *Hydro's* pier and Knut went aboard with two of his men. His third aide stood by at the get-away car.

They saw the crew gathered below deck, engrossed in a rather noisy battle of poker. The engine room was occupied. Two of Knut's men pushed through a hole and crept along the keel to the bow. Knut laid his charges in the bilge, coupling them to two separate time-delay mechanisms which he tied to the stringers on each side. The charge was big enough to sink the *Hydro* in five minutes.

Knut then set the time-delay charge, home-made from an old alarm clock, for 10:45 A.M. This was the time the boat was expected to arrive at the best place for its destruction. It was now only four o'clock in the morning, but the saboteurs were finished with the job. Knut and his partners crawled back through the bilge and escaped undetected. They got back into their car and drove away, and by nightfall were safe in Oslo, lost in the hustle and bustle of the Norwegian capital.

The *Hydro* sank at 10:45 sharp that morning just as planned. It went down with priceless machinery from Norsk Hydro and 3,600 gallons of heavy water on board. "So it was," the official report of this operation concluded, "that the manufacture of heavy water ceased in Norway; and so it was that all stocks available to German scientists from that source were lost."

Sabotage and the Cold War

The global battle of sabotage continued up to the very last hour of the Second World War, after which a new type of conflict descended upon the world, what we call the cold war. With it came a new phase in the war of wits, in which we are confronted with a different type of secret agent, the Communist operative to whom all means are justified, in peace as well as war.

Although little is published about them, considerable damage is done by Communist saboteurs. They are especially active in France where they hamper anything aiding the war in Indochina, especially ships and cargoes. In Britain, they boldly attack the vessels of the Royal Navy. The list of sabotage perpetrated against Her Majesty's ships is frighteningly long, and growing daily. It is even more alarming that British security organs seem incapable of coping with the problem. Some of the damage to the warships has been serious, indicating careful and painstaking organization, and none of the saboteurs have been found despite the narrow confines of their operations.

Maritime sabotage is the strongest arm of the Communist secret service, partly because it is regarded as vitally important, and partly because the Communists have genius guiding this type of work. He is the dean of saboteurs, the German Communist leader Ernst Wollweber. At the time of this writing, Wollweber is no ordinary outlaw, no roughneck, no lowly saboteur. He is Minister of the Interior in Eastern Germany, the Russian zone's top policeman directing law and order. He was appointed to the post—the first in his life that carries with it the slightest appearance of dignity—in the wake of the great patriotic uprising of June 17, 1953, that shook the Communist regime of Eastern Germany to its foundations. Wollweber is expected to prevent the recurrence of such outbreaks and to deal with them in his customary fashion—ruthless intolerance.

I knew Wollweber in Germany in the early thirties, at which time he conducted his world-wide sabotage activities as if they were a respectable business enterprise. He had his headquarters in Hamburg, in an office that masqueraded as a labor union of merchant seamen. From his office he engineered the mutiny of the Royal Navy at Invergordon and the rebellion of the sailors of the Royal Netherlands Navy. I have seen him there, sitting at his desk beneath a huge maritime map of the world on which colored pins marked the positions of the ships in which he had a personal interest. He had bloodshot, narrow eyes, and was a squat, dark, truculent, vulgar-looking man. When he laughed, he displayed a row of bad teeth stained by the tobacco from the pipe that was never missing from his mouth.

Wollweber's whole life had been wasted on violence. He was one of the "Kaiser's coolies," a sailor of the High Seas Fleet of Imperial Germany. Theodor Plivier wrote a classic book about him and about the mutiny Wollweber stage-managed at Kiel in 1918.

After the collapse of the Kaiser's Germany, Wollweber set himself up as a specialist in maritime sabotage. He formed Communist cells on innumerable merchant vessels sailing under the flags of all nations, and also on warships. He established sabotage schools where hand-picked sailors from many countries were trained as strike-makers, mutiny inciters, spies, and saboteurs. He organized merchant ships all over the world into a network for smuggling spies, transporting couriers, ferrying his gunmen, and shipping his prisoners to Soviet jails.

At that time, in 1930-33, Wollweber had a number of Americans on his staff: a tall, heavy-set, lazy Negro agitator named James Ford who later became the Communist candidate for the vice-presidency of the United States; George Mink, Thomas Ray, and Mike Pell, "activists" all; and a notorious triggerman known as Horseface, whose real name was Roy Hudson.

After Hitler's seizure of power in 1933, Wollweber moved his headquarters to Copenhagen, Denmark, and continued his global sabotage with even greater vigor. Today, although he occupies a position of apparent respectability, he still works at his old trade from the former German port city Stettin, given to the Poles at Yalta.

Wollweber is a Soviet agent of the worst type. His activities are directed and financed by the Kremlin. The not inconsiderable funds that he requires for his operations come from the treasury of the Sovtorgflot, the maritime trust of the Soviet Union, through the Profintern, the Communist center of labor conspiracy.

In fighting against men like Wollweber, the free world has been forced to invoke the doctrine of Zeno: knavery is the best defense against a knave. The spy and saboteur of the free world, operating in the countries occupied by the Communists, are remarkable for their courage and selfless devotion to their cause. Their sabotage, on however large a scale, is hardly more than a symbolic act under the circumstances. It is designed to remind both friend and foe that men are still willing to live dangerously and die heroically so that liberty shall not perish from the earth.

An example of this symbolic fight was supplied by saboteurs of the Hungarian underground in April, 1952, on the anniversary of the day of their country's occupation by the Red Army. It was a big day for the Communists, and they tried to make the most of it. Delegates from the whole Communist world converged on Budapest to attend the festivities. From the Soviet Union came Marshal Klementi Voroshilov, a powerful member of the Politburo. Top-ranking Communist leaders came from the other countries, from Czechoslovakia to China.

There were many overt acts the anti-Communist underground could have undertaken on that day. They could have sabotaged the train that carried the Soviet marshal or placed a time bomb under his reviewing stand. They could have committed innumerable acts to spoil the Communist fun by killing the guest of honor, but the Communists would have taken savage reprisals, killing hostages and exiling the innocent to forced labor camps. There was no point in defying the police state with useless, senseless, pointless acts of murder and sabotage, and the underground acting behind the

Iron Curtain was made up of sensible and responsible men and women.

And yet, Marshal Voroshilov's presence in Hungary was too good an opportunity to miss without at least a symbolic act of defiance. The underground leader in charge of the arrangements was a simple workingman known to his fellows only as Pete. He prepared his plan in great secrecy. Nothing leaked out to the secret police, despite the fact that this was to be a major demonstration at a time when Communist vigilance was increased in preparation for the marshal's visit.

Voroshilov's train reached the Hungarian frontier at 8 A.M. on April 20. A reception committee was on hand, and a band played the Communist anthems. Suddenly flames sprang up from the freight yard of the huge frontier station. Within a few minutes several warehouses were on fire.

At the same moment, a train carrying the French delegation reached the city of Györ and was received with the firing of a boxcar factory near the station. A power plant was set on fire to greet delegations from Czechoslovakia and Eastern Germany, while the Rumanian and Bulgarian delegations were greeted with fires in Hungary's great tobacco plant in Szeged.

The moment Marshal Voroshilov's train pulled into Debreczen, Hungary's third largest city, fire broke out in its biggest industrial plant, a sheet-metal factory. And as the trains arrived in Budapest, the capital, the city scarcely knew which spectacle to watch, the arrival of Voroshilov at the head of the foreign delegations, or the fire raging over several city blocks, consuming the Wolfner plant, Europe's biggest tannery and leather factory.

The honored guests could not sleep their first night in Budapest, for the city was kept awake by the sirens and bells of the fire-engines racing to the various conflagrations.

At the height of the fires the underground struck for a second time. It sabotaged the water works, forcing the firemen to stand by idly and watch helplessly as everything the patriot arsonists had put on fire burned out.

Operation Torch, as the demonstration was called, ended as planned. Nothing went wrong. The Hungarians showed the assembled Communists that the spirit of resistance was literally aflame in their land. Of all the men who participated in the demonstration, only the leader, Pete, had to flee. He reached the free world by way of Czechoslovakia and Austria. His comrades remained at their posts—to carry the torch for freedom.

PART IV

Counterespionage

Negative Intelligence

Negative intelligence is a generic term meaning three different things: security intelligence, counterintelligence, and counterespionage. By security intelligence, we mean the sum total of all efforts to conceal national policies, diplomatic decisions, military data, and any other information of a secret nature affecting the security of the United States from unauthorized persons. It is the effort to deny information to unauthorized persons by restricting it to those who are explicitly authorized to possess it.

The basis of security intelligence is concealment in general: the classification of documents according to the degree of their secrecy; various screening operations, which include the spreading of deliberately falsified or bogus information to mislead an enemy; the enactment of legislation to deter people from even trying to gain unauthorized possession of classified information; the selection and indoctrination of trustworthy and security-conscious personnel; and a protective plan designed to secure natural resources and industrial production against the intelligence, espionage, and sabotage efforts of an enemy.

A finely drawn line separates security intelligence from counterintelligence, which is the organized effort to protect specific data that might be of value to an opponent's own intelligence organization. One of its chief instruments is censorship. By censorship of the printed word, of correspondence, broadcasts, telecasts, telephone conversations, telegrams and cables, and other forms of communication, counterintelligence aims to prevent the dissemination of any information that might aid an opponent. Other instruments of internal security are the maintenance of files on suspects, the surveillance of suspects by observing their movements, reading their mail, listening in or recording their telephone conversations, and the infiltration of the enemy's intelligence organization to procure information about its methods, personnel, specific operations, and interests.

203

Up to this point, negative intelligence is a protective and anticipatory function. It is designed to prevent certain information from becoming public or from falling into unauthorized hands, whether accidentally or through the positive efforts of forces dedicated to its acquisition.

In counterespionage, negative intelligence becomes a dynamic and active effort. The purpose of counterespionage is to investigate actual or theoretical violation of the espionage laws, to enforce those laws, and to apprehend any violators, if possible before they succeed in compromising classified information by its delivery to foreign employers. To put it bluntly, the job of counterespionage is to catch spies.

Security intelligence and counterintelligence are essentially intellectual functions. Counterespionage is basically a police function. This fundamental difference is not generally understood, and the failure to understand it leads to confusion and misapprehension. Frequently, agencies charged with counterespionage are accused of failure to apprehend spies before the completion of their missions. Prevention of espionage and sabotage is not the fundamental function of counterespionage, but is properly the responsibility of the other protective services, of security intelligence and counterintelligence at the very source of the information.

Protection at the source is relatively simple. The apprehension of agents at large is a complex and difficult task. "A basic requirement of the secret agent is to disguise himself and his mission," Sir Basil Thomson, chief of Scotland Yard's Criminal Investigation Department, once told me. "Much of his training and basic skill is dedicated to concealment. His organization is supposed to supply him with a foolproof cover story and good documents. He knows how to handle himself because he is a man of exceptional ability, or else he would not be chosen for this intricate job. Because of this, and because the democracies often place more difficulties in the path of counterespionage agents than of the spies themselves, the trapping of the dark intruder is a formidable task."

In 1945, the Royal Canadian Mounted Police, whose assignments include counterespionage, were severely criticized for their failure to apprehend the espionage agents of the Soviet ring operating in Canada. This criticism was only partly justified. Atomic espionage in Canada was carried out between March and September of 1945. Five months is scarcely enough time for even the best counterespionage agency to pursue an investigation to a successful conclusion, unless it obtains information from inside the ring. Most of the Canadians involved in the case were known to the police as Soviet sympathizers, and their names were carried in police suspect files. But a man may be a suspect without being actively engaged in espionage. And he may be immune from prosecution for lack of evidence. Legally, he is not an espionage agent until he is proved one. In democratic countries, counterespionage agencies are bound by the provisions of existing laws. They are permitted to conduct their investigations only by legally sanctioned means. They are allowed to make arrests only when sufficient evidence is on hand, not simply to justify the arrest, but also to make it "stick" in a court of law.

The success of Soviet espionage in Canada was really due to a breakdown of security. A similar breakdown of security was the cause of espionage activity in the United States and Britain. Persons whose alien sympathies were either known or suspected were nevertheless allowed access to sensitive positions and information. Limited as counterespionage agencies are in their funds and personnel, it is physically impossible for them to keep every suspect under surveillance. In view of this, basic security must come from protection and anticipation rather than from counterespionage.

To illustrate this point with a practical example, we may cite the case of a potential "leak" in the United States. In this country, certain aviation maps which contain information useful to an enemy are on public sale. In a country where civilian and private aviation is widespread, such maps cannot be withdrawn from circulation without endangering safety in the air. It is physically impossible to record every purchaser of such maps and then to keep him under surveillance to discover what use he is making of them. Even if a purchaser actually delivered one of these maps to an agent of a foreign power, our counterespionage could do nothing about it. The information is, after all, in the public domain. And as long as a person can openly buy these maps, he can do anything he pleases with them without breaking the espionage laws in any way. Yet, these maps contain tremendously valuable information for any potential enemy of the United States.

The same is true in the case of the publications of the U.S. Government Printing Office and England's Stationery Office. Material printed by them may contain valuable information useful to an opponent, yet as long as it is unclassified it cannot be legally withheld even from spies. In order to protect such information, it must be classified and protected at the source. Arrests can be made only when all legal conditions of this step are clearly evident. The military and naval counterintelligence organs of the United States and Britain do not have the power of arrest or the facilities to conduct broad investigations. They may conduct preliminary inquiries and "shadow" suspects, but in the crucial moment they are not permitted to arrest them. They must call in a law-enforcement agency that has the power of arrest, to make the actual arrest. During the thirties, an American was found by the U.S. Navy to be spying for the Japanese naval attaché in Washington. The Navy's agent shadowed the man when he was known to be in possession of incriminating material and trailed him to a hotel room. The agent burst into the room just as the man was assembling the stolen documents in preparation for the visit of a Japanese officer. The agent had no power to arrest the man, but he did not want to lose him, and so he handcuffed the spy to the bed and went out to call the FBI. When the FBI agents arrived, they perceived that the spy's civil rights had been violated, and they refused to make the arrest. As it happened, the spy continued his surreptitious activities and was eventually arrested under legally proper circumstances.

The best way to hinder enemy espionage is, of course, to restrict the movements of possible agents and make impossible the acquisition of information valuable to an enemy. Although such iron-clad protection is not possible in a democracy, this is exactly what totalitarian regimes do. When the Nazis came into power in Germany all strategic maps were withdrawn from circulation. Picture postcards of aerial photographs were confiscated. The taking of pictures from planes was prohibited, and cameras had to be sealed before their bearers made a flight. Suspects were rounded up and detained in concentration camps.

Even more stringent measures of protection are practiced in the Soviet Union today. Virtually the entire country is off limits to foreigners. Every state paper, even if it contains only production statistics of a non-military plant, is regarded as classified. The exportation of books, newspapers, and periodicals is prohibited. The slightest shadow of doubt suffices to doom anyone suspected of espionage activity.

Similar measures are in force in Spain, Egypt, Syria, Iran, Iraq, Israel, and many other countries, some of which are not usually regarded as dictatorships and which, in fact, have strong democratic traditions. Sweden, for example, bans visitors from the city of Boden, where important military installations are located. Turkey bans unauthorized visitors from parts of Anatolia, and the taking of all photographs is prohibited between the Greek frontier and Istanbul. Similar restrictions exist in the United States, where unauthorized entrance is, for example, forbidden to the several atomic plants. In contrast, no restrictions are placed on visiting the atomic energy center of Norway.

The pattern of protection, therefore, has a clearly defined sequence. Concealment at the source of all "security information" must come first, protection and anticipation next. Action by counterespionage is the final security phase.

This is important to an understanding of the exact position and role of counterespionage in the over-all protection pattern, and to an appreciation of the difference between security intelligence and counterintelligence on the one side and counterespionage on the other. Virtually all countries keep counterintelligence separate from counterespionage in the organizational scheme of protection. Counterintelligence is an important part of the functions assigned to the various intelligence agencies. It is practiced vigorously, not only by Army, Navy, and Air intelligence organizations, but also by the Central Intelligence Agency of the United States. Yet the American law makes it very clear that their jurisdiction in this field is cautiously restricted, and that they are not permitted to perform any one of the police functions associated with counterespionage.

They are by their very nature unequipped to function as counterespionage agencies. They lack the machinery to deal with suspects. They have no technical laboratories needed for scientific detection work, and few of the complex apparatus needed for investigations. Their men cannot arrest suspects. They have no trained staffs to prepare prosecutions for the courts. The facilities needed to clinch a case and carry it to its logical conclusion are left entirely and exclusively in the hands of agencies designated primarily to conduct counterespionage. The security organs and counterintelligence branches of the various intelligence services are largely responsible for precautionary and anticipatory measures that will keep the work of counterespionage at a practicable minimum, but, when precaution and anticipation fail, counterespionage steps in to conclude a case.

In ninety-nine out of a hundred cases, the success of an espionage agent or saboteur is not due to any basic inefficiency of the counterespionage organs of a country, but rather to deficient security measures, especially in the handling of documents and the hiring of personnel. A good example of a protective measure that is inadequate is an American law called the "Foreign Agents Registration Act of 1938, as currently amended." It is the only law of its kind in the world, and it was originally devised to curb German propaganda in the United States. It is designed to set a legal trap for foreign agents, and to punish them for failure to register.

Under this act, "agents of foreign principals" engaged in the distribution of political propaganda must register with the Department of Justice and reveal the nature, sources, and contents of the material they disseminate. In addition, persons who have "knowledge of or have received instructions or assignment in espionage, counterespionage, or sabotage service or tactics of a foreign government or a foreign political party" are also expected to register. Theoretically, the law stipulates that every foreign propagandist and foreign espionage agent check in with the Department of Justice upon arrival in the United States.

In practice, however, the only people who comply with the provisions of the act are those who are not engaged in any surreptitious activity in the United States, or who have effectively severed all connection with foreign espionage organizations. In 1952, for example, a total of thirty-one persons registered as trained espionage agents: eighteen of them former Nazis, six former Soviet agents, one Japanese, two Hungarians trained by Soviet intelligence, one Pole, and one former member each of the Philippine, Danish, and Ukrainian undergrounds. Although it is certain that there are now in the United States at least a few trained British and French espionage agents, none of them is registered. It goes without saying that no practicing Soviet agent is registered, either. The closest this registration law ever came to exposing an espionage agent in the United States was in the case of a man named Hafis Salich, who was apprehended and convicted as a Soviet spy—more than fifteen years ago. While it is doubtful that the Foreign Agents Registration Act will identify many foreign agents by their own voluntary registration under the law, it does provide the legal basis necessary for the prosecution of persons engaging in espionage who have failed to register upon entering this country.

Although the United States is dependent upon such a weak safeguard as the Registration Act, and has outlawed censorship and wiretapping as an invasion of personal liberty, other safety precautions are in force, including internal security measures within government departments, strict screening of personnel in sensitive government and private jobs, and restriction of ingress to sensitive installations.

According to the *Internal Security Manual* published by the Foreign Relations Committee of the U. S. Senate, the

United States has on its statute books something like fifty laws to deal with subversion, sabotage and espionage. They include such major statutes as the Atomic Energy Act of 1946 whose Section 16(a) contains the death penalty for atomic espionage; the Civil Defense Act of 1950; the Communication Act of 1934 as amended; the Emergency Detention Act of 1950 which authorizes the Attorney General to apprehend and detain any person who "will probably engage or conspire to engage in espionage or sabotage" in any "internal security emergency" (as defined by presidential proclamation). In addition, these laws include the Internal Security Act of 1950; the Invention Secrecy Act of 1952; the Logan Act of 1948 which regulates private correspondence with foreign governments; the Magnuson Act of 1950 which controls foreign-flag vessels in American waters; the McCarran-Walter Act of 1952 with its stringent provisions concerning immigration; the National Security Act of 1939 as amended; the Neutrality Act of 1939 as amended; the Subversive Activities Control Act of 1950; and the Trading with the Enemy Act of 1917. Additional pertinent provisions are included in many other laws, such as the Air Force Act of 1942; the Hatch Act of 1939; the Taft-Hartley Act of 1947; the Legislative Reorganization Act of 1946; the Military Justice Code; the Mutual Security Act of 1951 as amended.

Even with this phalanx of protective and punitive laws, the pattern of protection remains incomplete. "Laws and orders are many," Senator Alexander Wiley of Wisconsin wrote in his introduction to the manual, "but effectiveness is uncertain. . . . As any serious student of the problem knows the sheer number of laws on this, or for that matter any other critical subject, is hardly a reliable index for the over-all effectiveness of those laws. . . . Time and again the legal framework in which our society operates and in which the Department of Justice, in particular, operates has unfortunately proven overly restrictive and has militated against the attainment of our national objective of self-preservation. Many laws have served as unnecessary and undesirable shackles and as obstacles to the FBI's and the Department's effectiveness." A democracy like the United States faces a grave dilemma when confronted with the conflict between its traditional civil liberties and the novel problems of defense against secret agents.

What frequently reduces the effectiveness of these laws is duplication in the negative intelligence efforts of the United States. According to Donald Robinson, who examined the problem critically in an informed article written for the

American Legion Magazine, there are as many as twenty-five separate agencies in the United States all involved in the fight for internal security. They often step on each other's toes both literally and figuratively, or cancel out each other's effectiveness.

Among the agencies, the FBI is paramount, but it has to contend with numerous other agencies "muscling in" on its responsibilities. In 1942, for example, the United States was in mortal danger for a fortnight because there were in the country eight skilled and trained German saboteurs with orders to blow up the key aluminum factories of this country and thus bring aircraft production to a standstill. One of the two groups of saboteurs, who came ashore from U-boats off Florida and Long Island, was spotted promptly by a young Coast Guardsman. But his superiors delayed several hours in notifying the FBI. The time that elapsed enabled the invaders to work their way inland and remain at large for two weeks, forcing the FBI to track them down through difficult investigation.

Early in the war an informant notified the FBI that an American scientist would dine with two Soviet consuls in a seafood restaurant on Powell Street in San Francisco. The FBI got ready to set up equipment in the place to monitor their conversation, but found agents of the Army's Counter-intelligence Corps already on the spot occupying the only booth where such monitoring appeared possible. "There were more investigators in that restaurant than customers," Robinson remarked. In the resultant confusion both the FBI and CIC proved incapable of getting anything but a jumbled unclear recording. If the conversation had been other than innocent, neither agency would have had recorded proof.

A similar situation exists in Great Britain where at least six separate agencies compete in the field. The Special Branch of Scotland Yard and MI-5 of the War Office share the responsibility for apprehending spies but their preventive work is hampered, both by deficient legislation which allows many loopholes, and by an injudicious distribution of responsibility among the pertinent agencies. There has been in recent years an alarming number of sabotage cases on Her Majesty's ships, but negative intelligence has succeeded neither in stopping the insidious practice nor in locating the culprits. It is known that Soviet atomic espionage had a ring operating in Britain, but to this day it remains unexposed despite clues supplied by Canadian, United States, and Swiss authorities in whose countries other branches of the network operated.

The work of negative intelligence is widely scattered

among a number of British agencies. Some of it is assigned to the Home Office which handles immigration and has jurisdiction over narcotics cases, explosives, and civil defense in general. Still other aspects of the work are assigned to the Ministry of Supply which maintains its own security branch combating espionage in atomic energy and guided missile projects. The Foreign Office is involved in internal security through the Passport Office which has several negative intelligence functions, and its own security branch for provision of armed protection for the Queen's Messengers and the diplomatic couriers while traveling in sensitive areas. Naval Intelligence has a negative branch dealing with matters of naval security and the protection of codes. The Air Ministry has its own Security Department handling the security problems of the RAF.

During the Second World War, Britain maintained a small organization called the Council of Three to coordinate all security matters and expedite the work of negative intelligence. It succeeded in streamlining British counterespionage to a remarkable degree. If such a coordinating agency exists today, nothing is known about it, although the current British *Who's Who* lists Sir Percy Sillitoe, formerly head of MI-5, as "director general" of an otherwise unidentified organization called "Security Services."

The existence of coordinating organs in the United States is a matter of public record. There were, in fact, two of them: one, the Interdepartmental Intelligence Conference (ICC), the other the Interdepartmental Committee on Internal Security (ICIS). They were set up by a 1949 directive of the National Security Council. The ICC consists of the director of the FBI; the chief of the Office of Naval Intelligence; the director of the Intelligence Division, Department of the Army; and the director of the Office of Special Investigations, Department of the Air Force. The ICIS is composed of representatives from the Departments of State, Treasury, and Justice, and the National Military Establishment. Both function as special committees of the National Security Council.

While the government of the United States has done everything in its power to insure this country's internal security, it cannot plug all loopholes without sacrificing democratic traditions and institutions. For this reason, the internal security of the United States—and that of the United Kingdom—remains somewhat deficient.

The consequences of this deficiency were illustrated in the case of Harry Gold, one of the Soviet agents engaged in atomic espionage in the United States. Harry Gold was a member of an espionage ring directed by a certain Jacob Golos, one of the chief organizers of Soviet espionage in this country. When Golos' secretary and mistress left the Communist fold in 1945 and supplied information about the Golos ring to the FBI, Harry Gold's name became known to the Bureau. But specific information about his activities was not immediately forthcoming.

In actual fact, Gold was even then the most efficient courier of the Soviet espionage ring operating in the United States. Under the alias "Raymond," he was detailed to act as the ring's cut-out between Anatoli A. Yakovlev, resident director of the ring in New York, and Dr. Klaus Fuchs, a member of Britain's scientific delegation to the United States working on the development of the atomic bomb.

The presence of Fuchs in the British delegation was in itself a case of faulty security. His Communist sympathies were known to British security organs, but this failed to prevent his assignment to one of the most sensitive jobs in the atomic project. Nor were his Communist sympathies communicated to American security organs. In the United States, Fuchs had absolutely no aboveground links with Communists. Harry Gold worked quietly and diligently in a civilian job, and there was nothing in his normal activities to justify surveillance or even suspicion on the part of the FBI.

Yet, underground, both Fuchs and Gold were exceedingly active. They met each other for the first time early in 1944, under the usual cloak of secrecy that Soviet intelligence arranges long in advance of such meetings. Fuchs was directed to go to a street corner on New York's lower East Side at a certain time on a Saturday, carrying a tennis ball in his hand. Gold was instructed to go to the rendezvous with a green-bound book in one hand, wearing gloves, and carrying an additional pair of gloves in his other hand. Contact was made as arranged and then, still following instructions, Gold and Fuchs went by taxi to a restaurant where Fuchs handed over to Gold certain information about the atomic bomb project.

After that, they met regularly, Fuchs giving Gold material in increasing quantities and importance. As soon as Gold left Fuchs, he would go around a corner and meet Yakovlev, handing him the material he had just received from Fuchs. Some of these meetings between Gold and Fuchs and Gold and Yakovlev lasted for less than a minute. During one of them, in the vicinity of the Brooklyn Borough Hall in June, 1944, Fuchs delivered to Gold the actual blueprint of a uranium bomb, a preliminary model of the A-bomb. Later, they met in Boston, where Fuchs supplied details of a plutonium bomb. Whatever information was still needed by the Russians to make a bomb of their own was supplied by Fuchs at 4 P.M. on June 2, 1945, at the Castillo Bridge in Santa Fe, New Mexico. After that meeting, Gold went to Albuquerque and met another spy, David Greenglass, from whom he received drawings of the device that was used to explode the bomb. This single journey was probably the most rewarding trip ever made by any espionage courier in the whole history of the profession.

Up to this point, the spies were strictly on their own. This was entirely positive espionage. Counterespionage had still not come into the act. Although security was strict in the Manhattan Project, nothing was discovered of Fuchs's extracurricular activities. Then on September 5, 1945, Igor Gouzenko, cipher clerk of the Soviet military attaché in Canada, revealed the existence of the Canadian ring and hinted that parallel rings were operating in the United States and the United Kingdom. On November 8, 1945, Miss Elizabeth Bentley gave corroborating evidence to Thomas J. Donegan, a special agent of the FBI's New York office. From then on, the wheels of counterespionage began to turn, but such is the nature of this delicate work that they could turn only very slowly. Nothing happened for almost two years. Then on May 29, 1947, the paths of the FBI and Gold crossed almost accidentally. The FBI was investigating a man named Brothman whom Miss Bentley had described as a member of the Golos ring. In Brothman's office in Elmhurst, Queens, two special agents of the FBI named Shannon and O'Brien came upon Gold himself.

The agents showed Gold a picture of Golos and Gold identified him promptly as a man for whom he worked. He seemed eager to unburden himself. After a brief conversation in the office, Gold and the two FBI men retired to the agents' car, and there, for two and a half hours, Gold talked. He revealed his real name and his real address in Philadelphia. He gave the details of his association with Golos who, incidentally, was listed in FBI files as an active Soviet espionage agent. Gold even talked of blueprints. "I kept those blueprints in my home in Philadelphia," he said, "and I never did turn them over to Golos."

Although Gold was extremely loquacious, he was also most cautious. He never incriminated himself. He represented his association with Golos as a business connection during which he supplied harmless information that was in the public domain and accessible to anyone. He was careful never even to suggest espionage in general, or atomic espionage in particular. The gist of his words was shrewdly designed to confuse the agents with useless and misleading information, and to divert them from the trail they were following.

At 7 P.M., the agents took Gold back to Brothman's office and typed out Gold's statement. Gold signed it readily. At 9 P.M., the men went their separate ways, the agents to their office and Gold back home to Philadelphia.

Shortly afterwards, two agents from the FBI's Philadelphia office visited Gold at his home. They asked about the blueprints he had mentioned to Shannon and O'Brien, but, when he told them that he had none, the agents left without searching the house. In actual fact, a closet in Gold's basement was full of incriminating material. In July, 1947, Gold was called before a New York grand jury which was following up some of Miss Bentley's leads and bits of material which the FBI investigations had developed. The grand jury took no action against Gold, although he conceded that his actions were at least irregular. The name of Klaus Fuchs was never mentioned. The question of atomic espionage never came up. Gold felt confident that the FBI had little information about his clandestine activities and that the special agents were just fishing.

On February 2, 1950, Klaus Fuchs was arrested in London, on a tip that Scotland Yard received from the FBI. Two FBI agents, Hugh Clegg and Robert Lamphere, were sent to Britain to question Fuchs. They asked him about hundreds of suspects. They finally came around to Gold and showed Fuchs a motion picture they had taken of Gold a short time before. In the meantime, the FBI had searched Gold's house in Philadelphia and found evidence of his trip to Santa Fe in 1944, the meeting that Fuchs described in detail to the FBI agents in England. On May 22, 1950, more than six years after his first contact with Fuchs in Manhattan and three years after his first interrogation by the FBI, Gold confessed and was placed under arrest.

My reason for relating this incident is to demonstrate how tedious and difficult any counterespionage activity is in its concluding stages. Counterespionage agents usually have to work from nothing more than suspicion. There is little they can rely upon, and much that they presume has to be substantiated to be of any value. The weaving of the rope that eventually hangs the espionage agent is a gradual and intricate process in which virtually all the advantages of deception favor the spy.

The Gold case illustrates some of the patterns of protection, but, even more than that, it points up some which were absent. Obviously nothing was known of the clandestine activities of Fuchs, whose own security was a responsibility of the agency for which he worked. Obviously, too, security was deficient at the source. There was no valid or evident reason to suspect Gold of any wrong-doing or to keep him under surveillance.

Yakovlev's assignment at the Soviet Consulate General was known, since his presence there had to be reported to the State Department. But it seems nothing was known of the fact that he was acting as resident director of the New York spy ring, else he would have been under constant surveillance. In turn, such a surveillance would have led the special agents to his contacts and resulted in the exposure of the entire ring. The failure to shadow Yakovlev was a serious omission, since it is an established fact that almost all Soviet nationals among the intelligence personnel work under the cover of diplomatic and trade agencies abroad. If it is not known who in an embassy or consulate is charged with the supervision of espionage, then every member of the Soviet diplomatic staff must be kept under surveillance. This requires a substantial apparatus at the defensive end of the affair, but such an apparatus is needed, no matter how large it may be, if the defenses are to be foolproof.

Thus counterespionage depends on numbers, so to speak, as well as on the efficiency of direct investigations. It will benefit from the false steps an agent occasionally makes, and from the deficiency of his own security. Moreover, it depends on the support that counterespionage receives from a vigilant public.

However, even the best counterespionage agency is bound to fail wherever parts of the protection pattern are omitted, either by inefficiency or incompetence, or by a country's failure to appreciate the danger that lurks in the presence of even a single spy and its refusal to understand the vital need for airtight defenses against what Sir Basil Thomson so aptly called "the dark intruders."

The Evolution of Counterespionage

It is evident that when a country is attacked it must defend itself against the invaders, whether they come in the form of armies or as espionage agents infiltrating a nation from abroad. The recognition that such a defense is needed against spies is not new, but it has taken a long time for nations to organize their special forces against them. For centuries, the task of apprehending spies was assigned to the standing secret services or to the police; and occasionally it was the responsibility of the intelligence services, which were then supposed to conduct negative as well as positive intelligence and espionage.

We meet such a fixed organization for the first time in England in the sixteenth century, when the agents of Sir Francis Walsingham were sent abroad to procure information in Spain, France, and Holland. Agents at home trapped conspirators, both native and foreign, who threatened the person and secrets of Queen Elizabeth. As the conspiracies multiplied, Walsingham enlarged his organization to cope with them, and, then, to justify his existence and to obtain the funds he needed, he invented threats where none existed.

Counterespionage, in the modern sense of the term, came into being with the American Civil War, which pioneered many institutions of the secret war. It was an outgrowth of the turbulence of the election campaign of 1860, and the answer to conspiracies that the bitter advocates of slavery plotted against Abraham Lincoln. Even so, it did not come into existence by the deliberate effort of a government threatened by conspirators. It was, in fact, created in 1861 in Baltimore, Maryland, by the directors of the Philadelphia, Wilmington, and Baltimore Railroad, who were afraid that their investment might suffer irreparable damage in the course of an attempt on the life of Lincoln, the president-elect, on his journey to Washington.

The directors of the P.W.B.R.R. got word that conspirators were planning to assassinate Lincoln on his way to the inauguration, stage a *coup d'état* on the European pattern in Washington, and isolate the capital by blowing up the bridges, tracks, and rolling stock of the railroad. When the directors of the railroad got wind of the plot, they called in Allan Pinkerton to do something about it. Pinkerton was an able Scotsman who had gained nationwide fame for his exploits as a private detective operating his own agency in Chicago.

Pinkerton went about the job in the most accomplished manner of modern-day counterespionage. He arrived in Baltimore under cover, using the alias E. J. Allen. He was accompanied by two of his operatives, Timothy Webster and Harry Davies, the latter turned counterspy after Jesuit training for the clergy. The three men were soon sitting in the bar of Barnum's Hotel, mingling with the conspirators and winning their confidence. Davies was, in fact, present at the meeting in which eight men were chosen by secret ballot to kill Lincoln as he passed through Baltimore. Pinkerton and his men had no power to arrest the conspirators, but they found out enough about the plot to devise a plan of their own that enabled Lincoln to reach Washington safely.

After that, Lincoln invited Pinkerton to organize a "secret service department" on a full-time basis, and the first counterespionage service worthy of the name was set up in a rented house on Eye Street in Washington. But such was the efficiency of the Southern spies, and so lacking was the support Pinkerton received from his own government, that his eventual failure was inevitable. Pinkerton was soon dismissed. But even in failure he pointed the way for others who were to follow.

In 1883, Britain established a "Special Branch" in Scotland Yard, initially to counter the plots of anarchists and nihilists, and subsequently to defend England from Irish Fenians who plotted the assassination of Queen Victoria during her jubilee celebration.

The next country to establish a counterespionage service on a full-time basis was France, in the wake of her disastrous defeat in the Franco-Prussian War of 1870-71. The Prussian campaign had been prepared by Chancellor Otto Bismarck, who employed 40,000 spies at a time when France had virtually none serving her own cause. The lessons of the war induced the French General Staff to build up its own intelligence services and to centralize them under one roof. The so-called Second Bureau was established within the General Staff and charged with both positive intelligence and counterespionage. A department for *Renseignements généraux* (general information) was added to the Directorate General of the *Sûreté Nationale*, the modern successor to the old political police, whose origins dated back to the fourteenth century.

The Second Bureau developed into a hotbed of domestic intrigue. It became best known, not for its successes in catching foreign spies, but for its despicable campaign against one of its own members, Captain Alfred Dreyfus. In that campaign, all the methods and paraphernalia of counterespionage were used to convict an innocent man, a victim of racial prejudice, while persons who actually served the Prussians as secret agents remained at large. The early history of the Second Bureau is a dark chronicle of intrigue and corruption. Its officers were selfish, devious, and callous men who undermined the efficiency of their own organization by treating their informants and agents in a contemptible manner.

217

Typical of the practices of the Second Bureau in those days was the case of Charles Lucieto, one of the Bureau's most loyal and useful informers. He was hired by the Bureau to serve as a double-agent, to offer his services to the Germans while actually spying for France. Lucieto performed well and loyally for France. But when his payment came due, the Second Bureau arrested him on charges of espionage for Germany to evade the obligation. The history of the Second Bureau abounds in such practices, one of several reasons why it never developed into a truly effective arm of counterespionage, and why France suffered more than any other country from the depredations of spies.

At the turn of the century, Russian spies made their appearance on the international scene and soon were swarming all over Europe. Counterespionage, practiced haphazardly until then, suddenly became an urgent necessity. The need was felt most keenly in Austria, where the Russians deployed their best operatives. In the face of this menace, the Austrians produced an exceptional counterspy in the person of Colonel Alfred Redl of their General Staff.

Although Redl was brilliant in positive intelligence as well, he really distinguished himself in counterespionage. Many methods still used today were originated by him. He was the first to place hidden microphones in rooms to record conversations. He concealed cameras in rooms and photographed suspects. He sprayed metal ashtrays with minium (red lead oxide) to obtain the fingerprints of suspects without their knowledge. He maintained a veritable museum of counterespionage in Vienna in which he exhibited all the tools of the trade and kept a collection of photographs of all the personalities in whom an agency of this nature could have even the remotest interest.

Yet Redl was himself an espionage agent—in the service of the Russians. They blackmailed him by threatening to expose him as a homosexual. Ironically, Redl was trapped in a remarkable coup of counterespionage by the very methods he himself had invented or developed. A clerk at the General Delivery window in the Vienna Central Post Office noticed the regular arrival of mysterious letters and reported the fact to the police. Some of the letters were surreptitiously opened and were discovered to be spy reports. The police set up a day-and-night watch in a precinct station across the street from the Post Office. The General Delivery counter was connected by wire to police station so that the clerk could alert the waiting detectives when anyone asked for mail addressed to "Opera Ball, 13." The police did not have long to wait. One day a man arrived and asked casually for letters addressed, "Opera Ball, 13." The police pounced. The man was Colonel Redl. When he was confronted with the evidence, he shot and killed himself.

The venality of the Second Bureau and the treachery of Redl illustrate some of the pitfalls of counterespionage. Enormous power is usually concentrated in the hands of men who head counterespionage agencies and they do not always use it judiciously. Instead of concentrating on foreign spies, they occasionally become involved in domestic intrigues and use their own conspiratorial apparatus to compound flourishing conspiracies. Such corruption not only jeopardizes their usefulness but actually sets them up as enemies of the countries they are supposed to serve. Necessary though counterespionage is in combating foreign agents, it is nevertheless imperative to circumscribe its powers and curb its chiefs. Otherwise, the services tend to become states within states, a greater menace than the espionage they were formed to counter.

After Redl's downfall the center of gravity shifted from Russia to Germany. Engaged in a bitter naval rearmament race with England, the Germans established an espionage network in the British Isles. There were twenty-two agents in their net, directed by a brilliant but erratic man named Gustav Steinhauer, who dubbed himself "the Kaiser's master spy." He had graduated to positive espionage from the German secret political police and then spent most of his time at the gambling tables of Belgian casinos. It was against such a spymaster and his motley crowd of agents, representing the German intelligence service, that England had to mobilize its own counterespionage forces. The urgent need for such a force was revealed by an accident.

In 1910, the Kaiser visited London to attend the funeral of Edward VII. His retinue included the acting chief of German naval intelligence, an officer well known to Scotland Yard's Special Branch. The officer was shadowed in the hope that he would lead agents of the Special Branch to some of his spies. One night the German left his hotel by a rear entrance and went to a modest house in a working-class district in London. The counterespionage agents trailed him there and established that the captain visited a hairdresser named Karl Gustav Ernst. After that, Ernst was kept under surveillance. It was soon learned that Ernst was receiving bulky letters from Germany. When Scotland Yard opened one of the letters, they found in it several sealed envelopes, addressed to individuals in various parts of Britain, properly franked with

219

English stamps. Then Ernst was observed mailing the letters one by one. Obviously, the man was a "letterbox." Obviously, too, the addressees were members of the German espionage network.

In due course, Scotland Yard obtained the names and addresses of all the twenty-two German agents in the British Isles and discovered that they were strategically placed in naval ports throughout all of England. It was decided to permit the men to remain at large, thereby initiating a method of counterespionage still used by most agencies today and known as "the long rope system." The term of course, is derived from the apothegm, "Give a man enough rope and he will hang himself."

In the "long rope system" counterespionage accepts the probability that once a spy is unmasked and arrested another one will take his place. Counterespionage is then obliged by a slow and tedious process to ferret out the replacement. Scotland Yard decided that it would be more productive to leave the original spy at his post, keeping him under constant surveillance, watching his mail and his contacts, and arresting him only in an acute emergency. An agent cannot do much harm when closely watched. But he can do his own cause harm if misleading information can be palmed off on him. Furthermore, an unmolested spy can lead watchful counterespionage to his associates and accomplices, and one by one the whole group can be arrested.

The morning after the outbreak of the First World War, Special Branch rounded up these known spies, together with about two hundred of their contacts and accomplices. At the very moment when Germany most needed them, not a single German spy was at large in England. After this brilliant coup, British counterespionage became known, respected, and feared throughout the world. It continued to function brilliantly throughout World War I, owing largely to the skill of Sir Basil Thomson, and to the aid he received from Admiral Reginald Hall, who was then reading the German cables as if they had been his own. One of Thomson and Hall's greatest scoops was the capture of Sir Roger Casement, who had been sent to Ireland by the German secret service to start a revolution in England's back yard.

Between the two world wars espionage flourished, chiefly because counterespionage was permitted to degenerate. An occasional German or Soviet agent was caught in Britain; German spies were caught in Japan; a few Japanese spies were caught in the United States. A cold war of espionage raged in central and eastern Europe, especially in Germany, where an intrepid Polish agent named Sosnovski managed to penetrate to the highest secrets of the German General Staff and obtained the deployment plan it had prepared for a war against Poland. Sosnovski was caught, not because he was incompetent, but rather because he was too good. He came to Berlin in 1934 with excellent credentials, to represent his father, a prominent international lawyer in Warsaw. Frequenting the most exclusive clubs, playing tennis, golf, and polo, he soon became the darling of Britain's highest society.

Before long he was carrying on a number of affairs simultaneously, as if trying to prove that a ladies' man is far more dangerous a spy than an ascetic. Although no one took particular notice of it, every one of his intimate women friends had close connections with the Reichswehr Ministry. At least two of them worked as confidential secretaries in the Ministry's Operations Department, one a middle-aged spinster whose affair with Sosnovski was the first love of an otherwise barren life, the other the nineteen-year-old daughter of a German general. They showed their gratitude by carrying their department's documents to Sosnovski, who copied them overnight and returned them the following morning in time for them to be replaced in the files before the offices opened for the day.

Sosnovski showered expensive gifts on his girl friends. He gave the youngest a fur coat which she paraded at home with the explanation that she had bought it herself with an increase she had received in her salary. Gratified by her daughter's rapid advancement, the girl's mother visited her superior to thank him for the raise. The officer acknowledged her thanks modestly, although he knew that the young fräulein had received no increase from his department. Then he promptly reported the incident to counterespionage, and the girl was placed under surveillance. Within four weeks, Sosnovski's secret was out, but by then Polish intelligence had copies of the German General Staff's highly classified and jealously guarded plans.

Counterespionage Agencies of Today

At the present time, most countries make a strict distinction between their counterintelligence and counterespionage organizations. Counterintelligence is usually assigned to military agencies, while counterespionage is conducted by civilian organizations that are either specially set up for the purpose or attached to existing agencies.

There are, of course, exceptions. In the Soviet Union, the Fourth Bureau of the Red Army General Staff deals exclusively with positive intelligence and has no negative function whatever. Counterespionage is assigned to the Ministry of the Interior, which is charged with all police functions and conducts counterespionage as part of its secret police work. During World War II, a special counterespionage agency was organized to serve in the field. It went by the abbreviated name of "Smersh," the telescoped syllables standing for the Russian words "Death to the spies." The name of the agency indicates the summary manner in which the Soviet Union deals with arrested foreign agents.

In France, the Second Bureau continues to function as the country's central counterespionage service. The General Staff now also has a Fifth Bureau, which handles cases of subversion both at home and in French territories overseas. Both of these bureaus are understaffed, employing between them only a few hundred persons. This shortage of personnel restricts their efficiency tremendously in a country where the danger of espionage, sabotage, and subversion is most acute.

There are no more than fifty detectives employed in that part of the *Sûreté Nationale* which is the counterespionage agency of France, conducting actual investigations on tips received from the Second and Fifth Bureaus and making arrests. The so-called General Information branch of the *Sûreté* is in charge of frontier defense, and, curiously enough, also of horse-racing and gambling. Its chief duty, however, is to collect political information for the heads of the administration and to defend the country from spies, saboteurs, and subversives. It is well equipped for the job so far as technical matters are concerned. The *Sûreté* has several police laboratories in the principal cities and a central laboratory in Lyon which is rated with the best in the world. It also maintains an excellent *Service de l'Identité Judiciaire*, which has on file photographs, fingerprints, and personal descriptions of innumerable espionage suspects.

Even so, counterespionage is hampered in France by the grave domestic difficulties of the country. The agencies are still politically inspired and often corrupt. They depend largely on the antiquated *dossier* system, the keeping of indiscriminate and unevaluated files. The system was inherited, together with its vicious implications, from the secret police of Joseph Fouché, Napoleon's ruthless and shrewd police minister. Some of Fouché's malicious methods still dominate counterespionage in France, although much of his comprehensive efficiency is lacking.

Western Germany, today a hotbed of espionage and the headquarters of innumerable spy rings, now has its own counterespionage agencies within the new *Bundeskriminalamt* (Federal Bureau of Crime Investigation), a relatively small branch of detectives with headquarters in Bonn. Its function is the protection of the president, the cabinet members, and the diplomatic corps, and also the operation of counterespionage. It has limited executive powers, but high technical efficiency.

Excellent counterespionage agencies exist in Switzerland, Italy, Belgium, the Netherlands, and the Scandinavian countries as well as in Israel, India, and Japan. All of these work within their respective police organizations and specialize in political police work and defense against espionage and subversion.

In Britain, the work of counterespionage is distributed between a branch of the War Office Military Intelligence Department, known the world over as MI-5, and the Special Branch of Scotland Yard's Criminal Investigation Department. Considering the tasks assigned to them, they are extremely small organizations. In 1939, when German espionage was at its peak, the Special Branch had only 156 detectives and administrative officers, and MI-5 had only a few investigators under its civilian head, Sir David Petrie. During the war, MI-5 was vastly enlarged to cope with the problems of the war waged on its secret fronts. But the Special Branch never had more than eight hundred employees. Today, MI-5 has only its normal complement of peacetime investigators, while the detectives assigned to the Special Branch number some two hundred. They are stationed at every airport and seaport and also serve as bodyguards for the royal family and prominent personages. Only a relatively small staff is then left to deal with movements regarded as subversive, and to track down espionage and sabotage suspects. Looking at it purely from the size of the organization, Britain's security is definitely limited. However, the numerical inferiority of the various British agencies in the field is compensated by their efficiency and by the exceptional competence of their personnel.

No matter how impressive past British scoops have been in the game of counterespionage, and no matter how elaborate similar organizations of other countries have been, they are all overshadowed by a relative newcomer to the game—the Federal Bureau of Investigation of the United States. Almost from the very first day in 1939 when the FBI joined the spy-hunters of the world as America's central counterespionage agency, it has functioned with unprecedented efficiency, and, what is even more important, with a scrupulous adherence to democratic processes.

In the business of counterespionage, the FBI represents the highest degree of competence. It is today, by any standard, the outstanding example of excellence in this field.

American Counterespionage and the FBI

Americans have every reason to be concerned about their security against conspirators who engage in espionage or sabotage. The safety of this republic was severely threatened by Benedict Arnold, whose subversive activities were calculated to defeat the American Revolution. A British spy named John Henry operated most efficiently in the United States in 1812 and succeeded in undermining the stability of President Madison's administration. Espionage complicated the efforts of the Union to defeat the Confederacy. Saboteurs caused substantial damage in World War I.

In World War II, a code clerk of the American Embassy in London betrayed some of this country's most valuable diplomatic secrets to the Germans and Italians. The espionage activities of native Americans helped the Soviet Union to acquire the atomic secrets of the United States.

Through its history, the United States has been on the receiving end of espionage, the target of positive intelligence. It has suffered considerably from the treachery of native agents and from the insidious activities of foreigners. Counterespionage, therefore, is an important responsibility of the United States government. But although the need has always existed, the recognition of it was rather late in coming.

The freedom with which espionage agents and saboteurs could formerly operate in the United States was only partly a result of the latitude that a democracy provides for such activities. To a far greater extent it was due to the fact that for 163 years of its existence, the United States had no properly organized, permanently functioning, central, counterespionage agency to deal with spies and saboteurs. The U.S. Army and Navy had counterintelligence branches within their intelligence organizations and the Army, in particular, had its own Counter Intelligence Corps and Criminal Investigation

Division. Other government agencies also had certain intelligence functions. But no coordinated effort or central agency existed. Most of the agencies active in the work were hampered by severe legal restrictions placed upon them, or suffered from shortages in funds and personnel. During the First World War, for example, counterespionage was assigned to the Secret Service, which was forced to prosecute this activity in addition to its numerous other commitments.

The result was that by the thirties the United States had become an open hunting preserve for spies. There would have been even more of them, except for the fact that the United States did not practice concealment on an efficient scale, but instead spread out virtually all its confidential affairs for anybody to read or observe. Actually it did not pay foreign countries to maintain extensive espionage organizations in the United States, since most of the information they wanted could be procured without the aid of spies.

Those who did work in America were inferior agents, left over after the better operatives were assigned to more important theaters. And if those who did come to the United States were rarely caught, it was chiefly because hardly an agency existed that could even follow their activities, much less catch them red-handed. Today there is a great deal of talk about belatedly exposed spies of bygone days. But such exposés must be viewed in perspective. It should be borne in mind that those spies were low-level, often untrained, agents, scrambling for largely unconcealed "secrets," and flourishing like mice in the absence of the cat. No serious damage to the United States accrued from their activities, no matter how much their work may now be magnified by self-seeking politicians or by ex-operatives who were themselves merely on the fringes of this espionage carnival.

The situation became serious only in the period beginning in 1938 and 1939 when aggressors in Europe and Asia compelled the United States to flex its own muscles. Then the foreign espionage services began to turn their earnest attention toward the United States. Spy rings of greater professional skill came into existence and began to expand. Better trained and more competent agents were dispatched to the United States. The recruiting of native agents was intensified.

Soviet espionage, in particular, became more interested in the United States. Originally, its only interest was in the so-called industrial "secrets" of this country, but it was quick to discover that most of these "secrets" were on the open market, available through regular commercial channels. They could be obtained simply by the payment of nominal fees at the U.S. Patent Office, or bought at somewhat greater expense from manufacturers themselves, who appeared most eager to do business with the U.S.S.R. These firms sold not only their products but also their secret formulas and special manufacturing processes. During those days, between 1924 and 1933, tanks, guns, planes, and warships were sold to the Soviet Union and exported openly with the proper licenses, issued by the State Department.

An occasional Soviet spy was uncovered in areas other than the industrial field. In 1931-32, an agent procured military data about the Panama Canal from a corporal of the U.S. Army. In 1932-33, another agent was found to be passing $100 Federal Reserve notes counterfeited under the direction of Soviet intelligence. The first espionage ring of any consequence was established in the United States in the mid-thirties by an agent named Gaik Badalovich Ovakimian. He managed to set up a large apparatus but found the pickings rather meager. His greatest achievement was the infiltration of the Justice Department in 1937 and 1938.

In 1938, a small net was discovered on the West Coast through a fortuitous accident. This ring had succeeded in infiltrating a naval district's intelligence office. In addition, a network of political espionage flourished in Washington. It was composed of starry-eyed dupes who held various positions in the United States government and supplied Soviet intelligence with information of such low value that most of it was not accepted by the collectors or, if it was, was never transmitted to Moscow.

The situation changed abruptly in 1938-39 with the appearance of German espionage agents on the scene. They were not particularly well organized and received only half-hearted support from Germany. A jurisdictional dispute raged among the various intelligence services in the Reich about the supervision of these agents. Moreover, because Hitler was anxious to maintain neutrality with the United States, the German Foreign Office opposed the utilization of espionage agents in this country.

Even so, it was left to a German spy to score the outstanding espionage scoop of those years. He was Hermann Lang, a simple technician employed in the Long Island plant of the C. I. Norden Company, which manufactured the famous Norden bombsight. At that time, the bombsight was widely publicized in the press as "America's No. 1 secret." Attracted by this publicity, the intelligence services of the world made energetic efforts to obtain its blueprints and, in the end, all of them did. But Germany was the first to succeed, through the efforts of Hermann Lang. Working at Norden as an expert draftsman and inspector in 1938, Lang memorized the bombsight's details, returned to Germany, and prepared a blueprint of the instrument from memory.

German intelligence was jubilant. The stocky, dark-haired Lang, a naturalized American with bushy eyebrows and sparkling brown eyes, was dined and wined. He was received by Hermann Göring, who thanked him personally for his great scoop and gave him 10,000 marks as a special bonus.

Lang was a member of one of the several German espionage rings that were set up one after another in the United States. They included a strange assortment of people. There were among them a notorious professional spy, several Nazi fanatics, and numerous beautiful women to give the drama its Hollywood touch. Although there is today a tendency to minimize the efficiency and effectiveness of German espionage in the United States shortly before World War II, the fact is that it was both efficient and effective. Every ship entering or leaving the port of New York, every military installation along the eastern seaboard, all fortifications, airfields, naval bases were reported by German agents to Berlin. A permanent card file maintained by one of the rings contained information about United States army camps, disposition of U.S. military forces, troop movements, and arms production. The information was accurate, detailed, and up to the minute. Still others sent data on so-called choke points in the United States to be sabotaged in the event of war. It was from such reports that Dr. Astor, chief of the Western Sabotage Section of German Military Intelligence, selected the targets for the "Pastorius" mission, Hitler's unsuccessful attempt to sabotage American industry with agents who were slipped ashore at night on Long Island and in Florida from German U-boats.

By 1939, the world situation had grown worse. War in Europe was imminent. There were indications that Japan also planned to intensify its espionage activities in the United States, and it was naturally expected that the Soviet Union would replace its amateurs with professional agents. The need for a central counterespionage agency in America was increasingly felt, especially when certain cases got tangled up between various competing agencies that were operating on shoe-string appropriations and with inadequate personnel.

On September 6, 1939, six days after the outbreak of the war in Europe, President Roosevelt issued a special directive in which he took cognizance of the danger and proclaimed the necessity of combating it with greater efficiency than had been shown previously by the scattered agencies. He was determined to end the bickerings and jealousies which interfered with the job. "To this end," the Presidential directive stated, "I request all police officers, sheriffs, and all other law-enforcement officers in the United States promptly to turn over to the nearest representative of the Federal Bureau of Investigation any information obtained by them relating to espionage, counterespionage, sabotage, subversive activities, and violations of the neutrality law." In the words of J. Edgar Hoover, the FBI became "a clearing-house for all matters concerning espionage, sabotage, and subversivism"—America's *central counterintelligence agency* in fact, if not in name.

Until then, the FBI was but one of several agencies engaged in counterespionage. Although normally eventual arrests in espionage and sabotage cases were made by FBI agents, and although the FBI was getting most of the newspaper publicity resulting from those exposés, the Bureau actually did little to develop espionage and sabotage cases. It was somewhat undermanned and far too busy for this extracurricular work. It had charge of "the investigation of all violations of Federal laws" with the exception of counterfeiting, postal violations, customs violations, and internal revenue matters. Even today, the FBI investigates violations of approximately 130 different Federal statutes, of which less than a dozen are concerned with "espionage, sabotage, treason, and other matters pertaining to the internal security of the United States." They include the Federal Kidnaping Statute, the National Bank Act, the White Slave Traffic Act, and the Atomic Energy Act of 1946—and also such statutes as, for example, the Migratory Bird Act.

In the past the FBI and its "G-men" were best known for their campaign against gangsters and racketeers, but today they are chiefly famous for their war against foreign spies. The appearance of the FBI in this specialized field brought an organization into counterespionage the likes of which had never existed before. Compared with its foreign counterparts, it has proved itself to be not only bigger but better, injecting practical, business-like American ideas and efficiency into a profession that in Europe had developed out of the musty past of a predatory secret political police.

With headquarters in Washington, D.C., it has 52 field offices throughout the United States, several training and technical installations and schools, and agents stationed abroad. More than 10,000 persons are permanently employed by the FBI. More than 5,000 of them are special agents, the majority of whom are today engaged in antisubversion work.

At the head of the Bureau, its director, J. Edgar Hoover, has stamped the mark of a remarkable personality not only on law enforcement in general but on counterespionage in particular. He is a dedicated scholar of crime detection. In the words of Alexander Holtzoff, a Washington judge, "Mr. Hoover himself represents the best type of career man in the government." He described Hoover as "a practical idealist," a man of an artistic temperament, and "highly sentimental not only in his own personal circle but also in his relations with all of his subordinates, and even at times in dealing with persons whom he has to arrest." But Hoover is also a strict disciplinarian, an able administrator, and a great educator.

Working under him are specially chosen subordinates who are capable of translating Hoover's theories into practice. The personnel of the FBI is chosen on the basis of careful selection, either for special skills or general aptitude for the job. A man's character and personal habits are dominant factors in selection. The FBI's personnel is not under the control of the civil service but is recruited and managed according to the principles laid down by its director and at his personal discretion. Efficiency methods developed by private enterprise are adopted by the Bureau, in addition to efficient police procedures developed within the organization itself, or imported from other services.

To supplement the work of its personnel the FBI maintains the world's most advanced technical criminal laboratories. Here and in special schools, agents are trained in cryptography, spectroscopic analysis, handwriting identification, fingerprinting methods, document identification, filing and indexing techniques, ballistics and explosives, general disguise and identification methods, communications equipment, photography, search and seizure methods, report writing, and the evaluation of information.

At headquarters, the Bureau maintains a filing system that contains the fingerprints and biographies of millions of people. Along with the data kept on law-abiding government and military personnel in this country as primary security measures, the FBI has at its fingertips similar data on espionage and sabotage suspects and potential alien subversives, both in the United States and abroad. Thanks to these files the FBI was able to round up or keep under constant scrutiny nearly every actual and potential German espionage agent in the United States in December, 1941. So thorough was the list that no effective German spy was left at large, and none showed up for the remainder of the war.

The honesty and integrity of the FBI are legendary. Agents are kept under strict discipline, and the slightest infraction of Bureau regulations may lead to dismissal. The result is that throughout its history this organization has been free of prejudice, corruption, and malfeasance in the course of law enforcement.

The FBI is extremely ethical and democratic. These qualities, naturally taken for granted by Americans as characteristic of any police force, point up a great distinction between the FBI and many foreign espionage agencies. The civil rights of individuals, including those accused of criminal actions, are stringently observed. Special agents are indoctrinated in the need for staying strictly within the law when conducting investigations, even though the law itself may frustrate their primary objective. The idea of a "secret police" or a "political police" is stressed as an abhorrent condition, and the fact that the agency is designed to *defend* democracy is emphasized.

The fact that it is publicly popular is an important element in the over-all efficiency and success of the Bureau. With the exception of Scotland Yard and MI-5, which are also popular with the general public, no other counterespionage agency of the world enjoys as much public confidence and cooperation as the FBI.

When, in September, 1939, the Federal Bureau of Investigation was established as the central counterespionage agency of the United States, it brought to its new task of detecting and trapping spies a wide experience in criminal investigation. The application of certain anticriminal methods to counterespionage is not always effective, and the FBI is striving to develop what Director Hoover himself calls "intelligence methods" to increase the Bureau's efficiency in this particular field. However, counterespionage, as distinct from security intelligence and counterintelligence, is an investigative activity whose methods are not much different from those of criminal investigation. In the final analysis, the spy and saboteur, whatever his motivations may be, is a violator of laws and therefore a criminal. Accordingly, counterespionage has the three phases that characterize modern police science: identification of persons, field work, and laboratory work to examine and analyze clues and traces discovered in the course of investigations.

Like modern criminal investigation, counterespionage also inquires into the methods and techniques the law violator has used in his approach to and perpetration of the crime. It apprehends the criminal, and gathers and collates information

230

on the facts and circumstances necessary for the prosecution of secret agents. The basic methods of finding a fugitive spy are not different from tracing a fugitive criminal. Interrogation has identical techniques in both investigations, as have surveillance and trailing. Like the police, counterespionage agencies also work with informers, plants, confidential informants, and denouncers. Both use the same methods to detect deception, and identical precision instruments for laboratory work. However, although all of this is true, there still remains a vast area of difference between criminal investigation and the detection of secret agents. Criminal investigation invariably begins at the scene of the crime, where it expects to find vital clues. At the same time, it tries to establish specific motives which presumably induced the criminal to his action. In espionage, there is rarely a "scene of the crime." The motive, if any can be found, hardly ever provides a decisive clue.

Even when espionage investigation uses the orthodox methods of criminal investigation, it applies them in its own special way. The three basic methods of counterespionage are identification, shadowing, and what is colloquially called "roping," the criminological jargon for worming oneself into a suspect's confidence, also called penetration or infiltration.

Identification is based on registration work, the maintenance of extensive files on as many potential secret agents as possible, as well as on authorized persons who have access to classified information in their regular daily work. Such files usually include the suspect's fingerprints, his photograph, and whatever biographical data is available. These records are ingeniously cross-indexed and so arranged as to be readily accessible when needed. They provide the basic clues which in routine criminal investigation would be present in a physical form at the scene of the crime. International exchange of information about suspects is designed to facilitate identification still further. Countries linked by mutual interest cooperate closely in the registration and identification of secret agents. This was shown in the case of Klaus Fuchs, who was arrested on a tip from the FBI, while the arrest of a "maildrop" in Scotland during the thirties resulted in the breaking of a German espionage ring in the United States.

Shadowing is the term used to describe the process of following an espionage or sabotage suspect wherever he goes. In a broader sense, this is done to keep him under constant surveillance, either to catch him in an incriminating act, or to uncover other members of his net or ring, as well as to obtain evidence needed for arrest and prosecution. Surveillance of a suspect often includes the tapping of his telephone, although espionage agents nowadays rarely use the phone. When they resort to it at all, they conduct their conversations in code to prevent anyone listening in from obtaining the clues or leads he seeks. It also includes the examination of a suspect's mail and the observation of his contacts. Counterespionage agents often work with concealed cameras and hidden microphones to obtain legally admissible documentation for subsequent prosecution.

Surveillance requires ingenuity and extreme patience. Secret agents are trained in the methods of the enemy and know how to shake off "shadows" and to conceal their activities even from the most ingenious methods of direct observation. Complications that counterespionage agents encounter during surveillance work make their effort a long and tedious process, occasionally enabling secret agents to perpetrate their crimes and to escape even when under active, day-and-night surveillance.

Probably most rewarding among the investigative methods of counterespionage is roping, or the infiltration into the agent's confidence and the penetration of his ring. This may be accomplished by counterespionage agents in disguises but usually is done by special go-betweens, called informers, plants, or double-agents.

The overwhelming majority of cases solved in counterespionage begin with a tip from an informant or plant. When such a tip is received the person denounced is usually put under surveillance. Experience shows that unless an agent himself commits some glaring blunder, counterespionage cannot by itself detect and develop a case absolutely from scratch without outside information. It is therefore ridiculous to detract from the efficiency of Scotland Yard or the FBI by pointing out that their most eminent successes were essentially due to outside efforts, and that they received undeserved publicity for the independent efforts of some other agency or individual. The eventual arrest of a secret agent is usually a long process, starting with the original tip that first brings him to the attention of the counterespionage agency. Enormous and complex effort is needed to prove espionage against a suspect in a democracy.

Even the testing of the initial tip is a serious matter, especially in agencies which receive virtually thousands of these denunciations every year. The weeding-out process is by no means foolproof. Irresponsible accusations consume much of the time of counterespionage agents, while often a tip that proves valuable in the end may appear useless when first received. No counterespionage agency has the staff necessary to track down every tip it receives. Perfunctory investigation and part-time surveillance usually do not yield the results in counterespionage frequently achieved in criminal investigation. During the first ten months of the Second World War, the FBI received 5,246 complaints of sabotage. When these complaints were investigated, it developed that most of them came, as Clyde A. Tolson, assistant director of the FBI, expressed it, "from disgruntled employees, cranks, persons who had grievances." In 1941, for example, the FBI succeeded in convicting 177 persons indicted, but only ten of them were what Tolson described as "actual sabotage cases."

Internal efficiency and technical competence are the two essential attributes of counterespionage. Scotland Yard and the FBI possess both to a high degree. But no matter how efficient and competent a counterespionage agency is, it cannot operate effectively without outside aid. Such cooperation must be forthcoming from all agencies of the government, and in particular from such intelligence and law enforcement agencies as the counterintelligence branches of Army, Navy, and Air Intelligence, the Central Intelligence Agency, regional or local police, and other Federal, state, and municipal law enforcement agencies as the Bureau of Customs, the Bureau of Internal Revenue, the Narcotics Bureau, the Post Office Department, and the Immigration and Naturalization Service.

Of equal, if not greater, importance is the collaboration of an intelligent, enlightened, and patriotic public free of hysteria. In this connection, J. Edgar Hoover once said: "The biggest job facing the American people in their protection of the home is the necessity for the average citizen to do something about his own protection. . . . If his home is safe, it will be safe only when he protects it. This does not mean armed force or physical effort; it implies, however, constant vigilance."

In counterespionage, informants and informers are of exceptional importance. All counterespionage agencies make widespread use of both. An informant is any person who occasionally or regularly reports observations of possible interest to the counterespionage service. An informer is a professional aide of the agency, who may or may not be paid for his services. He is planted under false pretenses within an opponent's organization or where he can deal personally with a suspect.

In addition, counterespionage agents make use of so-called provocateurs and double-agents. The former's job is that of a catalyzing agent, to provoke certain overt acts that will bring the conspiracy into the open and enable the law-enforcement agency to strike. Double-agents are used to give their services to an opponent while in fact they are informing on their activities, contacts, and associations to their own counterintelligence or counterespionage organizations. The job of the informer may not be completely ethical or admirable, but it is essential and often crucial. It may be stated categorically that, without such informers and double-agents, a counterespionage agency would be doomed to failure.

The FBI, in particular, is conscious of the pitfalls involved in the employment of informers, agents provocateurs, and double-agents. It goes to extreme lengths in screening and choosing them. A former Attorney General of the United States once outlined the principles that guide the Department of Justice in the selection and use of its informers. "I have taken personal pains," he said, "to inquire and satisfy myself as to the character, ability, and general worth of every one of the so-called undercover agents of the Department of Justice. . . . They are men of splendid character, of unusual intellectual attainments, and of a wonderfully high order of physical courage . . ."

In the course of its own evolution from a general law-enforcement agency preoccupied with criminal investigation to a central counterespionage agency, the FBI incorporated in its own work all these methods. Today it stands as the outstanding example of a counterespionage service centrally conducted, completely separated from all positive intelligence efforts. The whole complex of counterespionage, then, and in particular the FBI's method of executing it, may be illustrated by a case that typifies counterespionage at its best.

The Case of William G. Sebold

Shortly after World War I, a young veteran of the Kaiser's army came to the United States to escape the turmoil of postwar Germany and to try his fortune. His name was William G. Sebold. A mechanic by profession, he did not find it difficult to get a job. In due course, he became prosperous and established himself as a respected member of the California community in which he lived.

In 1939 he was working for the Consolidated Aircraft Company's San Diego plant and was earning enough to afford a vacation to visit relatives in Germany. He was anxious to go, and he feared that the coming war in Europe would force him to postpone his trip. Sebold's American passport listed his occupation as "airplane mechanic," and the German frontier authorities, who examined the passports of all German-Americans scrupulously, reported his arrival to the Nazi espionage organizations.

A few days after his arrival in Mülheim, his birthplace, Sebold received a visitor. The stranger was suave and polite, but his conversation was very much to the point.

"You are an airplane mechanic," the man said. "We can use men like you, especially in the United States."

"But I'm an American citizen," Sebold countered.

"What difference does that make?" the man said. "You're a German and we expect you to conduct yourself accordingly." The man demanded that Sebold surrender his U.S. passport and departed, leaving the confused German-American to ponder the next step. Sebold was confronted with a dilemma typical in such situations. If he agreed he would forfeit his right to regard himself as an American citizen, and if he refused to cooperate he would not be allowed to return to the United States. He decided to act as an American. He went to Cologne and called on the American consul, telling him everything that had happened. To his surprise, the consul advised him to do as the Germans proposed, to accept the offer and then wait for developments.

Still confused, but somewhat fortified by the assurances he received in Cologne that he would do a great service to his adopted country by spying against it for his native land, Sebold returned to Mülheim to await further instructions from the German espionage agency. He did not have long to wait, and, his acceptance completed, Sebold was sent surreptitiously to an espionage school in Hamburg where he was trained in special photography for the production of microfilm. He was taught codes, telegraphy, the operation of short-wave transmitters, and the use of secret inks. It was obvious that the Germans were training him to serve as the transmitter of a spy ring, the member whose job it is to transmit the information that others collect.

On January 27, 1940, Sebold was called to the office of Nicholas Fritz Ritter, a Gestapo officer who functioned as the principal of the spy school.

"Are you familiar with the Norden plant on Long Island which manufactures the secret American bombsight?" Ritter asked.

"I never heard of it," Sebold said on first impulse, but then

235

corrected himself. "Of course, I could probably find out everything about that bombsight. Perhaps I could even get its blueprints."

"You don't need to exert yourself," Ritter said. "We already have the blueprint. You will work for us in America as a radio operator." He handed Sebold a slip of paper with four names and addresses on it. "These are the collectors for whom you will work," Ritter said. "Here, memorize their names and addresses."

Sebold was then given an American passport made out to "William G. Sawyer," and a cover story to go with the name. He was handed five long documents reduced to the size of postage stamps and told to conceal them in the back of his watchcase. They were instructions for the collectors in New York. He was paid an advance of $1,000 and was told that $5,000 was awaiting him in a Mexican bank. Finally, he was given detailed instructions: "Upon arrival, you will open an office in midtown Manhattan where you will meet the collectors and receive from them their material. You will set up your transmitter in a house somewhere on the Long Island coast and transmit the information by radio."

A few weeks later, traveling on the S.S. *Washington*, Sebold arrived in New York and went to work at once to carry out his instructions. He formed a company he called Diesel Research Company, and rented an office on 42nd Street in New York. In his house in Centerport, Long Island, he installed his short-wave transmitter. Then on May 31, 1940, Sebold locked himself in the room where his radio stood and, at 6 P.M. sharp, prepared the machine to transmit the first information he had received from his collectors.

"CQDXVW-2 calling AOR." Sebold tapped out the prearranged signal.

"Go ahead CQDXVW," an operator at AOR in Germany replied.

"I'm ready to send," Sebold tapped out.

"Splendid," Germany answered, when Sebold had completed his message, and continued with new instructions for the American ring. "Need urgently from all friends data on monthly production of aircraft factories, exports to all countries, especially to England. Number, type, date of delivery by steamer or air. Payment cash-and-carry or credit."

Sebold confirmed the message.

"Rose has money for you," the man in Germany signaled.

Sebold acknowledged and signed off.

For months afterward messages went out from CQDXVW-2 in Centerport, U.S.A., to AOR in Hamburg, Germany, from

Sebold alias Sawyer to Rittler alias Rankin. But there was someone else listening to the signal, too. It was the FBI. From the moment Sebold went to the American consul in Cologne, he was a spy, but only nominally for the Germans. He was what is known as a double-agent, actually a trusted key figure in the American counterespionage network. Sebold was in daily touch with special agents of the FBI. They drafted most of the messages he sent to Hamburg, and his radio was actually operated by communications specialists of the Department of Justice. In his office on 42nd Street, the FBI set up concealed microphones to record the conversation of all his visitors. Cameras were hidden to photograph them. The collectors with whom Sebold worked were placed under surveillance, and the whole ring of German spies was firmly under control.

This game went on for more than a year. Then, on the evening of June 28, 1941, the FBI struck. The entire ring that Sebold serviced with his radio was rounded up. They in turn led the FBI to another ring, and its members were also taken into custody. The Germans were astounded. They had become convinced that their intricate system was invulnerable, and they could not imagine where the leak was. At their trial they got the answer. The FBI produced a witness whose detailed testimony sealed their fate. He was, of course, William G. Sebold.

The Sebold case is a classic example of counterespionage. It proves again the importance of having an informer within a spy ring. It shows how a single informer, if strategically placed, can lead counterespionage agents to a whole ring. It showed, too, how an informer or double-agent serves as a decoy to trap other agents who are not immediately connected with his own network.

The discovery of these rings eliminated virtually all German espionage agents working in the United States in 1941. The period between the arrest of these men and women and the bombing of Pearl Harbor was not great enough to permit their replacement before America imposed wartime counterespionage measures. The action of the FBI in this one major case was manifold in its consequences and, although there occurred isolated cases of espionage and sabotage in the United States during the war, all organized efforts by the enemy to these ends failed.

In wartime, espionage is confronted with added difficulties, one of which is, of course, the intensification of counterespionage. The defensive forces of the battle of espionage are enlarged and broadened, and certain agencies are brought into existence which, in most countries, exist only in wartime to cope with the specific problems of espionage in war. The small counterintelligence forces of the armed forces are expanded. The Army's CIC and CID are given police powers. Naval Intelligence enters the picture more energetically and the Coast Guard also adds its forces to the defensive network of a country organized to combat spies and saboteurs.

Of the agencies specially established or enlarged to cope with the problems of wartime espionage one of the most important is the Office of Censorship. Strictly speaking, censorship is a counterintelligence or security measure, rather than a counterespionage function; it functions preventively, it conducts no investigations of its own. Whenever a suspicious piece of correspondence turns up, censorship forwards it to the proper authorities to determine what is behind it. Even so, censorship is appropriately dealt with here as a counterespionage activity, if only because censorship is regarded as an auxiliary arm of the defensive forces organized against espionage agents.

Censorship

The scope of censorship may be shown by a few figures. During its brief stay in Europe during the First World War, the military censors of the American Expeditionary Force received 30,846,630 letters, of which more than six million pieces were actually examined. Although a secret-ink laboratory was established in France only three months before the war ended, it nevertheless examined 53,658 suspicious documents referred to it by censors. During World War II, the British postal censors had 800,000,000 pieces of mail referred to them, of which more than two million pieces had to be subjected to some kind of scientific analysis in the laboratory. In the First World War, Britain employed more than 5,000 persons in censorship. The number of military censors was more than 10,000 in the Second World War. In the United States, too, thousands worked in the Office of Censorship, examining millions of documents.

A distinction must be made between censorship on the home front and that in the active theaters of operation. The military censor examines mail of overseas personnel, while the home front censor today examines all branches of communication, including the press, radio, and television. Censors work in close cooperation with the security organs and counterespionage agencies of their countries, and receive from them so-called suspect lists, composed of the names and aliases of persons who are suspected of espionage, sabotage, or subversion. Often the names of very highly placed personages appear on suspect lists. In the First World War, for example, the queens of Greece, Sweden, and Spain were included in all Allied suspect lists, as was General Wille, chief of staff of the Swiss Army, known for his pro-German sympathies.

While the democracies maintain censorship bureaus only during war or national emergencies, totalitarian countries maintain them on a permanent basis. The censorship office of Czarist Russia, known as the Black Cabinet, attained conspicuous notoriety. Headed by an infamous double-agent named Karl Ziewert, an Austrian by birth, it examined the correspondence of the political opponents of the czar, and also of his own statesmen, generals, grand dukes, and the czar himself. Ziewert is remembered as an ambitious and ingenious censor, and some of the tools still used in censorship to detect concealed messages were invented by him.

Today censors have delicate instruments which enable them to steam open envelopes and seal them again without leaving a trace. Wax seals can be lifted from envelopes with heated blades or hot wire, and with an intricate little machine originally invented by Ziewert. Censors subject suspicious documents to thermal examination and to chemical or stereoscopic analysis to bring out invisible writings. They also examine certain pieces under ultraviolet or infra-red rays. Censors have means of detecting photographs which have been reduced to microscopic size, simply by enlarging them until they become easily legible.

When a clue is found by censors, it is forwarded to the agencies that conduct counterespionage through investigation. Such clues are extremely useful, since they often contain concrete evidence in the franking and other postmarks, and in the signatures and names of addressees, although the latter are usually concealed mail-drops. These clues enable counterespionage agents to start from a definite premise and, in many cases, help them in tracking down an espionage agent who has compromised his own security by entrusting his message to the mails or other media of open communication.

There is a saying in counterespionage circles that for every spy caught ten remain at large. Some are living on borrowed time, enjoying the temporary benefit of the "long rope." Others are working successfully and without fear of exposure, their identities and missions unknown to the agencies trying to counter them.

If secret agents take risks, so do the countries against which they work so insidiously. Espionage is a game of give and take. Positive espionage is enormously important and no present-day power can afford to neglect it. But for the defense and survival of a country, counterespionage is probably even more important. It is in the truest sense of the word a country's first line of defense.

PART V

Propaganda

What Is Political Warfare?

Intelligence operations frequently transcend the narrower confines of the intelligence service and resort to intrigue in more subtle form, with far greater emphasis on the intellectual potential than in those phases we have previously witnessed. That aspect of intelligence in which information is used aggressively to manipulate opinion or to create special conditions by purely intellectual means is called political warfare. In recent years, political warfare has come to be regarded as a permanent addition to the established forms of human conflict.

According to Sir Robert Bruce Lockhart, wartime director-general of Britain's superbly efficient Political Warfare Executive, this phase of intelligence practices every form of overt and covert attack that can be called political, as distinct from military. It is that form of intelligence operations that uses ideas to influence policies. It deals with opinions and with their communication to others. It is organized persuasion by non-violent means, in contrast to military warfare in which the will of the victor is imposed upon the vanquished by violence or the threat of it.

Political warfare is a British term. In other countries the activity is known by different names. In Germany, for example, it is called *geistige Kriegführung*, intellectual warfare, to stress the fact that it is war waged primarily in the intellectual or spiritual sphere, a contest of ideas. In the Soviet Union where, under the influence of Clausewitz, all warfare is considered political, this particular form of aggression is called propaganda and agitation. In the United States, it is called psychological warfare or morale operations, the former to indicate that it is the application of psychology to the conduct of war, the latter to suggest that it is aimed at the morale of an opponent.

In actual fact, none of these terms expresses the real scope of political warfare. The terms used in the particular countries mentioned above mean chiefly propaganda, the organized effort to influence the attitudes of people on controversial issues. However, political warfare is a more comprehensive concept than that, since in addition to propaganda it may also include diplomatic action and economic moves used in a coordinated manner to attain a nation's ends.

Diplomacy may be used, for example, to persuade nations to enter into alliances or remain neutral; or to break up opposing alliances. It can be applied to terminate wars by negotiations even while military operations continue undiminished. Diplomacy was used in this manner in 1945, when efforts were made to conclude hostilities with Japan in the diplomatic rather than the military sphere.

Aside from diplomacy, political warfare may also involve specific economic moves, the blockading of enemies, the withholding from them of essential raw materials by so-called preclusion buying, the special manipulation of tariffs. In 1935, when Britain endeavored to persuade Italy to refrain from attacking Ethiopia, it exerted diplomatic influence through the League of Nations and also applied to Italy economic pressures in world trade. At the present time, the United States restricts trade with Communist countries, while simultaneously providing lavish economic aid to its allies. This is essentially political warfare. However, both diplomatic and economic warfare are independent activities. They are conducted by special agencies, such as the diplomatic corps or organizations dedicated specifically to economic warfare. They are designed to affect large numbers of people, but they make no direct appeals to those people. Diplomacy in particular is conducted within its own confines, often in secrecy, and without directly approaching the masses.

What Is Propaganda?

In the sense in which we understand the relation between all intelligence operations, propaganda alone is the major implement of political warfare. The term is used comprehensively here, to include what the British call political warfare, the Germans intellectual warfare, and we in the United States psychological warfare or morale operations. It is the deliberate and organized effort to spread ideas, doctrines, and principles for the distinct purpose of gaining adherents, followers, or allies; to persuade people of the justness and logic of one's cause and the erroneousness and injustice of the opponent's cause; and especially to make others act in a manner advantageous to one side and detrimental to the other.

The ultimate purpose of propaganda is to make others act exactly as we want them to act or to think exactly as we want them to think. It is essentially a totalitarian effort, since it imposes ideas on people without allowing disagreement. In fact, propaganda strives to exclude all opposing arguments, never permitting its objects an alternative. It expects its audience to accept its argument without qualification or equivocation, in contrast to the theory of education and information in which the audience is permitted to study all sides of an issue without bias.

Propaganda is never objective. Although today much is said about "truth in propaganda," the fact is that propaganda is always biased and subjective. Since it is a functional effort with a utilitarian purpose, it is subordinate to selfish design. It goes without saying that propaganda must give the appearance of truthfulness, since mendacity, invented "facts," and palpably spurious arguments are certain to defeat the very purpose of propaganda. However, even the most truthful propaganda is slanted, if only to the extent of the effect of what it leaves unsaid. In the final analysis, propaganda need not be actually truthful as long as it is plausible.

The Germanic theories of warfare and the Communist principles of revolution are strange and repugnant to Americans and Britons, since they do not conform to accepted ideas of moral human conduct. Yet what to us appears as unjustified and barbaric is acceptable to large numbers of people. What may seem false to some may still appear true to others, or, as W. I. Thomas expressed it, "If men define situations as real, they are real in their consequences."

We distinguish between spiritual propaganda, which promotes faith and religious ideologies, and temporal propaganda, which has political designs and aspirations. Spiritual propaganda long preceded temporal propaganda as an organized activity. It was an important instrument of the Roman Catholic Church long before nations used it for their own purposes. The famous sermon in which Pope Urban II called for the First Crusade in November, 1095, at Clermont, France, was a monumental act of propaganda. In 1622, Pope Gregory XV founded what may be called the world's first "propaganda agency," the *Congregatio de propaganda fide,* to propagate the Catholic faith.

Temporal propaganda has become an organized activity of nations only in recent years, but in its primeval form it is as old as man's ability to communicate his ideas. It was used by

243

Gideon when he succeeded in convincing the Midianites that his own force of only three hundred warriors was superior in numbers to their big army. It was utilized by Wang Ming in China and by the Athenian Themistocles, whose shrewd use of propaganda Herodotus described as follows:

"Themistocles, having selected the best sailing ships of the Athenians, went to the place where there was water fit for drinking, and engraved upon the stones inscriptions, which the Ionians, upon arriving the next day at Artemisium, read. The inscriptions were to this effect, 'Men of Ionia, you do wrong in fighting against your fathers and helping to enslave Greece. Rather, therefore, come over to us or, if you cannot do that, withdraw your forces from the contest and entreat the Carians to do the same. But if neither of these things is possible, and you are bound by too strong a necessity, yet in action, when we are engaged, behave ill on purpose, remembering that you are descended from us and that the enmity of the barbarians against us originally sprang from you.'"

In the American War of Independence and again in the Civil War, propaganda played a strong role. In the archives of the Department of the Army there is preserved a long leaflet addressed by "An Old Soldier" to the British redcoats about to embark for the Colonies, pleading with them to lay down their arms; there is a leaflet inviting the British at Bunker Hill to desert. They lie side by side with the famous surrender leaflets of World War II, which were typically short and to the point.

It was not until late in World War I that the potential of the cunningly chosen word was recognized as often superior to the potential of the physical weapon. A German general of infantry wrote: "We expend a lot of costly ammunition trying to destroy the gun in the hands of a soldier. Would it not be cheaper to devise means whereby we might paralyze the fingers that pull the triggers of those guns?"

Propaganda crept into the strategems of World War I until it became a "bluff barrage." Its basic aim was then, and is now, to minimize defeats and magnify victories, to establish one's own cause as just and certain to triumph, and to depreciate the cause of the enemy, doomed to failure.

The first in World War I to lay down this "bluff barrage" were the British. They introduced systematized propaganda as a full-fledged implement of war and assigned Lord Northcliffe, the British newspaper publisher, to organize and conduct it. His work was so effective that the Germans announced, "The enemy has founded a 'Ministry for the Destruction of German Confidence' at the head of which he has put the most thoroughgoing rascal in all the Entente—Lord Northcliffe." The results of British propaganda during World War I were strange indeed. Most of it was aimed at the enemy's troops in the field, yet it served to impair and then crush the morale of the whole German nation. While most often defeatism begins on the home front and then spreads to the troops, it was the other way around in the First World War. Every soldier on leave from the front became an unwitting agent of Northcliffe's. He repeated slogans and assertions of British propaganda and talked of Germany's defeat as if it were an accomplished fact. The German General Staff was scandalized and frightened. "Instances like these," General Erich Ludendorff complained, "drag the honor and respect of the individual and of the whole army into the mud, and have a disastrous effect upon the morale of the people at home."

American propaganda in 1917-18 was confined to the dissemination of the truth everywhere. "You could not keep our people long supporting a war," General Dennis E. Nolan, chief of intelligence of the American Expeditionary Force, said, "unless they knew what was happening." The same method was applied to the enemy. The American chief of staff insisted that public announcement be made regularly of what would normally be regarded as a closely guarded military secret: the number of American soldiers landed in France. He properly expected that such announcements would go far in discouraging the enemy in the sight of this ever-growing force, while his own strength was diminishing by the hour.

The climax of the Allied propaganda effort in World War I was the proclamation of President Woodrow Wilson's Fourteen Points. These promised much to victor and vanquished alike and assured the enemy of humane treatment in defeat. It was not designed as propaganda but evolved from Wilson's humanitarian and civil approach to the whole issue of war and peace. However, it became propaganda in its effect and did speed the end of German resistance.

The Propaganda Effort

Within the propaganda spectrum we distinguish between so-called white, grey, and black propaganda. White propaganda is the open and undisguised activity of a country which clearly identifies itself as the source of the effort. The mass of information going out of the United States today under the auspices of the government's information program is white propaganda.

In grey propaganda the source is clearly identified, but the appeal is slanted to serve a definite propaganda purpose. The operation of Radio Free Europe is in the category of grey propaganda. This is a broadcasting network maintained with private funds by an organization called the National Committee for a Free Europe for beaming appeals to the countries in eastern and southeastern Europe (Poland, Czechoslovakia, Hungary, Rumania, Bulgaria, and Albania) which are under Communist domination. The purpose of these broadcasts is to counter Communist propaganda in those countries, to provide a platform for exiled politicians, and to supply information about events in the free world, the sort of news that is not otherwise available to people living in countries where no freedom of information prevails. Although the source of all material emanating from Radio Free Europe is clearly identified, it uses intelligence in the preparation of its appeals and so slants it as to be most effective in the war of wits. Radio Free Europe is an effective instrument of the cold war, if only because it succeeds in undermining the propaganda monopoly of the Communists in the countries occupied by them, and because it serves as a constant reminder to the listener behind the Iron Curtain that he is neither forgotten nor forsaken. The very existence of this major propaganda instrument indicates to him that Communist occupation in those countries is of a temporary nature and that the free world uses whatever means are available to it to bring about the eventual liberation of oppressed peoples.

A major wartime example of grey propaganda was a campaign run by the mythical Commander Robert Norden of the United States Navy, who talked to officers and men of the German Navy in their own language. It fell into the grey category, despite the fact that its source was clearly identified, chiefly because it depended entirely on intelligence material in the formulation of its appeals, and because it was conducted in support of and in cooperation with conventional military operations. A similar campaign was conducted by Captain Ellis M. Zacharias, of the United States Navy, with the purpose of persuading the Japanese high command to seek peace by unconditional surrender. Captain Zacharias tried to provide arguments for a peace party within Japan's highest echelons and to convince his audience that further resistance was hopeless. Both operations were conducted within an intelligence agency of the United States Navy and were clearly labeled as intelligence operations.

Black propaganda is a fundamental intelligence operation, not only because it uses intelligence material solely as its ammunition, but because it is an independent maneuver conducted in an atmosphere of surreptitiousness. Black propaganda never identifies its real source. It pretends to originate within or close to enemy or enemy-occupied territory, and to be conducted by subversive elements in the enemy's midst. This is a highly secret activity, since its exposure would terminate its usefulness. Today there are several agencies conducting black propaganda on both sides of the Iron Curtain, but they flourish mostly in times of war. Britain is particularly adept at conducting black propaganda. The two most successful such efforts to date were both conducted by British agencies during World War II. One of them was a clandestine radio station called *Geheim Sender Eins* or "Secret Transmitter No. 1," over which the broadcasts of a propagandist called *Der Chef*, The Boss, were beamed. The Boss was a British journalist named Sefton Delmer. He became one of the authentic men of mystery of World War II when he suddenly vanished from sight. Even his name became taboo. His colleagues called him "the Beard," because of the whiskers he cultivated. In the United States, we used to refer to him as "Henry VIII," because this corpulent, bearded, whimsical, quarrelsome Briton reminded some of us of that long-dead king. His skill was universally admired, and today Delmer is regarded as one of the outstanding exponents and practitioners of black propaganda.

On the air, Delmer pretended to be a senior officer of the Wehrmacht with a good record in World War I. He was intensely "patriotic" in a rather petulant German way, but he was against everything. He hated the British, the Jews, the Russians, the Nazis, everybody in the world. This lively combination of boisterous hatred made him irascible and truculent, and soldiers, usually full of beefs of their own, loved to listen to someone who seemed to echo their collective grievances. There was something else that attracted listeners to The Boss. He was the most profane and obscene broadcaster ever to soil the air waves. He bandied about the usual words of trench lingo, but in his scathing delivery they sounded like so many words of endearment.

The Boss went to extreme lengths to gain the confidence of his German audience. At one point he picked a notoriously inefficient German officer whose blunders had resulted

247

in the annihilation of a battalion, and had him denounced on one of the regular "white" B.B.C. broadcasts beamed to Germany. Later he learned that the denunciation had drawn blood. The German High Command had the officer arrested and made him face a court martial. At this stage The Boss decided to intervene. He launched into a bitter denunciation of the German High Command for acting on a tip from the British radio. "Since when are we taking our orders from those confounded British?" he asked with pathos. "Who are they, anyway, to tell us what to do with our own officers? If this goes on, we'll soon have all our officers before court martials—and isn't that exactly what the bloody Englander wants? To err is human, isn't it? Most of our officers err once in a while and they cannot help it if it results in the annihilation of a battalion. Such is war!"

Several times each week the ribald Boss went on the air to hammer at the Germans with his blasphemies, obscenities —and extremely interesting information in which propaganda was shrewdly concealed. He supplied the most intimate details of Hitler's private life. He revealed controversies within the German High Command over operational plans. He mongered gossip and peddled scandal. This, in a sense, was as much a triumph of intelligence as propaganda. It showed the excellence of the intelligence material on which The Boss had based his uncouth, vulgar rantings.

Although the German soldiers listened regularly to *Der Chef*, they rarely doubted the fact that it was an enemy broadcast. Incidentally, until June, 1942, even the U.S. Military Intelligence Service had no positive proof that *Geheim Sender Eins* was where it was. The British let no one in on the secret and conceded their parentage of this fabulous intelligence-propaganda operation only when a couple of American intelligence specialists confronted them with conclusive evidence obtained through a smart piece of detective work the details of which cannot be discussed.

In addition to radio, black propaganda employs a great variety of media. They include underground newspapers which imitate the appearance of well-known dailies. A famous example of this medium was the imitation of the mass-circulation *Soir*, which the Belgian underground published during World War II. Another means of black propaganda is the smuggling of subversive material to specific addressees through the mail. German operations in this field included the sending of letters to French soldiers from their home towns, alleging that their wives were committing adultery. The Nazis sent enormous quantities of their propaganda through the

U.S. mail, and similar material was disseminated by the Japanese, most of it from clandestine sources.

Mass-mailing of propaganda material is practiced with the realization that many of the communications may never reach their addressees. It is still effective however, because it overburdens censorship and ties up the regular mail and thus interferes with morale.

Black leaflets and pamphlets are most effective when properly composed and efficiently distributed. This is an art in which the Communists excel because they were dependent on leaflets and pamphlets as news media for so long before the radio was available for propaganda.

The means of black propaganda are many. Some of them represent bold violations of international law but cause endless embarrassment to the enemy. Among these more violent forms are the counterfeiting of enemy currencies and the forging of ration cards and identification papers. If nothing else is gained, the enemy's bureaucratic apparatus is tied up and his secret police is kept busy conducting investigations. The essence of this, as of all black propaganda, is to confuse the enemy authorities.

The Media of Propaganda

Propaganda—white, grey, and black—depends on established conventional means of communications. Chief among these media is the radio, and the time may not be far off when television will also be used. Although it probably seems as if radio propaganda has been with us always, it is only a little more than twenty-five years old. The Soviet Union was the first and the United States the last to employ radio as a propaganda carrier. Germany began broadcasting propaganda appeals to foreign audiences within a few weeks of Hitler's seizure of power. France responded almost immediately with the establishment of Radio Strasbourg, which beamed propaganda appeals to Germany. It was operated by a few refugees from Nazi persecution.

After that the empire and overseas services of the British Broadcasting Corporation were instituted with a two-fold propaganda aim: to tie the empire closer to the mother country and to serve as an instrument of British foreign policy. Throughout the propaganda contest, in peace and war, the B.B.C. has retained uncontested leadership in this effort, chiefly because it succeeds in concealing the propaganda aim of its broadcasts behind a civilized and seemingly objective form of delivery. The B.B.C. is remarkable for the accuracy of its broadcasts and for their high intellectual level. During the war, it served as Britain's most important link with the world at large. The chief ammunition of B.B.C. propaganda was the news, presented with a conspicuous show of objectivity.

Gradually other countries followed suit, and the United States designated the National Broadcasting Company, the Columbia Broadcasting System, and a firm called the World Wide Broadcasting Foundation to conduct international propaganda by broadcasts. During the Second World War the United States established a Coordinator of Information, later an Office of Facts and Figures, and eventually the Office of War Information, for broadcasting to the world, to both friend and foe. The Coordinator of Inter-American Affairs conducted propaganda to Latin-American countries.

During the Second World War the air waves were overcrowded with propaganda broadcasters operating on both sides of the global front. There was Tokyo Rose, the collective name of a number of Japanese propagandists who specialized in tactical intelligence, often identifying American units which had just arrived in the Pacific to create a sense of superior Japanese intelligence, an important feature of effective propaganda. There was Axis Sally, the Nazi Lorelei, who cooed her way into GI hearts. And Lord Haw Haw, an expatriate Anglo-Irishman named William Joyce who deserted to the Nazis with his chief asset, a thick British accent in which he tried to shake the morale of the British people. The Free French operated a radio station in Brazzaville, on the Congo River in French Equatorial Africa. The Russians conducted their radio propaganda on an enormous scale, using Radio Moscow on innumerable wavelengths, broadcasting in scores of languages.

Next to radio, the printed word is the chief medium of propaganda dissemination. In this category are newspapers and periodicals, books, brochures, and leaflets. Leaflet propaganda in particular is widespread in times of war, and it is used today by the National Committee for a Free Europe which sends leaflets by balloons to the satellite countries of Europe. During the First World War the number of leaflets prepared by the belligerents were dropped by the millions, and in the Second World War the total number of leaflets dropped amounted to billions. During one single week in September, 1951, the National Committee for a Free Europe sent to Czechoslovakia thirteen million leaflets, approximately twenty-five percent of the total number of leaflets the Allies dropped on Germany in World War I.

The motion picture is another medium of propaganda dissemination, and today both the United States and the Soviet Union make the most of it. According to C. D. Jackson, one of the foremost proponents of American propaganda, "more people see American films in Europe and in the rest of the world than at home." Audiences totaling 110,000,000 people see American movies abroad every week, while the total weekly audience at home is 90,000,000. Behind the Iron Curtain, much of the Soviet propaganda appeal is carried by motion pictures, since all movies made in Communist countries must carry propaganda messages.

Propaganda Manipulations

Whatever media are used, propaganda must be painstakingly prepared with seven specific principles in mind. The basic principle requires that whenever it is used aggressively it must be aimed at personalities rather than issues. Concentration on personalities simplifies the problem, since underlying issues are usually complex and cannot be handled with the simplicity that propaganda basically requires to be effective and widely understood. It is generally accepted in the newspaper world that "names make news"; the same principle prevails in propaganda.

Second, it must be carefully camouflaged so as not to appear as propaganda. Conducted in the name of propaganda it is bound to fail. It cannot be conducted in a detached manner.

Third, propaganda must be based on intelligence and knowledge, on evaluated information, and especially on a close familiarity with the political, intellectual, military, economic, and emotional trends of the country and the people to which it is directed. A fluent knowledge of the language in which the propaganda is conducted is a prime condition, since audiences resent the misuse of their native tongue by foreign speakers.

Fourth, propaganda must never appear to create issues, but instead must recognize existing issues and treat them in a manner most advantageous to the propaganda cause. Communist propaganda rarely uses Communism as an issue, but concentrates instead on issues prevalent in the target countries, such as unemployment, internal dissension, or political unrest. It exploits the issues by twisting them. It then bases its argument on the twisted interpretation.

Fifth, propaganda must never be rigid or stationary, but must be adaptable to daily developments, always prepared to shift its interpretation of an issue to conform to a changing scene.

Sixth, propaganda cannot be conducted by remote control. While directives and instructions may come from a central propaganda authority, the actual tenor of propaganda material must be left to the discretion of the men who disseminate it.

Seventh, propaganda must utilize all existing facilities, especially the citizens of the countries to which the propaganda is directed, by winning them over to function as its unwitting carriers.

In developing a propaganda plan, it must be borne in mind that it must be simple and repetitious, without being monotonous, harping on the same ideas over and over again. While it is sometimes aimed at reason, it is usually directed at the emotions. In emotional appeals propaganda pits love against hatred, justice against injustice, truth against lies. In order to enhance the effectiveness of a propaganda theme, it should be boiled down to a slogan, which then is repeated relentlessly. A brutal quality is frequently regarded as an important element of good propaganda, not only because it shows strength, but because it is provocative and is most likely to attract attention. "Propaganda and terror are not opposites," the German expert Eugen Hadamovsky wrote. "Violence, in fact, can be an integral part of propaganda." The role of violence, he added, is "the lightning-like effect of exciting attention and manipulating it at the propagandist's will."

According to the best qualified experts, the most effective propaganda is the show of power and success. Victory is infinitely more effective than the promise of victory. When the aim of propaganda is to promote peace, it is by no means sufficient only to talk about peace; it is necessary to put forward some concrete plan designed to promote peace. If the aim is to terrorize, threats are insufficient in effective propaganda; there must be actual terrible deeds to exploit.

Propaganda does not try to make direct converts to the doctrine it is designed to propagate. It is only supposed to undermine resistance to the acceptance of new ideas by using whatever argument is most likely to influence those to whom it is addressed. In good radio advertising, the merchant rarely describes his product in physical detail but instead stresses the advantages it provides. Soviet propaganda rarely advertises in terms of Communist theories, but endeavors to win adherents by promising the solution of economic and social inequalities and the improvement of unpopular conditions.

Rumor as a Propaganda Weapon

Word-of-mouth spreading of news and rumor is a widely recognized and effective channel of propaganda. There are those who believe that rumor has almost as great an influence on public opinion as the radio or press. Rumor can be used positively to enhance the position of those who spread it, or to promote favor for their claims. Negatively, it can be used to drive a wedge between the people and their government, to make them doubt the justness of their cause, and especially to influence them against the claims of the opposition.

The spreading of rumor is a part of human nature, and this peculiarity of man is frequently intentionally exploited by what are called "directed rumors." The generals of Genghis Khan, for example, employed this technique to exaggerate their strength and confuse their enemies. They planted spies in the headquarters of their foes where they reported that the armies of Genghis Khan "seemed like grasshoppers, impossible to count." Other spies warned, "They breathe nothing but war and blood, and show so great an impatience to fight that their generals can scarcely moderate them." As a result of such rumors the frightened Europeans described the Khan's cavalry as "a numberless horde," although in reality it was numerically far inferior to their own forces.

"How much of human history, we may reasonably ask, can be regarded as the reactions of important groups of people to current rumor?" This question was posed by Professor Gordon W. Allport of Harvard University, one of the great rumor experts of the world. And he himself answered it, "A great deal, we suspect, for until very recent times the inhabitants of the world had little to rely on other than rumored information." But, despite the increased circulation of newspapers, despite the invention of the telegraph, telephone, radio, and television, the net role of rumor in molding public opinion is even greater in our time than ever before.

Rumor became a problem of grave national concern during the years of 1942 and 1943. Within six weeks of Pearl Harbor malicious rumors flew so thick and fast that President Roosevelt had to repudiate them in a special "fireside chat." Even then they did not subside. During the summer of 1942 Dr. R. H. Knapp of Harvard University collected some thousand different rumors then current throughout the country. Most of them (65.9 percent) were "wedge-driving" rumors which tried to pit people against each other within the United States. They promoted anti-Semitism, and fanned distrust of the Army, the Navy, and the Red Cross. They tried to stimulate draft evasion, suspicion of the Roosevelt administration, opposition to the purchase of war bonds, anything that weakened the war effort.

Many of them (25.4 percent) were "fear" rumors, which distorted or magnified our initial military setbacks, invented tales about fifth-column activities and sabotage, exaggerated the enemy's strength and cunning, invented atrocities, and stressed our shipping losses.

A few of them were "pipe-dream" rumors about the imminence of peace, the discovery of destroyed enemy submarines all along our coasts, or unscored victories. Wedge-driving rumors were prevalent in the Middle West, fear rumors in the South, "pipe-dream" rumors along the Atlantic seaboard, possibly reflecting the attitudes and sentiments of the population of those regions.

The rumors which Dr. Knapp found most widespread were about the Navy dumping three carloads of coffee into New York harbor and the Army destroying whole sides of good beef. Another insisted that the Russians were getting most of our butter and using it for the lubrication of their guns. In another, the Red Cross was accused of charging soldiers in Iceland outrageous prices for sweaters knit at home.

Political Warfare and the Cold War

After 1943 when victory seemed more certain and more information could be broadcast about the actual conduct of the war, the deluge of rumors subsided.

When the Second World War was followed by the cold war, intelligence operations suddenly came into their own. There is nothing remarkable in this sequence. The cold war is merely a synonym for intelligence operations. Military means are used only occasionally, and then at the periphery of the conflict. In a large measure, diplomats and propagandists are used to wage its hottest battles.

For the Russians the coming of the cold war represented no problem, since they did not have to create new agencies to wage it. They had only to revive a few old ones. The place of the Comintern was taken by the Communist Information Bureau, the Cominform. The Amsterdam-Pleyel peace movement was revived almost without change in the organization called "Partisans of Peace." Radio Moscow, the first to engage in the propaganda war of the air, never ceased to exert its subtle influence on the listening world.

In the United States, Britain, and France, new offensive and defensive networks had to be organized almost overnight. This is how the Central Intelligence Agency came into being. This is why the Voice of America was changed from an information to a propaganda organ, as was the B.B.C. in Britain to some extent, and the international radio services of France, Turkey, Yugoslavia, and Spain. Special cold war agencies were formed, including Radio Free Europe, Radio Liberation (beamed to the Soviet Union), and Radio Free Asia.

Despite the fact that the cold war is nothing but an intelligence operation on a monumental scale, the West is still reluctant to regard the conflict as a war of wits and to shift operations from the military to the intellectual field. Emphasis remained on conventional military means, on rearmament revolving largely about the Air Force and atomic and thermonuclear weapons. This failure to place emphasis on intelligence operations led to the loss of China, to the consolidation of Soviet rule in eastern and south-eastern Europe, and to the prolongation of peripheral wars in Indochina, Malaya, and Korea.

After a number of skirmishes, the cold war reached a climax on June 17, 1953, when rebellions flared up against the Soviet Union in Czechoslovakia, Poland, and on an impressive scale in Eastern Germany, especially in the Soviet zone of Berlin. As they had on July 20, 1944, in rising against Nazism, the Germans again acted on their own initiative, and without foreign aid. In both revolts, they rose against the power of greatest resistance, against the entrenched security forces of a totalitarian regime. Throughout eastern Europe the 1953 risings were spontaneous. They were engineered by workers. The forces of an unorganized populace were thrown against the tightly organized security forces of the oppressor.

The intelligence operations listed in this book represent certain definite patterns of non-military warfare as it is waged in our own days. Each has its own motivations, strategies and tactics, weapons, special local characteristics.

Different though these operations are, there is something common to all of them. They represent a new form of warfare, and common to all of them is a new force that propels these conspiracies. It is a force that wages war without military means.

For what is war? It is merely the continuation of a nation's policy by physical means, or, as Clausewitz defined it, "an act of violence designed to compel our opponent to fulfil our will." Although Clausewitz's theories of total military destruction of an enemy influenced many nations and led to the increased use of violence in war, an old concept that conflict need not be violent at all is beginning to manifest itself in the foreign policies of some nations today.

"The popular idea that war is a mere matter of brute force, redeemed only by valor and discipline," wrote George F. R. Henderson, "is responsible for a greater evil than the complacency of the amateur. It binds both the people and its representatives to their bounden duties. War is something more than a mere outgrowth of politics. It is a political act, initiated and controlled by the government, and it is an act in which the issues are far more momentous than any other."

Clausewitz formulated his famous tenet at the beginning of the nineteenth century. Those were interesting years in the life of mankind. Thinkers were puzzled by the direction in which society was moving and tried to apply the lessons of this evolution to the age-old problems of war.

At the start of the last century, wars were no longer what they used to be. Neither was man any longer the helpless automaton that circumstances had compelled him to be for centuries. After the dark ages of oppression, the citizen began to emerge as Aristotle envisaged him, the possessor of political power. He began to sit on juries and in assemblies. The oligarchs, monarchs, and tyrants found that their influence was waning as the influence of their subjects grew. Gradually the old order was broken, in England by political philosophers, in America by indignant patriots, and then in France by the mob whose way to the Tuilleries was led by intellectuals. It was obvious that after centuries of helpless obscurity the people could no longer be ignored, much less oppressed. They themselves were the dominant factors when it came to the molding of their own destinies.

Before Clausewitz had established himself as a military theorist, a strange figure appeared in Prussia. He was Dietrich Heinrich von Bülow, black sheep of a famous Prussian family of high officials and generals, younger brother of a field marshal. He had been in turn soldier, writer, actor, trader, and adventurer, and had proved a failure at everything.

Yet this apparently worthless scion of a famous family occupies a far more important role in the history of conflict than his successful brother or some of the celebrated generals whose names survive in the annals. For Heinrich von Bülow was the first to define the enormous influence that the gradual change of society exercised on war. He became the originator of the concept that today finds its way into all thinking dedicated to the problems of human conflict.

Bülow regarded war as "organized disorder" in which organization was vastly overstressed while the nature of the disorder was overlooked. He thought that war itself, the actual clash of arms, was far less important than the "friction" that preceded and caused it. Years before Clausewitz came to his conclusion that war is never an isolated act but rather the continuation of policy by other means, Bülow maintained that military strategy was but a subordinate instrument in human conflict, the extension and not the substance of political strategy and action.

Bülow examined closely the nature of frictions and then sought their solution, not in the mobilization of the obtuse and regimented mass, but in the manipulation of the sensitive and informed individual. He went further than that. He regarded man as fully capable of solving the problems created by "frictions" by intellectual rather than military means.

To be sure, the power of intellect was never completely neglected in war. But while former wars had shown the value of a trained general, the wars of the new era began to show the value of an educated army and an educated people. The people have gained a direct influence on war, not only on its conduct, but also on the events which precede it. The progress of enlightenment suggested alternatives to the solution of frictions. War was but one of the alternatives. Diplomacy was another.

Bülow spelled out his ideas in his major work, which he called *The Spirit of a New System of War*. They were brilliant ideas but, when he first proclaimed them in 1799, they were far too original and far too premature for his times. His principles shocked his contemporaries steeped in the traditions of warfare, for Bülow was contemptuous of the callous military system of Frederick the Great, and he thought little of Napoleon's aggressive military strategy. He advocated the humanization and intellectualization of war, and suggested that it be waged in the political rather than military sphere.

Many observers of our own contemporary scene have stated in so many words that human conflicts need not necessarily be resolved by the violence of armed action. They have recognized the intellectual progress of mankind, the spread of knowledge and information, the growing participation of the masses in public affairs.

They have recognized the gradual growth of political thinking which has enabled man to devise alternatives to the customary traditional solution of conflicts by arms. They have pointed out the mental poverty of the political philosophers and military scientists who see in war the only agent for social and political change, and they have concluded that man is capable of imposing his will on others by outsmarting or outthinking rather than outgunning his opponent.

What we have called intelligence operations represent a long step on the road that leads gradually away from the old-fashioned war to a resolution of differences in the intellectual sphere. Today we begin to see that wars can be waged without actually sending armies into the field. We call it cold war. It is conflict, yes. But it is directed by statesmen and diplomats rather than generals. It is waged by intelligence specialists and propagandists rather than soldiers.

But even as we witness this evolution, we still fail to recognize the cold war for what it is, a war of wits. And since we fail to recognize it, we continue to spend billions on arms. Between 1776 and 1781, George Washington spent approximately eleven percent of his entire military budget on intelligence operations. The fact that today we spend less than one percent of our peacetime military budget on these same activities shows how little the function of intelligence is appreciated and supported, how little effort is being made to solve the "friction" by intellectual means rather than brute force.

The Roman Seneca was sensible to the degradation of man when he exclaimed that only men wage wars—no beasts ever do. Since his time, every age has merely improved the art and instruments of rage.

Now for the first time, man is exploring the means of waging war without resorting to violence. Instead of flexing his muscles, he is trying to use his head. It is not to be expected that all nations will recognize the efficacy of this philosophy simultaneously, for indeed they will not. However, this fact does not minimize the responsibility of those who do see it for making a relentless effort to replace physical conflict with the war of wits. To this end intelligence activities occupy a position of tremendous importance and can contribute immeasurably.

Source Notes and References

These notes and references are offered as documentation of the material presented in the text. The starred titles are suggested as a selective bibliography of the subject. The figures to the left designate the pages and lines of text to which the notes refer.

6:46   Henderson, G. F. R. H., "War," in *Encyclopaedia Britannica*, 11th ed., 1911, v. 28, p. 305.

7:9   Ludendorff, E., *Kriegführung and Politik*, (Berlin), 1922, pp. 320-342.

7:24   Blau, A., *Geistige Kriegführung*, (Potsdam), 1938; Münzenberg, W., *Propaganda als Waffe*, (Paris), 1934.

7:35   *Aston, Sir G., *Secret Service*, (London), 1931, p. 29.

8:11   New York *Times*, 1954, March 5, p. 7.

8:25   For definitions of the term "intelligence" in its social scientific connotation, see Young K., *Sociology*, (New York), 1942, p. 355.

8:32   *Kent, S., *Strategic Intelligence for American World Policy*, (Princeton), 1949, pp. 3-10, 209-211; *Pettee, S. G., *The Future of American Secret Intelligence*, (Washington), 1946, pp. 95, 102-108.

8:45   *Department of the Army Appropriations for 1955*, Hearings, (Washington), 1954, p. 47.

9:16   Spaulding, O. L., Nickerson, H., Wright, J. W., *Warfare*, (Washington), 1937, p. 7.

9:27   In his preface to Hoy, H. C., *40 O.B.*, (London), 1926.

9:30   13 Numbers 1-33.

9:35   Frontinus, Sextus Julius, *Stratagematica*, (London), 1816.

9:36   Saxe, Maurice de, *Reveries on the Art of War*.

10:6   Muir, Sir W., *Life of Mahomet*, (London), 1861, v. 4.

10:10   Mohammed ibn Omar al-Waqidi, *Mohammed in Medina*, abr. tr. by Wüstenfeld, (Berlin), 1882.

10:12   The battle of Badr was fought on Ramadan 19 in the second year of the Hegira, usually made to synchronize with March 17, 624. In the *Koran*, the date is called the "Day of Deliverance."

10:22   Wells, H. G., *The Outline of History*, (New York), 1931, pp. 606-607.

11:4   The overwhelming importance of meteorological information is presented dramatically in Eisenhower, D. D., *Crusade in Europe*, (New York), 1948, pp. 116, 239, 248-250, 253, 261-263.

11:28   According to A. W. Dulles, about 20 percent of total intelligence handled by CIA is economic information; the rest is political, military, psychological, scientific and technical intelligence. See interview in *U.S. News and World Report*, 1954, March 19, pp. 62-68.

11:35   *Sweeney, W. C., *Military Intelligence. A New Weapon of War*, (New York), 1924, pp. 13-29.

12:27   *Ibid.*, pp. 146-149.

13:2   Elmer, A., *Napoleons Leibspion, Karl Ludwig Schulmeister*, (Berlin), 1931, p. 107.

13:4   Urbanski, A. V., "Aufmarschpläne," in *Lettow-Vorbeck, P. V., *Die Weltkriegsspionage*, (München), 1931, pp. 85-88.

13:8   *Thompson, J. W., Padover, S. K., *Secret Diplomacy. A Record of Espionage and Double-Dealing*, (London), 1937, pp. 42-50.

13:19   Breasted, J. H., "The Battle of Kadesh," *Decennial Publications*, University of Chicago, 1904, First Series, v. 5, pp. 81-126; Erman, A., *Life of Ancient Egypt*, (London), 1894, pp. 41-46, 526.

13:36   Aston, *op. cit.*

13:46   *Dept. of the Army Appropriations for 1955*, (q.v.,) p. 323.

14:15   *Ibid.*, p. 323.

14:22   *Department of the Navy Appropriations for 1955*, Hearings, (Washington), 1954, p. 893.

14:45   *Zacharias, E. M., *Secret Missions*, (New York), 1946, pp. 334-335. Also see his "The Inside Story of Yalta," *United Nations World*, 1949, v. 3, no. 1, pp. 12-18, where he wrote: "My estimate . . . was based on an extremely careful study of Japan's conscription system, including draft statistics, physical fitness reports, and on intelligence reports revealing the rapidly increasing manpower difficulties of the Japanese Imperial Army." The study mentioned above was conducted by the present writer.

15:24   London, K., *How Foreign Policy is Made*, (New York), 1949, pp. 16-36, 39-74, 99-130, 140-150, 155-165.

15:33   Nicolson, H., *Diplomacy*, (London), 1939, pp. 3-27.

15:35   Maskelyne, J., *White Magic. The Story of the Maskelynes*, (London), 1936, pp. 83-86.

16:4   It was the present writer who, in December 1945, called the attention of Mr. Byrnes to certain pertinent passages in V.v.I. Lenin's *Collected Works*, (Russian Edition), v. 27, pp. 84-85, reprinted in *Strategy and Tactics of the Proletarian Revolution*, (New York), 1936, pp. 57-61.

16:8   For the Soviet's use of diplomacy in intelligence operations, see Stalin, J. V., "Report on the immediate tasks of the Party in connection with the national problem," printed in *Marxism and the National Question*, (New York), 1942, pp. 98-110, where Stalin said: "The whole purpose of the existence of the People's Commissariat of Foreign Affairs is to take account of these controversies [between the imperialist states], to use them as a point of departure, and to maneuver within these contradictions."

16:13   Goltz, H. V. D., "Politische Spionage," in *Die Weltkriegsspionage*, (q.v.), pp. 153-157; Kent, *op. cit.*, pp. 35, 49.

16:27   *Nazi Conspiracy and Aggression*, (Washington), 1946, v. 3, pp. 19-27, 32-35.

16:45   Jones E., "The psychology of quislingism," *International Journal of Psychoanalysis*, 1941, v. 22, no. 1, pp. 1-6.

17:18   Possony, S. T., *Strategic Airpower*, (Washington), 1949, pp. 116-118.

17:26   Calkins, C., *Spy Overhead. The Story of Industrial Espionage*, (New York), 1937.

17:27   *Enc. Brit.*, (q.v.), pp. 492-493.

17:44   Goldenberg, H., "Das Wissen vom Gegner," *Soldatentum*, (Berlin), 1938, pp. 259-263.

18:3   Blau, *op. cit.*, pp. 43-57; Farago, L. (ed.), *German Psy-*

chological Warfare, (New York), 1942, pp. 264-270.

18:13 Beck, W., "Amerikanisches Soldatentum," Soldatentum, 1936, pp. 137-141.

18:41 Keilhacker, M., "Grundzüge des englischen Volkscharakters, etc.," Beihefte, Zeitschrift für angewandte Psychologie, (Berlin), 1938, v. 79, pp. 187-208.

19:15 Sayers, M., Kahn, A. E., Sabotage, (New York), 1942, pp. 16, 26, 28-30, 32-34, 41, 121.

19:35 Goudsmit, S. A., Alsos, (New York), 1947, pp. 14-25.

19:43 Ibid., pp. 50-56.

20:15 *Miksche, F. O., Secret Forces, (London), 1950, pp. 134, 138-142.

20:35 Eisenhower, op. cit., pp. 233, 296.

21:41 Erfurth, W., Surprise, (Harrisburg), 1943, p. 195.

22:21 The events related here are described on the basis of the author's first-hand experience. Also see, Stimson, H. L., Bundy, McG., On Active Service in Peace and War, (New York), 1948, pp. 617-633; Baldwin, H. W., Great Mistakes of the War, (New York), 1949, pp. 88-108.

23:3 Statement of W. Averell Harriman, Hearings, Military Situation in the Far East, (Washington), 1951, v. 5, pp. 3328-3342.

23:16 Zacharias, Secret Missions (q.v.), pp. 332-341.

23:27 Zacharias, E. M., "The A-Bomb Was Not Needed," United Nations World, 1949, v. 3, no. 8.

24:3 Zacharias, Secret Missions, (q.v.), pp. 332-350. For General Marshall's attitude to non-military operations, see Carroll, W., Persuade or Perish, (Boston), 1948, p. 385: "General George C. Marshall, the wartime Chief of Staff, had been as responsible as anyone for the obsession with military ends which put the United States in such an unfavorable position for the post-war political struggle."

25:23 The incident was related to the author by its participants. Cf., Cant, G., The Great Pacific Victory, (New York), 1946, pp. 118, 125, 162-163.

27:3 Farago, op. cit., pp. 153-155; London, op. cit., pp. 81-89.

27:34 For a typical sample of such an official biographical study prepared by an intelligence agency, see the estimate of Malenkov's personality, Ostprobleme, 1953, April.

27:42 Perkins, F., The Roosevelt I Knew, (New York), 1946, pp. 82-84. Upon the sudden death of President Roosevelt in 1945, the chancelleries of the world were flooded with "biographical estimates" of the new President, Harry S. Truman. On April 16, 1945, Lord Halifax, the British Ambassador in Washington, cabled Mr. Churchill: "It may be of interest that Truman's hobby is history of military strategy, of which he is reported to have read widely. He certainly betrayed surprising knowledge of Hannibal's campaigns one night here. He venerates Marshall." Churchill, W. S., Triumph and Tragedy, (Boston), 1953, p. 481. On the same day, Foreign Secretary Anthony Eden cabled to the Prime Minister: "My impression from the interview is that the new President is honest and friendly. He is conscious of but not overwhelmed by his new responsibilities. His references to you could not have been warmer." Ibid., p. 484.

28:44   °*The Report of the Royal [Canadian] Commission,* (Ottawa), 1946, pp. 123-161.

29:24   °*Soviet Atomic Espionage,* (Washington), 1951, pp. 13-59.

30:31   *Activities of Soviet Secret Service,* Hearing, (Washington), 1954, pp. 24-25.

30:37   *Foreign Office List,* (London), 1946.

30:44   Kent, *op. cit.,* pp. 58-61.

31:10   *Wells, op. cit.,* pp. 958-959.

31:27   °Nicolai, W., *Geheime Mächte,* (Berlin), 1921, pp. 10-11.

31:30   °Pinkerton, A., *The Spy of the Rebellion,* (New York), 1883.

32:4   °Rowan, R. W., *The Story of Secret Service,* (New York), 1938, pp. 274-283.

32:14   *Enc. Brit.,* (q.v.), v. 4, pp. 791-792.

32:19   Aston, *op. cit.,* pp. 13-42, 293-300. The War Office Intelligence Branch was established in 1873 in the office of the Adjutant General of the Forces, as a result of the lessons learned in the Crimea where blunders and hardships were largely due to a woeful lack of information about the enemy. The first "MI" was housed in an abandoned coach house on Adelphi Terrace. Later it was moved to a secluded and shuttered house at Queen Ann's Gate which for decades became the hush-hush center of British secret intelligence.

32:21   When the huge new Admiralty Building was erected off Trafalgar Square, the planners allocated only two small rooms to accommodate the budding intelligence department.

32:32   °Mashbir, S., "What is intelligence," in *I Was an American Spy,* (New York), 1953, pp. 41-56.

33:4   °Cookridge, E. H., *Secrets of the British Secret Service,* (London), 1948, pp. 1-9; Firmin, S., *They Came to Spy,* (London), 1946, pp. 144-150.

33:8   °Hagen, W., (pseudonym of Dr. Wilhelm Höttl), *Die geheime Front,* (Linz), 1950, pp. 9-12.

33:15   °Willoughby, C. A., *Shanghai Conspiracy,* (New York), 1952, pp. 170-172.

33:43   *Hearings,* Subcommittee of the Committee on Appropriations, House of Representatives, 81st Congress, 2nd Session, part 1, (January 9, 1950), pp. 1-15; Phillips, C., "The supercabinet for our security," New York *Times Magazine,* 1954, April 4, pp. 14-15, 60-63.

34:12   *United States Government Organization Manual 1953-1954,* (Washington), 1953, pp. 62-63.

34:34   °Baldwin, H. W., *The Price of Power,* (New York), 1947, pp. 203-219; Pettee, *op. cit.,* pp. 102-118.

35:1   Hagen, *op. cit.,* p. 12.

35:4   Görlitz, W., *Der deutsche Generalstab,* (Frankfurt), 1950, p. 427.

35:8   *Congressional Record,* 83rd Congress, 2nd Session, (1954), v. 100, part 45, pp. 2811 ff.

35:19   Seid, A., "Der englische Geheimdienst," *Schriften des Deutschen Instituts für Aussenpolitische Forschung,* (Berlin), 1940, no. 23.

35:21   For the public part of PID's table of organization, see the 1946 edition of the *Foreign Office List*. In the 1954 list, Political Intelligence appears as part of Research and Library, headed by Ernest James Passant as Director of Research and Air Commodore K. C. Buss as Deputy Director. Mr. Passant is an eminent historian who taught at Cambridge and served in Naval Intelligence, combining erudition with practical experience.

35:23   The actual director of PID, or more accurately, of Her Majesty's Secret Service, is shielded from the public by ironclad secrecy. In *The Fourth Seal*, Sir Samuel Hoare called him "the nameless spyking of the British Secret Service Organization." Sir Paul Dukes recalled with some awe: "It was eighteen months before I was allowed to know his real name and title, and even then I was careful never to use it." Sir George Aston remarked: "He wears many well-earned decorations, few people know how well. His name is—shall we say 'X,' the 'Unknown Quantity.'"

35:28   Cookridge, *op. cit.*, pp. 4-7.

35:45   *Whitaker's Almanac*, 82nd Annual Volume, (London), 1950, p. 370.

36:11   Testimony of Ismail Ege (Colonel Ismail Gusseynovich Akhmedoff), former chief of Soviet Intelligence's Fourth (Technological) Section, before the Senate Internal Security Subcommittee, on October 28-29, 1953. Also see Richard Sorge's description of the organization in Willoughby, *op. cit.*, pp. 171-172.

36:13   *Rep. R. [Can.] Com.*, (q.v.), pp. 20, 26-27, 733.

36:21   The "Center" has four major branches: Operations, Information, Training, Auxiliaries. Within its Operations Branch, it maintains eight "strategic intelligence sections." Section 3 is concerned with the United States. Section 4 collects technical and scientific data. Section 5 conducts intelligence operations, organizes terroristic acts, kidnapings, assassinations, uprisings. Section 6 handles such technical details as authentication, the development of special intelligence weapons and instruments. Section 7 is charged with tactical military intelligence and Section 8 with cryptography and cryptanalysis. The Navy has its own intelligence administration, a far smaller, but reputedly efficient service.

36:35   °Alsop, S., Braden, T., *Sub Rosa. The OSS and American Espionage*, (New York), 1946, p. 9-26.

37:9   °MacDonald, E. P., *Undercover Girl*, (New York), 1947, pp. 5-36.

37:19   "The CIA: Who Watches the Watchdog," Richmond (Va.) *News Leader*, 1953, March 30; "About Which You Actually Know Nothing," *ibid.*, 1953, July 17.

37:26   According to A. L. Miller, *Congr. Rec.*, 81st Congress, 1st Sess., v. 95, part 13, pp. A1663-A1664.

37:38   The table of organization presented here is the author's idea of an efficient secret service. It is not based on any existing tables of organization, certainly not on that of the CIA.

39:27   Zacharias, *Secret Missions*, (q.v.), pp. 302-316.

40:16   Urbanski, A. V., "Was kostet die Spionage," in *Die Welt-kriegsspionage* (q.v.), pp. 165-166; "Battle Order of Espionage," *United Nations World*, 1949, v. 3, no. 6; *ibid.*, 1949, v. 3, no. 7.

40:20   *Enc. Brit.*, (q.v.), v. 28, pp. 293-294.

40:31   According to Dr. Mynors Bright's researches in the Pepysian Library, Magdalene College, Cambridge, *cf.*, Rowan, *op. cit.*, p. 104.

40:40   *Hansard*, 1954, pp. 1307-1308.

41:7   Farago, L., "England's secret government," *Ken* magazine, 1938, v. 1, no. 1, (April 7), pp. 46-48.

41:11   Cookridge, *op. cit.*, p. 5.

41:22   Rowan, *op. cit.*, pp. 489, 712.

41:36   Kisch, E. E., *Der Fall des Generalstabschefs Redl*, (Berlin), 1924.

41:39   Foote, A., *Handbook for Spies*, (New York), 1950; *Neue Zürcher Zeitung*, 1953, November, 3, 4, 5, 6.

41:43   *Rep. R. [Can.] Comm.*, (q.v.), p. 68.

42:9   Army Appropriations, (q.v.), pp. 317-346.

42:19   According to *The Reporter* magazine, the National Security Agency, "known until recently as the Armed Forces Security Agency is . . . believed to have somewhere between four and eight thousand employees, engaged, it has been said, in breaking foreign codes." v. 10, no. 13, June 22, 1954, p. 23.

42:22   *Congr. Rec.*, 83rd Congress, 2nd Sess., v. 100, part 45, p. 2814.

42:27   *Ibid.*, pp. 2811-2813.

42.46   Sweeney, *op. cit.*, pp. 141-161.

43:6   Pratt, F., "That real spy, the researcher," New York *Times Magazine*, 1948, August 15, p. 10.

43:13   Baldwin, *op. cit.*, p. 204.

43:22   London, *op. cit.*, pp. 85-88.

44:16   Pettee, *op cit.*, pp. 39-46; Kent, *op. cit.*, pp. 9, 157, 164-168.

45:9   New York *Times*, 1935, March 21, September 19, 23. The account of Herr Jacob's adventure is related here on the basis of the author's on-the-spot investigations at the time of the incident.

48:44   Alsop and Braden, *op cit.*, pp. 17-18.

49:12   Zimmermann, J. L., *The Guadalcanal Campaign*, (Washington), 1949, pp. 14-19.

49:19   Cookridge, *op. cit.*, pp. 19-36.

50:3   Interview with A. W. Dulles, *U.S. News and World Report*, 1954, March 19, pp. 62-70.

50:11   Zacharias, E. M., "What is wrong with our spy system," *Real* magazine, 1953, v. 2, no. 2, pp. 14-17, 78-81.

50:32   *World Almanac*, (New York), 1954, pp. 724-734.

50:45   Sweeney, *op. cit.*, p. 86.

51:3   For a typical question concerning Her Majesty's Secret Service, see *Hansard*, 1950, 480, pp. 1166-1167.

51:39   Information supplied by the editors of the *Current Digest of the Soviet Press*.

52:33   Speier, H., Kris, E., *German Radio Propaganda*, (New York), 1942, pp. 103-107, 289-325.

53:9   Hoy, H. C., *op cit.*, pp. 21, 181-184, 192.

54:29   Cookridge, *op. cit.*, pp. 19-21.

55:11   Aston, *op. cit.*, pp. 28-38.

56:15   MacDonald, *op. cit.*, pp. 248-251.

57:18   The system of personal observations by professional intelligence officers was introduced into the British secret service by General Sir Henry Wilson when he was commandant of the Camberley Staff College. He encouraged his aides to make "holidays trips" to the Continent. On one of his own bicycle tours, Sir Henry succeeded in obtaining information from which he deduced the basic details of the Schlieffen Plan.

57:20   Görlitz, *op. cit.*, p. 453.

57:27   Bismarck, B. V., "Der Militärattache im Nachrichtendienst," in *Die Weltkriegsspionage*, (q.v.), pp. 104-110; Beauvais, A. P., *Attaches Militaires, Attaches Navales et Attaches de l'Air*, (Paris), 1937; Schweppenburg, G. V., *Erinnerungen eines Militärattaches*, (London) 1933-1937, (Stuttgart), 1949, pp. 9-25.

57:35   Nicolai, *op. cit.*

57:41   Zimmermann, *op. cit.*, pp. 14-16; Pratt, F., *The Marines' War*, (New York), 1948, pp. 3-30.

58:36   *Ibid.*, pp. 8, 9-10, 38.

58:41   *Feldt, E. A., *The Coast Watchers*, (New York), 1946, pp. 78-103.

59:29   Cant, *op. cit.*, p. 138.

60:12   Spaulding, Nickerson, Wright, *op. cit.*, pp. 14-16.

60:40   Schwien, E. E., *Combat Intelligence. Its Acquisition and Transmission.* (Washington), 1936, pp. 57-60; *Thomas, S., *S-2 in Action*, (Harrisburg), 1940.

61:6   *World Almanac*, 1954, p. 732. The grand total of all mobilized forces in the First World War was 65,038,810 officers and men. Of the 7,995 U.S. combatants reported as missing in Korea, 4,631 prisoners of war were returned by October 23, 1953. The Republic of Korea reported 459,429 as missing. Of them only 7,848 prisoners of war were returned.

61:21   For the emotional trends among prisoners of war, see Strong T., (ed.), *We Prisoners of War*, (New York), 1942, pp. 32-37, 38-40, 78-83.

61:24   *Enc. Brit.* (q.v.), v. 32 (1922), pp. 150-162.

61:39   Moorehead, A., Montgomery, (New York), 1946, pp. 143-144.

62:7   "Information obtained from prisoners should be priced at the right value; a soldier sees nothing beyond his company, and the officer at most can give an account of the movements and position of the division to which his regiment belongs. The general in command should not consider confessions torn from prisoners, except when they square with reports of the outposts, to justify his conjectures as to the position the enemy occupies." Sweeney, *op. cit.*, p. 162.

62:20   Einsiedel, H., *Tagebuch der Versuchung*, (Berlin-Stuttgart), 1950, pp. 17-78; Hahn, A., *Ich Spreche die Wahrheit*, (Esslingen), 1951, pp. 14-29, 130-136.

62:23   Liddell Hart, B. H., *The German Generals Talk*, (New York), 1948.

62:29 *The Battle of the Atlantic. The Official Account of the Fight Against the U-Boats 1939-1945*, (London), 1946, p. 57.

63:2   The incident was related to the author by the officer who conducted the interrogation.

64:12 Schwien, *op. cit.*, pp. 59-60.

64:33 *The Confidential Records of the French General Staff*, (Berlin), 1940.

65:7   Pratt, *op. cit.*, pp. 44-46.

66:2   *Documents on German Foreign Policy 1918-1945*, (Washington), 1949, *cf.* General Introduction, pp. VII-XIII, where the editors state: "Never had three victorious powers set out to establish the full record of the diplomacy of a vanquished power from captured archives 'on the basis of the highest scholarly objectivity.'" The captured archives went back to 1867. Similarly, the papers of the German Army, Navy and Air Force were captured and published. Martienssen, A., *Hitler and His Admirals*, (New York), 1949. According to Martienssen, "during the final stages of the Second World War, enemy State documents were captured on a scale which was unique in history." The largest haul of documents was made at Schloss Tambach, near Coburg, where some 60,000 files of the German naval archives were captured, relating to the German Navy from 1868 until the date of their capture, April 1945.

66:29 This incident was related to the author by one of the persons directly involved in the capture and exploitation of the order.

66:36 Wilmot, C., *The Struggle for Europe*, (New York), 1952, pp. 18-34.

68:15 Arnold, H. H. and Eaker, I. C., *Winged Warfare*, (New York), 1941, pp. 128-130.

68:45 Bley, W., "Luftspionage und Fernzerstoerung," in *Die Weltkriegsspionage*, (q.v.), pp. 140-152; Urbanski, A. V., "Flugzeug und Spionage," *ibid.*, pp. 635-647.

69:24 Rowan, R. W., "Something German in Denmark," in *Spy Secrets*, (New York), 1946, pp. 89-92.

69:34 Dornberger, W. R., *V2 Der Schuss ins Weltall*, (Esslingen), 1952, pp. 263-271; Churchill, W. S., *op. cit.*, pp. 50-53.

70:32 Sweeney, *op. cit.*, pp. 162-187; Fell, H. W., "Die Auswärtung und das Ergebnis der Agentennachrichten," in *Die Weltkriegsspionage*, (q.v.), pp. 158-164; Pettee, *op. cit.*, pp. 25-38; Schwien, *op. cit.*, pp. 61-67.

71:10 Kent, *op. cit.*, pp. 170, 172-173. Letters to and including "F" may be used to indicate the trustworthiness of a source, and numerals up to six to rate the probability of information. Material from the public domain is similarly rated or marked with the word "Documentary."

71:40 Churchill, W. S., *The Grand Alliance*, (Boston), 1950, pp. 355-356.

72:35 *Military Situation in the Far East*, Hearings, (Washington), 1951, pp. 18, 84-86, 122, 157, 239-241, 350, 436, 545, 639, 758, 1035, 1190, 1429, 1436, 1778, 1832, 1859, 1990, 2113, 2267, 2273, 2583, 2629, 2914, 3581.

72:45 Dulles, A. W., New York *Herald-Tribune Book Review,* 1950, October 29, p. 5.

73:18 Baldwin, *op. cit.,* p. 210.

73:25 Sweeney, *op. cit.,* pp. 188-205.

74:1 *Executive Order 10501* of November 5, 1953 (18 F.R. 7049), safeguarding official information. It established various classification categories; limited authority to classify; regulated declassification, downgrading and upgrading; and the storage, transmission, disposal and destruction of classified documents. Also see *Atomic Energy Act* of 1946 as amended, Section 10.

74:9 Ingersoll, R., *Top Secret,* (New York), 1946, p. 104.

75:20 Based on the author's personal experience.

75:46 The material in this section reflects the author's own concepts and theories. Part of the nomenclature developed here is original.

76:14 Farago, L., *Axis Grand Strategy,* (New York), 1942, p. 60.

76:39 Lasswell, H. D., "Policy and the intelligence function," in *The Analysis of Political Behavior,* (New York), 1947, pp. 120-131.

77:5 The evolution of the policy of His Majesty's Government between 1935 and 1939 is described on the basis of Wilmot, *op. cit.,* pp. 34-40, 49, 53-54.

77:10 *Nazi Conspiracy and Aggression,* (q.v.), v. 3, pp. 11-13.

79:29 Sontag, R. J., Beddie, J. S. (eds.), *Nazi-Soviet Relations 1939-1941,* (New York), 1948, pp. V-VIII.

79:44 *Ibid.,* pp. 217-254, 258-259; Rossi, A., (pseudonym of Jean-Ange Tasca), *Deux ans d'alliance Germano-Sovietique,* (Paris), 1949, pp. 166-180.

80:37 *Assistance to Greece and Turkey,* Hearings, (Washington), 1947, p. 11; Acheson, D. G., *The Pattern of Responsibility,* (Boston), 1952, pp. 139-144.

82:8 See note 91:23, v. 4, pp. 2668-2677.

82:37 Zacharias, "The Inside Story of Yalta," (p.v.), pp. 12-16, based on the present writer's source material.

82:44 Sherwood, R. E., *Roosevelt and Hopkins,* (New York), 1948, pp. 843-845.

83:29 Stettinius, E. R., Jr., *Roosevelt and the Russians. The Yalta Conference,* (New York), 1949, pp. 90-91.

83:37 Harriman, *op. cit.* On pages 3338-3340 of the document, several pertinent memoranda prepared by the Joint Chiefs of Staff are reproduced verbatim. Also see, Byrnes, J., *op. cit.,* pp. 42-43, 92, 205-207, 208-213, 263. *The Forrestal Diaries,* (q.v.), pp. 57-58.

83:39 Deane, J. R., *The Strange Alliance,* (New York), 1946, pp. 47, 60, 107, 223.

84:12 "Most of the Japanese troops [defeated on Saipan and Tinian] were veterans of the Manchurian campaign," Karig, W., Harris, R. L., Manson, F. A., *Battle Report. The End of an Empire,* (New York), 1948, pp. 261-262, 272. The 18th Infantry Division under Lieutenant General Renya Matagushi, including the crack 114th Regiment, was annihilated in New Guinea, the 5th Imperial Guards and the 24th Division were destroyed elsewhere. They formerly formed part of the Kwantung Army and were carried as such in the Order of Battle.

85:5   Forrestal, *op. cit.*, p. 31.

85:20 *Ibid.*, p. 70. Also see Leahy, W. D., *I Was There*, (New York), 1950.

86:39 Stimson, Bundy, *op. cit.*, pp. 617-618, 624.

87:4   Schwien, *op. cit.*, pp. 27-40.

87:12 Baldwin, *op. cit.*, p. 206.

87:36 Gilbert, V., *The Romance of the Last Crusade.* (New York), 1923, pp. 183-185.

89:25 Baldwin, *op. cit.*, p. 206.

90:34 Reid, O. R., Bird, R. S., "Are we inviting disaster?", *Congr. Rec.*, 81st Congress, 2nd Sess., v. 96, part 16, pp. A5623-A5624.

91:15 Forrestal, *op. cit.*, p. 360.

91:25 *Congr. Rec.*, 81st Congress, 2nd Sess., v. 96, part 8, p. 10086.

92:4   Washington *Evening Star*, 1951, May 10.

92:36 Entry dated November 7, 1942, *The Ciano Diaries, 1939-1943*, (New York), 1946, p. 540.

93:14 Reid and Bird, *op. cit.*

94:33 *Ibid.*

95:9   Taylor, T., "To improve our intelligence system," New York *Times Magazine*, 1951, May 27, p. 12.

96:28 Sulzberger, C. L., in New York *Times*, 1950, April 10, November 4.

97:9   Marshall, *op. cit.*, pp. 13, 15, 45-47; Lüdecke, *op. cit.*, p. 89; °Baden-Powell, R. S. S., *My Adventures as a Spy*, (London), 1915; Dukes, P., *The Story of ST-25*, (London), 1938; Lawrence, T. E., *Seven Pillars of Wisdom*, (New York), 1935.

97:15 Sweeney, *op. cit.*, pp. 248-259.

98:6   Thompson and Padover, *op. cit.*, pp. 46-50, 83-85, 93; *Enc. Brit.*, (q.v.), v. 26, pp. 902-903.

98:22 °Abshagen, K., *Canaris, Patriot und Weltbürger.* (Stuttgart), 1949; Colvin, I., *Chief of Intelligence*, (London), 1951.

98:23 Willoughby, *op. cit.*, pp. 166-167; Deane, *op. cit.*, pp. 56-63; °Kriwitsky, W., *In Stalin's Secret Service*, (New York), 1940.

98:39 Pennypacker, M., *General Washington's Spies on Long Island and in New York* (Brooklyn), 1939.

98:41 *Time* magazine, 1953, August 3, pp. 13-14.

98:46 Alsop and Braden, *op. cit.*, pp. 9-13.

99:24 Hendrick, B. J., *The Life and Letters of Walter H. Page*, (New York), 1925, v. 3, pp. 360-384; also Hoy, *op. cit.*

99:35 °Thomson, Sir B., *My Experiences at Scotland Yard*, (London), 1923.

100:3 Bardanne, J., *Le colonel Nicolai, espion de genie*, (Paris), 1947; °Nicolai, W., *Nachrichtendienst, Presse und Volksstimmung*, (Berlin), 1920.

100:21 "Time to re-examine CIA leadership," *Christian Century*, 1952, v. 67, November 12, p. 1308.

100:39 Baldwin, *op. cit.*, pp. 203-219.

101:6 Sweeney, *op. cit.*, pp. 120-140, 248-259.

102:27   MacDonald, *op. cit.*, pp. 246-261. Also see, E.7, *Women Spies I Have Known*, (London), 1939.

103:10   Picker, H. (ed.), *Hitler's Tischgespräche in Führerhauptquartier 1941-1942*, (Bonn), 1951, p. 327.

103:17   New York *Times*, 1934, June 17-21.

103:23   Zacharias, *Secret Missions*, (q.v.), pp. 4-5.

103:28   Nicolai, *op. cit.*

104:9   Schmidt, D. A., *Anatomy of a Satellite*, (Boston), 1952, p. 52.

104:26   New York *World-Telegram*, December 11, 1941.

104:33   °Busch T. (pseudonym of Arthur Schütz, *Entlarvter Gehemdienst*, (Zürich), 1946, p. 456.

105:15   *Ibid.*, pp. 456-457.

105:25   Donovan, W. J., "Military intelligence," in *Enc. Brit.*, (1952), v. 12, pp. 459-462.

105:28   Dodd, M., *Through Embassy Eyes*, (New York), 1939, pp. 96-129.

105:36   New York *Times*, 1953, March 5, p. 2.

106:13   *Memoirs of M. de Blowitz*, (London), n.d.; Sir William Howard Russell of *The* [London] *Times* rendered equal service in military intelligence, *cf.* Woodham-Smith, C., *The Reason Why*, (New York), 1954, pp. 148, 172, 187-189, 265, 270.

106:19   Hesse, F., *Das Spiel um Deutschland*, (München), 1953, pp. 38, 59, 81, 203.

107:19   °Maclean, F., *Escape to Adventure*, (Boston), 1950.

108:15   About "the clever young men at the British universities," see Wells, H. G., *op. cit.*, p. 1062.

109:26   Marshall, *op. cit.*, *pp.* 17-18, 26-27, 37, 41-48, 50-62, 85, 91, 93-100.

109:32   Farago, L., "The murder that shocked the world," in *Real* magazine, 1953, v. 2, no. 3, pp. 68-71.

110:23   Alsop and Braden, *op. cit.*, pp. 18-26.

110:29   Mashbir, *op. cit.*, pp. 53-56.

110:41   In a speech to the American Legion, New York *Herald-Tribune*, 1953, June 17, p. 1.

111:3   Coffin, T., "America has ace spies, too," *Coronet* magazine, 1951, v. 30, August, pp. 37-41.

111:14   Mitchell, W. A., *Outlines of the World's Military History*, (Harrisburg), 1940, p. 203.

111:28   Baldwin, *op. cit.*, pp. 204-205; Pratt, F., "How not to run a spy system," *Harper's* magazine, 1947, pp. 195, 241-246.

113:26   General Marshall said: "It is a rather touchy subject, particularly because it takes a long time to develop an effective intelligence service such as we intend for the CIA under General Smith, and one of our great difficulties as I see it is the amount of public discussion in regard to it, because all of that detracts against it. I think those special agencies, notably Great Britain and others, you never hear of them, I doubt if you even know the designation of the unit. It is just kept entirely out of discussion, comment, and we have a long way to go to reach the point where we have more authoritative sources." During the MacArthur hearings, see note 91:23, v. 1, p. 640.

114:41   Vansittart, Lord, *Lessons of My Life*, (New York), 1943.

115:14   Davis, F., "The secret history of a surrender," *Saturday*

Evening Post, 1945, September 22, pp. 9-11; 29, p. 17.

116:1 °Ronge, M., Kriegs und Industriespionage, (Zurich), 1930.

122:9 Lettow-Vorbeck, P. V., Die Weltkriegsspionage, (q.v.), a monumental anthology. No comparable work exists in the English language.

122:10 Bullock, A., Hitler. A Study in Tyranny, (New York), 1954, pp. 572-598. The Barbarossa operation order was issued on December 13, 1940, as Führer Directive No. 21. It is available as Document no. 446-PS among the Nuremberg papers (q.v.).

122:15 The significant episode is presented here on the basis of material supplied by Dr. Wilhelm Höttl, a former high official of Germany's wartime secret service. Further documentation came from Flicke, W. F., Agenten Funken Nach Moskau, (Kreuzlingen), 1954, pp. 47-61, and Foote, op. cit.

123:17 Flicke, W. F., Spionagegruppe Rote Kapelle, (Kreuzlingen), 1953, part 3, pp. 191-261.

123:22 Stalin's fantastic refusal to accept the corroborated intelligence of his own secret service was described in dramatic detail by Colonel I. G. Akhmedoff, an eyewitness. According to Akhmedoff, on April 17, 1941, the section of Military Intelligence (RU) which he then headed received a report from one of its chief sources in Czechoslovakia, a vice president of the Skoda Works named Shkvor, that "the Germans are concentrating their troops on the Soviet frontiers and that the German High Command [had] stopped all Soviet military orders in the Skoda plant." Akhmedoff regarded this as the most important report ever received by RU. Because of its importance, the report was taken immediately to Stalin by Major General Panfilov, deputy director of Military Intelligence. That same night, Panfilov showed Akhmedoff the original report, with Stalin's handwritten marginal note which read: "This information is English provocation. Find out who is behind this provocation and punish him." Colonel Akhmedoff was sent to Germany to track down the provocateur. After that, reports continued to pour in, including the two explicit ones mentioned in the text. But Stalin persisted in dismissing them as "English provocations." Then, on June 21, 1941, while still in Germany, Colonel Akhmedoff received information that the Wehrmacht would begin operations against the Soviet Union on June 22. He presented the report to Ambassador Vladimir G. Dekanosov, who was at that time Stalin's right-hand man. (He was liquidated in the great Beria purge in 1953-54.) Dekanosov refused to believe the information and continued preparations for an Embassy outing he was arranging for next day, a Sunday. "But that picnic did not take place," Akhmedoff concluded, "because at 3 A.M., Sunday morning, Dekanosov was called to von Ribbentrop and delivered the note about the declaration of war by Germany." Cf., Interlocking Subversion in Government Departments, Part 15, (Washington), 1953, pp. 1005-1006.

124:2   Kaledin, V. K., *The Moscow-Berlin Secret Service*, (London), 1940, by an agent who worked in both.

124:21   °Maugham, W. S., *Ashenden or the British Agent*, (London), 1927.

124:28   Tolstoi, L. N., *War and Peace*, tr. Louise and Aylmer Maude, (New York), 1942, p. 709.

124:43   Lüdecke, *op. cit.*, pp. 119-170.

125:11   This section is based in part on the author's conversations with former high-ranking officials of the Soviet secret service who escaped to the West; also on Richard Sorge's memoirs, printed in Willoughby, *op. cit.*, pp. 134-230, one of the most important documents of intelligence literature; °Gouzenko, I., *The Iron Curtain*, (New York), 1948, pp. 102-118; °Foote, A., *Handbook for Spies*, (New York), 1949, pp. 61-91; the *Report of the Royal Canadian Commission*, (Ottawa), 1946; and on exhaustive firsthand information supplied by Colonel Issmail Gusseynovich Akhmedoff, former chief of Section IV of the Military Intelligence Department of the Red Army General Staff.

127:31   Willoughby, *op. cit.*, pp. 23-132.

128:13   *Rep. R. Can. Com.*, (q.v.), pp. 12-13.

128:16   Foote, *op. cit.*, pp. 48-60.

128:38   Massing, *op. cit.*, pp. 163-180, 206-211.

129:10   °Hirsch, R., *The Soviet Spies*, (New York), 1947.

130:42   *Rep. R. Can. Com.*, (q.v.), pp. 447-458.

131:16   Such dependence on espionage is by no means exclusive with the Communists in Russia. During the First World War, for example, Austrian espionage succeeded in apprehending only a single French spy, two British agents, and a total of 16 Italian operatives, while catching as many as 323 Russian spies. *Cf.*, Ronge, *op. cit.*, p. 393.

132:9   Knebel, F., "Red spies. The inside story of the people who betrayed their country," *Look* magazine, 1951, vol. 15, no. 13, (June 19), pp. 31-37.

132:27   "Der Ostspionagefall vor dem Bundesstrafgericht," *Neue Zürcher Zeitung*, 1953, November 5, Section 7, Also, *ibid.*, no. 2576, a summarization of the charges against Rudolph Roessler and Dr. Xavier Schnieper.

132:36   Based on a tabulation of espionage cases reported in the New York *Times* between 1917 and 1954.

132:40   Burnham, J., *The Web of Subversion*, (New York), 1954.

133:26   Picker, *op. cit.*, pp. 87, 139.

134:3   Roscoe, J., *The Ethics of War*, (London), 1914.

134:10   Maugham, *op cit.*, p. 4.

134:17   Mennevee, R., *L'espionnage international en temps de paix*, (Paris), 1929, two vols.

135:7   For examples of such operations instruction, see Marshall, *op. cit.*, pp. 19, 49; for a characteristic operational scheme of an espionage network, see Foote, *op. cit.*, pp. 63, 81; and Landau, H., *All's Fair*, (New York), 1934, pp. 48-57.

135:20   Sweeney, *op. cit.*, pp. 206-208.

135:42   Cookridge, *op. cit.*

136:4   Churchill, W. S., *Triumph and Tragedy*, (Boston), 1953, p. 49.

136:14   *Rep. R. Can. Com.*, (q.v.), pp. 15, 20-21.

137:17 Gouzenko, *op. cit.*, pp. 181-195, 262-279.

137:29 Foote, *op. cit.*, pp. 80-91.

138:3 Willoughby, *op. cit.*, pp. 25, 33-38, 45, 78-79, 90-92, 108-110, 117, 120-124.

138:19 Turrou, L. G., *Nazi Spies in America*, (New York), 1938, pp. 3-30, 275-299; Hynd, A., *Betrayal from the East*, (New York), 1943, throughout.

138:29 °Best, S. P., *The Venlo Incident*, (London), 1950; Hagen, W., *Die geheime Front*, (q.v.), pp. 43-44. Additional information was supplied by Mr. H. B. Gisevius, a prominent member of the German anti-Nazi underground.

138:45 Sweeney, *op. cit.*

139:11 Mashbir, *op. cit.*, pp. 127-150, 188-208. The only recorded attempt at direct espionage by the United States prior to the Second World War was the mission of Lieutenant Colonel Peter Ellis of the Marine Corps to a closed Japanese island in the Pacific. Colonel Charles E. Burnett, American Military Attache in Tokyo, made this comment to Mashbir on Colonel Ellis' impending journey: "Colonel Ellis here, after many years of study, has suddenly conceived an intense and irrepressible desire to study the flora and fauna of the island of Jaluit. Now undoubtedly the Ambassador is being deceived by this, and I am being completely deceived by this, but the question is: Do you think it will also fool the Japanese." Ellis died mysteriously during the journey. (*Cf.*, Mashbir, *op. cit.*, pp. 103-104.)

139:23 Based on the author's examination of pertinent documents.

139:35 Willoughby, *op. cit.*, p. 116.

140:10 Weisenborn, G., *Der lautlose Aufstand*, (Hamburg), 1953, pp. 203-217, an authoritative and authentic account.

140:18 Gisevius, H. B., *To the Bitter End*, (Boston), 1947, pp. 480-483; Hagen, *op. cit.*, pp. 455-458.

140:28 Dulles, A. W., *Germany's Underground*, (New York), 1947, pp. XI-XII.

141:10 Sweeney, *op. cit.*, pp. 211-212.

141:31 The "Müller" incident is based on an unpublished wartime narrative.

142:30 Altmann, L., "Zur Psychologie des Spions," in *Die Weltkriegsspionage*, (q.v.), pp. 37-52.

143:13 The most famous homosexual espionage case was that of Colonel Alfred Redl of the Austro-Hungarian General Staff, (*Cf.*, Kisch, E. E., *Prager Pitaval*, (Berlin), 1928, pp. 67-108). The other was that of the 18th century French diplomatic agent, Chevalier d'Eon de Beaumont; (*cf.*, Rowan, *op. cit.*, pp. 128-137).

144:17 °*Assessment of Men. Selection of Personnel for the Office of Strategic Services*, (New York), 1948, pp. 230-315, 450-493; MacDonald, *op cit.*, pp. 39-52.

145:23 For the unhappy ending of espionage missions, see Baumann, F., "Wie sie starben," in *Die Weltkriegsspionage*, (q.v.), pp. 53-61; Ott, K. A., *Der Mensch vor dem Standgericht*, (Hamburg), 1948; Pölchau, H., *Die letzten Stunden*, (Berlin), 1949.

146:2 Tickell, J., *Odette*, (London), 1939, pp. 102-117.

146:8 °Churchill, P., *Of Their Own Choice*, (London), 1951. No human activity has as many occupational hazards as the game of espionage. A study of the case histories of sixty Allied agents who operated in France during World War II showed that only 24 managed to escape the hunters. Six died in action, eleven by execution. Of the 60 agents, 30 were captured.

147:31   *Assessment of Men*, (q.v.), pp. 58-63.
148:40   *Ibid.*, pp. 63-202.
149:4   *Ibid.*, pp. 91-92, 310-311, 343-344.
149:16   *Ibid.*, pp. 133-138.
150:12   Urbanski, A. V., "Spionageschulen," in *Die Weltgriegs-spionage*, pp. 99-103.
150:12   Sweeney, *op. cit.*, pp. 255-260.
151:28   Dioneo, "The republic of spies. How Soviet 'shadowers' and 'scouts' are taught their work," *New Russia*, 1920, v. 3, pp. 175-178.
151:40   Zacharias, E. M., Farago, L., *Behind Closed Doors*, (New York), 1950, pp. 96-98; *House Report No. 1920*, p. 71. *Hearings*, Special Committee on Un-American Activities, 1939, v. 9, pp. 6984-7025.
152:19   Snowden, N. (Pseudonym of Miklos Soltesz), *Memoirs of a Spy*, (New York), 1933, pp. 1-9.
152:22   For the only reliable account of Dr. Schragmüller's activities, see Rowan, *op. cit.*, pp. 557-564.
154:20   MacDonald, *op. cit.*, pp. 37-52; Ford, C., MacBain, A., *Cloak and Dagger. The Secret Story of the OSS*, (New York), 1946.
154:45   *Ibid.*
155:21   Gouzenko, *op. cit.*, pp. 168-180.
156:11   Lüdecke, *op. cit.*, pp. 15-16.
156:18   *Ibid.*, pp. 17-18.
156:36   Baden-Powell, *op. cit.*, pp. 61-69.
160:16   Chambers, W., *Witness*, (New York), 1942, pp. 319, 724.
160:26   For a classic example of such an operation, see Moyzisch, L. C., *Operation Cicero*, (New York), 1950, pp. 48-64.
161:10   Chambers, *op. cit.*, pp. 422-423.
161:44   *Rep. R. [Can.] Comm.*, (q.v.), pp. 120, 125.
162:8   *Ibid.*, p. 14.
162:15   *Ibid.*, pp. 454-455.
163:8   Willoughby, *op. cit.*, pp. 179-180, 194-199.
163:42   °Weyl, N., *The Battle Against Disloyalty*, (New York), 1951, pp. 209-212, 214-216.
164:1   Willoughby, *op. cit.*, pp. 231-242; Lüdecke, *op. cit.*, pp. 19-21.
164:18   Sweeney, *op. cit.*, pp. 159-161.
164:24   Lüdecke, *op. cit.*, pp. 19-21.
164:42   °Koop, T., *Weapon of Silence*, (Chicago), 1946.
165:4   Hoover, J. E. "Enemy's masterpiece of espionage," *Reader's Digest*, 1946, April, v. 48, pp. 1-6.
165:6   Rowan, *op. cit.*, pp. 636-642; Busch, *op. cit.*, pp. 111-118.
165:23   Sayers and Kahn, *op. cit.*, pp. 32-34.
165:38   Silber, J. C., *The Invisible Weapon*, (New York), 1926.
166:8   Foote, *op. cit.*, pp. 61-79.
166:38   Firmin, *op. cit.*, pp. 62-68, 123-129.
167:7   Foote, *op. cit.*, pp. 48-60.
167:32   Miksche, *op. cit.*, pp. 30-41, 119.

167:42   *Schreider, J., *Das War das Englandspiel,* (München), 1950, pp. 61-68, 149-161, 212-225.

168:38   Willoughby, *op. cit.,* pp. 62-63, 73.

169:11   *Ibid.,* pp. 117-120.

169:13   *Enc. Brit.,* 1911, (q.v.), v. 7, pp. 565-566.

169:32   Busch, *op. cit.,* pp. 176-192.

171:31   Pratt, F., *Secret and Urgent,* (Indianapolis), 1939.

172:42   Count Ciano noted in his diary: "You never know with cipher. We are reading everything the British send—are we to believe that other people are less good at the game than we are?" In *Ciano's Hidden Diary* 1937-1938, (New York), 1953, p. 49.

173:7   Rowan, *op. cit.,* pp. 601-603.

173:12   Levine, I. D., "Execution of Stalin's spy in the Tower of London," *Plain Talk,* 1948, v. 3, no. 2, (November), pp. 21-25.

173:32   *Yardley, H. O., *The American Black Chamber,* (Indianapolis), 1931.

173:33   Hoy, *op. cit.,* pp. 23-107.

174:8   Zacharias, *Secret Missions,* (q.v.), pp. 84-89, 97-98.

174:27   For a description of the agencies mentioned in this section, see Theobald, R. A., *The Big Secret of Pearl Harbor,* as reprinted in *U.S. News and World Report,* 1954, April 2, pp. 59, 67.

174:30   Rowan, R. W., *Spy Secrets,* (New York), 1946, pp. 110-112.

174:45   Aston, *op. cit.;* Busch, *op. cit.,* pp. 193-195.

175:27   New York *Times,* 1945, September 10, p. 6; 12, p. 1, 2; 13, p. 5; 16, p. 36.

178:23   Busch, *op. cit.,* pp. 239, 260-264; Firmin, *op. cit.,* pp. 36-38.

180:2   Busch, *op. cit.,* pp. 474-475.

180:28   *Moorhouse, A., *The Traitors,* (New York), 1952, p. 1.

181:1   Smith, W. C., *Sabotage. Its History, Philosophy, Function,* (Spokane), 1913.

181:15   Tompkins, D. C., *Sabotage and its Prevention,* (Berkeley), 1942, a comprehensive annotated bibliography. Also see, Söderman, H., O'Connell, *Modern Criminal Investigation,* (New York), 1952, pp. 436-444.

181:21   Miksche, *op. cit.,* pp. 124-125.

181:28   Trautman, W. E., *Direct Action and Sabotage,* (Pittsburgh), 1912.

181:34   Saunders, H. A. St. G., *The Green Beret,* (London), 1950.

181:36   Lenin, V. I., "Partisan warfare," in *Proletariat,* 1906, October 13. Skorzeny, O., *Geheimkommando Skorzeny,* (Hamburg), 1949.

182:4   Söderman and O'Connell, *op. cit.,* pp. 408-435, Farren, H. D., *Industrial Guard's Manual,* (New York), 1942, pp. 55-64; Sayers and Kahn, *op. cit.,* pp. 3-7, 99-105, 110-119.

182:21   Merker, P., *Revolutionäre Gewerkschaftsstrategie,* (Hamburg), 1929; Miksche, *op. cit.,* p. 127; Flynn, E. G., *Sabotage. The Conscious Withdrawal of the Workers' Industrial Efficiency,* (Chicago), 1916.

182:39   Busch, V., *Modern Arms and Free Men,* (New York), 1949, pp. 149-150.

183:3 Farren, H. D., *Sabotage*, (New York), 1941.

183:14 Miksche, *op. cit.*, pp. 134-135; Rowan, *op. cit.*, pp. 520-524.

183:15 Valtin, J., *Out of the Night*, (New York), 1941, pp. 121-137, 209-226, 233, 344-374.

183:39 Rowan, *op. cit.*, pp. 518-525, 715-716.

184:8 Palat, E. B., *La Ruee sur Verdun*, (Paris), 1921.

184:21 °Rintelen, F. V., *The Dark Invader*, (New York), 1931; Hall, W. R., Peaslee, A., *Three Wars With Germany*, (New York), 1944, pp. 71-194; Papen, F. V., *Memoirs*, (New York), 1952, pp. 29-52.

184:32 "Im Rücken des Feindes," *Die Wehrmacht*, 1939, April 26.

184:34 *Nazi Conspiracy and Aggression*, (q.v.), v. 2, pp. 264-265, 390, v. 5, pp. 390-392.

184:42 *Ibid.*, v. 3, p. 320.

185:25 *Ibid.*, v. 5, pp. 507-508.

185:29 Abshagen, *op. cit.*, chapter called "Sabotage der Sabotage," pp. 286-301.

185:31 Skorzeny, *op. cit.*, pp. 219-256.

185:39 Marshall, *op. cit.*, p. 13.

186:6 °Kovpak, S. A., *Our Partisan Course*, (London), 1947; Ignatov, P. K., *Partisans of Kuban*, (London), 1945; Vinogradskaya, Y. A., *A Woman Behind the German Lines*, (London), 1944.

186:17 The incident in Israel was related to the author by Major Lou Lennart who served as chief of staff to the Israeli officer in charge of the operation.

186:23 Pearlman, M., *The Army of Israel*, (New York), 1950, pp. 129-133.

187:43 Yerxa, F., Reid, O. R., *The Threat of Red Sabotage*, (New York), 1950.

188:21 Miksche, *op. cit.*, pp. 129-142.

189:5 *Ibid.*, p. 142.

190:7 Alsop and Braden, *op. cit.*, pp. 116-225.

190:9 Abshagen, *op. cit.*, pp. 273-285; Erhardt, A., *Kleinkrieg*, (Potsdam), 1944.

190:12 Marshall, *op. cit.*, pp. 12-16; Davidson, B., *Partisan Picture*, (Bedford), 1946.

190:17 *Guerilla Warfare in the Occupied Parts of the Soviet Union*, (Moscow), 1943.

190:30 Charts in Miksche, *op. cit.*, pp. 81, 110, 112, 117.

191:19 Lawrence, *op. cit.*, pp. 188-196; Garnett, D. (ed.), *The Letters of T. E. Lawrence*, (New York), 1938, pp. 181-258.

191:21 Buckmaster, M. J., *Specially Employed. The Story of British Aid to French Patriots of the Resistance*, (London), 1952.

192:14 Miksche, *op. cit.*, pp. 85, 142-156; °*Kompani Linge*, (Oslo), 1948, pp. 37-116; *Assessment of Men*, (q.v.), pp. 268-279, 372.

192:27 Rintelen, *op. cit.*; Papen, *op. cit.*

192:37 Firmin, S., *op. cit.*, pp. 96-100.

192:41 Miksche, *op. cit.*, pp. 103-105.

193:33 As quoted, *ibid.*, pp. 14-15.

194:1   *Kompani Linge,* (q.v.), v. 1, pp. 169-193; Laurence, W. L., *Dawn Over Zero,* (New York), 1946, pp. 94-112.

199:25   Yerxa, Reid, *op. cit.,* pp. 3-5.

200:1   Valtin, *op. cit.,* pp. 230-232, 235, 558-565.

200:30   Plivier, T., *Des Kaisers Kulis,* (Berlin), 1930.

200:44   Valtin, *op. cit.,* pp. 358-368.

201:23   Stowe, L., *Conquest by Terror,* (New York), 1952, pp. 265-266.

201:27   The narrative of the Hungarian sabotage operation is based on the private report of "Pete."

203:1   Kent, in *op. cit.,* pp. 209-210, regards "security intelligence" as the foundation on which all intelligence functions rest and from which positive intelligence evolves. His is a novel and interesting approach, fully justified by the realities of today's intelligence complex. My own approach to this present discussion of negative intelligence was stimulated by Kent's premise. The subdivision of negative intelligence as proposed in this section is an original attempt to introduce specialization into what used to be a monolithic structure. The idea of such specialization developed from a careful study of the over-all security problem in the face of internal subversion and the mass attack of espionage agents.

203:10   For the problems of internal security, see Weyl, N., *The Battle Against Disloyalty,* (New York), 1952, pp. 179-197, 339-342; Barth, A., *The Loyalty of Free Men,* (New York), 1952, pp. 99-136, 137-153; *Report of the President's Temporary Commission on Employee Loyalty,* (mimeographed release), 1947, March 22; Nikoloric, L. D., "The government loyalty program," in *The American Scholar,* 1950, Summer.

203:24   Koop, *op. cit.,* pp. 16-30, 47-58; for press censorship, Thomson, G. P., *Blue Pencil Admiral,* (London), 1947; for radio censorship, Saerchinger, C., "Radio, censorship and neutrality," *Foreign Affairs,* 1940, 18, pp. 337-349.

204:6   Heinz "Spionageabwehr," *Jahrb. d. deutschen Heeres,* (Leipzig), 1938, pp. 129-127; Ronge's classic work, (q.v.); and Sulliotti, I., *L'armata del silenzio.* (Milano), 1931.

206:7   Zacharias, *Secret Missions,* (q.v.), pp. 166-172.

207:20   Section 102 (d) 3 of the *National Security Act* (Public Law 253, 80th Congress).

207:25   Thomson, Sir B., *The Story of Scotland Yard,* (New York), 1937, pp. 225-234.

207:44   *Report of the Attorney General,* (mimeographed), 1953, May, pp. 1-11, 119-120.

208:45   "Provisions of Federal Statutes, Executive Orders, and Congressional Resolutions relating to the internal security of the United States," (Washington), 1953.

209:26   *Ibid.,* pp. 3-4.

209:44   Robinson, D., "Our comic-opera spy set-up," *American Legion Magazine,* 1951, February.

210:8   Thorwald, J., *Der Fall Pastorius,* (Stuttgart), 1953, pp. 8-18.

210:20   Robinson, *op. cit.*

211:15   Firmin, *op. cit.,* pp. 55-61.

211:44   Moorehouse, A., *op. cit.*, pp. 87, 90-92, 94-95, 98-99, 203; *Soviet Atomic Espionage*, (q.v.), pp. 3-4, 145-152; *The Shameful Years*, (Washington), 1951, pp. 67-70.

213:14   Gouzenko, *op. cit.*; *Interlocking Subversion in Government Departments*, (Washington), 1953, pp. 1-3, 17-19.

213:23   *Pilat, O., *The Atom Spies*, (New York), 1952, pp. 57-78.

214:22   Moorehouse, *op. cit.*, pp. 144-145, 155-156.

215:6   Pilat, *op. cit.*, pp. 43-47, 80-82, 174-176, 280-281.

216:9   *Enc. Brit.*, (q.v.), v. 28, pp. 293-295.

216:17   Rowan, *op. cit.*, pp. 276-277.

216:38   Pinkerton, A., "History and evidence of the passage of Abraham Lincoln from Harrisburgh, Pa., to Washington, D.C. on the 22nd of February, 1861," (Chicago), 1891.

217:6   Pinkerton, *The Spy of the Rebellion*, (q.v.).

217:14   Moylan, Sir J., *Scotland Yard*, (London), 1935; Prothero, M., *The History of the C.I.D.*, (London), 1934.

217:19   Rowan, *op. cit.*, pp. 326-335, 349-353.

217:36   Steinthal, W., *Dreyfus*, (Berlin), 1928.

217:44   Lucieto, C., *On Special Missions*, (London), 1924.

218:20   Redl, A., *Organisation der Auskundschaftung fremder Militärverhältnisse und die Abwehr fremder Spionage im Inlande*, (Wien), 1903.

218:33   Renwick, G. "The Story of Colonel Redl," in Nicolai, W., *The German Secret Service*, (London), 1931.

219:23   Steinhauer, G., Felstead, S. T., *Steinhauer. The Kaiser's Master Spy*, (London), 1924.

220:32   Hoy, *op. cit.*

221:1   Steele, J. in New York *Times*, 1935, February 18, p. 1; 19, p. 5.

222:6   *Activities of Soviet Secret Service*, (Washington), 1954: the testimony of Captain Nikolai Evgenyevich Khokhlov before the Senate Internal Security Subcommittee, on May 21, 1954. According to Khokhlov, domestic counterespionage is the job of the First Chief Directorate of the Ministry of the Interior (MVD); while counterespionage abroad, including infiltration of enemy espionage organizations is assigned to the Second Chief Directorate whose Section 9 is charged with terroristic action, kidnapings, and the assassinations of enemy agents.

222:9   *Sinevirskii, N., *Smersh*, (New York), 1950.

222:23   Söderman and O'Connell, *op. cit.*, pp. 15-17; Belin, J., *Secrets of the Surete*, (New York), 1950, pp. 88-110, 166-178, 223-240, 258-277.

223:11   Political counterespionage was assigned to a special agency called Federal Bureau for the Protection of the Constitution. In July 1954, this Bureau attained notoriety when its chief, Dr. Otto John, deserted to the Communists. Cf. *Die Zeit*, (Hamburg), v. 9, no. 30, 1954, July 29, pp. 1-3, for an authoritative account of the strange case.

223:18   Cookridge, *op. cit;* Firmin, *op. cit.*

224:11   Van Doren, C., *Secret History of the American Revolution*, (New York), 1941, pp. 143 ff.

224:13   "Documents of Henry, the British Spy," in Singer, K., *Three Thousand Years of Espionage*, (New York), 1948, pp. 76-87.

224:16   Rowan, *op. cit.*, pp. 252-258.

224:19   Busch, *op. cit.*, pp. 274-289.

225:13   "It was my impression that, at that time—I mean before the war—when I was in the Soviet Union, the Soviet Intelligence was more interested not in the United States of America, but in Japan and other countries which were in direct conflict with the Soviet Union." Testimony of Colonel Igor Bogolepov, reprinted in *Institute of Pacific Relations,* Hearings, (Washington), 1952, part 13, p. 4590.

226:8   *The Shameful Years,* (q.v.), pp. 5-21.

226:20   Zacharias, *op. cit.*, pp. 203-205.

226:25   Chambers, *op. cit.*, pp. 425-426. "The volume of production was high . . . But Bykov was continuously exasperated by their material and distrustful of them. . . . At times Bykov convinced himself that he was being cheated. . . . Yet I was in the curious position of agreeing with Bykov about the value of the material, but for different reasons. . . . I concluded that political espionage was a magnificent waste of time and effort—not because the sources were holding back; they were pathetically eager to help—but because the secrets of foreign offices are notoriously overrated."

226:37   Sayer and Kahn, *op. cit.*, p. 26.

227:27   Thorwald, *op. cit.*, pp. 18-22.

227:35   Zacharias, *op. cit.*, pp. 147-212.

227:43   *Annual Report of the United States Attorney General, 1939,* p. 153; p. 152; Hoover, J. E., "Stamping out the spies," *The American* magazine, 1940.

228:13   Lysing, H., *Men Against Crime,* (New York), 1938, pp. 9-20, 123-136, 145-196.

228:24   *United States Government Organization Manual 1953-54,* (Washington), 1953, pp. 180-181; interviews with J. Edgar Hoover, *U.S. News and World Report,* 1950, August 11, pp. 30-33; 1951, March 30, pp. 32-37.

228:32   °Collins, F. L., *The FBI in Peace and War,* (New York), 1940.

229:4   *Congr. Rec.*, 87th Congress, pp. A2466-A2472.

229:14   °*The Story of the FBI, Look* magazine, (New York), 1947.

230:24   I am indebted to Dr. Harry Söderman for invaluable advice in the preparation of this section.

233:5   N.Y. *Times,* 1942, June 9.

233:9   Schwarzwalder, J., *We Caught Spies,* (New York), 1946; Spingarn, S. J., Lehman, M., "How we caught spies in World War II," *Saturday Evening Post,* 1948, November 27, pp. 214-216; December 4, pp. 42-43; December 11, p. 28.

233:28   Quoted in Lysing, *op. cit.*, p. 242.

234:13   *Hearings,* House of Representatives, Committee on Rules, 66th Congress, 2nd Sess., 1920, v. 1, p. 49; v. 2, p. 212.

234:32   Sayers and Kahn, *op. cit.*, pp. 23-34.

238:20   Koop. *op. cit.*, pp. 16-30, 47-58; Busch, *op. cit.*, pp. 636-642.

239:13   Rowan, *op. cit.*, p. 486.

241:1   °Lerner, D., *Propaganda in War and Crisis,* (New York), 1951.

241:3   Lasswell, H. D., "The rise of the propagandist," in *The Analysis of Political Behavior*, (q.v.), pp. 173-179.

241:11 *Lockhart, Sir R. H. B., *Comes the Reckoning*, (London), 1948, pp. 125-224.

241:21 Speier, H., "Psychological warfare reconsidered," in *The Policy Sciences*, (Stanford), 1952.

241:25 Farago, L., "Soviet propaganda," *United Nations World*, 1948, v. 2, no. 8, pp. 18-24.

241:33 Lasswell, H. D., "Political and psychological warfare," in *Propaganda in War and Crisis*, (q.v.), pp. 264-266.

242:36 Doob, L., *Propaganda. Its Psychology and Technique*, (New York), 1944, pp. 71-154.

243:23 Young, K. in *German Psychological Warfare*, (q.v.), pp. XV-XXII.

243:37 According to Carlton Hayes (*Enc. Brit.*, q.v., v. 27, p. 790), "it is well established that Urban preached the sermon which gave the impetus to the crusade." The sermon was written out by Bishop Baudry. It can be found in J. M. Watterich's *Pontif. Roman. Vitae.*

243:39 See Ranke's *Popes*, v. 2, pp. 468 ff.

243:41 De Martinis, *Juris pontificii de Propaganda Fide*, (Rome), 1888. In 1627, Urban VIII founded the College of Propaganda for the education of missionaries and the printing of polyglot press.

243:43 *Linebarger, P. M. A., *Psychological Warfare*, (Washington), 1948, p. 3.

244:3   *Ibid.*, p. 7.

244:20 Davidson, P., *Propaganda and the American Revolution*, (Chapel Hill), 1941.

244:21 Linebarger, *op. cit.*, p. 20.

244:31 Geyer, H., "Uber die Zeitdauer von Angriffsgefechten," *Militärwissenschaftliche Rundschau*, 1939, v. 4, no. 4, pp. 179-186.

244:35 Rowan, *op. cit.*, pp. 643-646.

244:42 Fyfe, H., *Northcliffe. An Intimate Biography*, (New York), 1930, pp. 238-256.

245:30 Wellesley, Sir V., *Diplomacy in Fetters*, (London), 1944, pp. 9, 30, 42, 54.

245:39 Kris, E., Leites, N., "Trends in Twentieth Century propaganda," *Psychoanalysis and the Social Sciences*, (New York), 1947, v. 1.

245:40 *Overseas Information Programs of the United States*. Part 1: Report of the Committee on Foreign Relations; part 2: Hearings, (Washington), 1953.

246:7   Stowe, L., *op. cit.*, pp. 85, 141, 259, 281, 284-287, 289; Barrett, E. W., *Truth is Our Weapon*, (New York), 1953, pp. 96, 214, 276-277, 281.

246:33 Zacharias, *op. cit.*, pp. 307-311; Barrett, *op. cit.*, pp. 9-10; Carroll, *op. cit.*, p. 366.

246:41 Zacharias, *op. cit.*, pp. 332-383.

247:3   Linebarger, *op. cit.*, pp. 44, 88-89.

247:15 Farago, L., "British propaganda," *United Nations World*, 1948, v. 2, no. 9, pp. 22-25. Lochner, L. P., *What About Germany?*, (New York), 1942, pp. 234-235. Mr. Lochner, long-time AP correspondent in Germany, accepted "the Boss" as a genuine representative of the German anti-

Nazi movement, but appeared scandalized by his obscenities.

247:17   The other effective British clandestine radio operation was the so-called *Soldatensender Calais*, transmitting black propaganda virtually around the clock.

248:35   Linebarger, *op. cit.*, p. 206.

249:12   Warburg, J. P., *Unwritten Treaty*, (New York), 1946, pp. 151-161.

249:22   Siepmann, C. A., *Radio, Television and Society*, (New York), 1950, pp. 117-154, 292-316.

249:29   Sington, D., Weidenfeld, A., *The Goebbels Experiment*, (New Haven), 1943, pp. 139-140, 149, 181-193.

249:34   Katz, D., "Britain speaks," in Childs, H. L., Whitton, J. B., *Propaganda by Short Wave*, (Princeton), 1943, pp. 109-150.

250:12   Thomson, C. A. H., *Overseas Information Service of the United States Government*, (Washington), 1948, pp. 17-192.

250:19   Ettlinger, H., *The Axis on the Air*, (Indianapolis), 1943; Linebarger, *op. cit.*, pp. 81-88.

250:38   Herz, M. F., "Some lessons from leaflet propaganda," *Public Opinion Quarterly*, 1949, Fall.

251:6   Jackson, C. D., "Assignment for the press," in Markel, L. (ed.), *Public Opinion and Foreign Policy*, (New York), 1949, pp. 180-187.

251:15   Stern-Rubarth, E., *Propaganda als politisches Instrument*, (Berlin), 1921.

252:29   Hadamovsky, E., *Propaganda und nationale Macht*, (Oldenburg), 1933.

253:6   Allport, G. W., Postman, L., *The Psychology of Rumor*, (New York), 1947.

253:29   *Ibid.*, p. 161.

254:2   Knapp, R. H., "A psychology of rumor," *Public Opinion Quarterly*, 1944, pp. 22-37.

254:32   Stone, S., "Chart of the cold war," in Markel, *op. cit.*, pp. 143-155; Carroll, *op. cit.*, pp. 371-392; Barrett, *op. cit.*, pp. 219-300.

255:1   Barghorn, F. C., *The Soviet Image of the United States*, (New York), 1950, pp. 3-38, 103-290.

255:29   Riess, C., *Der siebzehnte Juni*, (Berlin), 1954.

255:34   Zeller, B., *Geist der Freiheit*, (München), 1952; Görlitz, *op. cit.*, pp. 647-672.

256:8   Clausewitz, C. V., *On War*, (London), 1940, v. 1, pp. 2-3.

256:16   *Enc. Brit.*, (q.v.), v. 28, p. 306.

256:44   *Ibid.*, v. 4, pp. 794-795.

257:2   Bülow, P. V., *Familienbuch der v. Bülow*, (Berlin), 1859.

257:12   Cämmerer, V., *Development of Strategical Sciences*, (London), 1905.

258:1   Mannheim, K., *Man and Society in an Age of Reconstruction*, (London), 1940. Also see, Kennan, G. F., *American Diplomacy 1900-1950*, (Chicago), 1951, pp. 58-62; Lippmann, W., *The Cold War*, (New York), 1947, pp. 58-62; Werfel, F., *Star of the Unborn*, (New York), 1946, a utopian novel in which conflict is transferred into what Werfel called "man's astromental sphere."

258:25   Rowan, *op. cit.*, p. 682.

Index of Names

283